THE
KNOWLEDGE
CAFÉ

THE KNOWLEDGE CAFÉ

Create an Environment for Successful Knowledge Management

Benjamin C. Anyacho, MBA, PMP

BK

Berrett–Koehler Publishers, Inc.

Berrett-Koehler Publishers, Inc.
1333 Broadway, Suite 1000
Oakland, CA 94612-1921
Tel: (510) 817-2277
Fax: (510) 817-2278
www.bkconnection.com

ORDERING INFORMATION
Quantity sales. Special discounts are available on quantity purchases by corporations, associations, and others. For details, contact the "Special Sales Department" at the Berrett-Koehler address above.
Individual sales. Berrett-Koehler publications are available through most bookstores. They can also be ordered directly from Berrett-Koehler:
Tel: (800) 929-2929; Fax: (802) 864-7626; www.bkconnection.com.
Orders for college textbook / course adoption use.
Please contact Berrett-Koehler: Tel: (800) 929-2929; Fax: (802) 864-7626.

Distributed to the U.S. trade and internationally by Penguin Random House Publisher Services.

Berrett-Koehler and the BK logo are registered trademarks of Berrett-Koehler Publishers, Inc.

Printed in the United States of America

Berrett-Koehler books are printed on long-lasting acid-free paper. When it is available, we choose paper that has been manufactured by environmentally responsible processes. These may include using trees grown in sustainable forests, incorporating recycled paper, minimizing chlorine in bleaching, or recycling the energy produced at the paper mill.

Library of Congress Cataloging-in-Publication Data
Names: Anyacho, Benjamin C., author.
Title: The knowledge café : create an environment for successful knowledge management / Benjamin C. Anyacho, MBA, PMP.
Description: 1st Edition.. | Oakland : Berrett-Koehler Publishers, 2021. | Includes bibliographical references and index.
Identifiers: LCCN 2021008222 | ISBN 9781523089512 (paperback) | ISBN 9781523089529 (adobe pdf) | ISBN 9781523089536 (epub)
Subjects: LCSH: Knowledge management—Technological innovations. | Virtual reality in management.
Classification: LCC HD30.2 .A589 2021 | DDC 658.4/038—dc23
LC record available at https://lccn.loc.gov/2021008222

First Edition

27 26 25 24 23 22 21   10 9 8 7 6 5 4 3 2 1

Book production by Westchester Publishing Services
Cover design by Jimmy Chan

Dedicated to all project managers and knowledge managers around the world.

Contents

Preface

My dad, Isaiah Anyacho Njoku, was a carpenter, a spiritual man with strong leadership skills. My mom still tells me about his shrewd knowledge today, around 50 years after his passing.

His carpentry was not the most sophisticated, but all of his works have a remarkably unique signature, witnessed in every door and every chair crafted by his capable hands. His pieces stirred my imagination and curiosity for knowledge transfer. One of my greatest regrets was not having the opportunity to cross-fertilize ideas, learn, and share knowledge with him because I was a baby when he passed on.

Like everyone on the planet, my father didn't have control over his death. But, he most definitely had control over his knowledge.

Grasping this awareness inspired me to make knowledge exchange or transfer one of my career's ethos (driving forces), and I've been walking on air since I came to this realization. I have set my face like a flint to share that all knowledge is useless if it goes to the grave unshared. In fact, most of the concepts I'm sharing in this book are what I have done or am currently doing daily. Knowledge must be managed and transferred to others like a priceless legacy—and live! In the most simplistic terms, shouldn't knowledge exchange be like a father–son relationship, nonthreatening and congenial? Sure, journals and notes may be concise. However, what would you say if someone asked, "Do you want to read a book about Scotland, or would you prefer to meet someone from Scotland?"

A few conversations are best in a formal setting; the rest are possible in a café!

Managing knowledge begins with curiosity within human interactions, rather than being driven by process or technology. As important as technology is in knowledge management (KM), it would be useless without people and the right culture accelerators. Technology like AI should be given a seat at the table—and be managed as a stakeholder, because machine learning and AI will play a prominent role in the next knowledge-centric organization and human-machine collaborations will be key. People and conversation shall be the chief in all knowledge management and stewardship.

My emphasis shall rest on two cardinal points: simplicity and people side of KM enabler while recognizing process, technology, and content management enablers. Café conversation and mindset sit at the center of KM enablers. Human interaction is key in KM; conversation is king. The Knowledge Café paradigm is the people's side and environment, with little emphasis on other enablers. The Knowledge Café mindset is an attitude of knowledge exchange or management that could be structured, but mostly unstructured, agile, and conversational.

In fact, some of the simplest ways to stir knowledge in an organization are to minimize knowledge transfer hierarchical structures—create Knowledge Cafés, pool and share every knowledge worker's knowledge, and incentivize folks for sharing their knowledge.

The Knowledge Café construct is learning agile in knowledge management. The café can be a virtual or face-to-face gateway for conversation, knowledge transfer, and knowledge exchange. It fills our desire to connect and communicate with others and transcends IT tools, repositories, and complicated processes. Knowledge management is the responsibility of us all—and most importantly, people rather than machines. A café may be a one-off or a continuous event.

Two fundamental questions must be asked and answered about knowledge management: "Why is it needed?" and "How can an organization cultivate an environment in which it will thrive?" Café is all about asking questions.

To successfully answer these questions, you must first accept the uncomfortable truth that people cannot be forced to share their knowledge. Or better put: knowledge is value and people need an incentive to exchange it. To overcome this challenge or fear, an organization must build, espouse, and support an ecosystem in which all workplace stakeholders are invited to share their experience, skill, and wisdom joyfully. This will intentionally promote within the culture that knowledge transfer is welcomed and embedded into the organization's culture.

When knowledge transfer is intentional, regularly implemented, and encouraged at every organization level, people take pride in transferring their professional knowledge. Knowledge is the principal capital of knowledge workers—all employees that think, solve problems with their knowledge, give meaning to information, and apply knowledge. They are the knowledge creators and sharers who champion the cause of knowledge management, thus improving an organization's current practices and future processes. Organizations will experience the benefits of KM as more employees naturally rise to leadership roles and compete to share what they know. Rewarding knowledge exchange and the transfer encourages cultural transparency, increases trust, and reduces the frustration of those who have previously shouldered the bulk of the organization's knowledge transfer and exchange. Practitioners in the Knowledge Café ecosystem naturally are supposed to share their knowledge and have fun doing it. "Aha!" moments happen at the café.

Knowledge transfer comes through genuine relationships where knowledge transfer and exchange become reciprocal, iterative, and interactive. A relationship is an incentive for the café construct.

The predominant aspect of knowledge is the intellectual capital in the minds of people. Understanding process and technology is not as complicated as understanding people. The minds of knowledge workers need to be ignited and not filled with more one-directional information. Winston Churchill said, "The empires of the future are the empires of the mind." The most significant knowledge transfer or exchange doesn't happen in the classrooms or conference rooms but in conversation—in the café, the mind is ignited, and knowledge is transferred. In fact, classrooms are becoming experiments for a café style of learning.

> Conversation is king. Content is just something to talk about.
> —Cory Doctorow, Canadian-British writer

Loss of employee knowledge through employee turnover and employee retirement is another reason to curate an atmosphere of knowledge sharing and transfer.

The Knowledge Café is the ecosystem in which everyone—educated or not, certified or not, experienced or not—can find common ground by exchanging information and brainstorming solutions. Imagine an environment in which new employees, and indeed every knowledge worker, have a common source of truth with easy access to indexed and searchable knowledge assets such as storytelling, oral history recordings of previous project stakeholders, knowledge interviews, and the café style processes. The Knowledge Café concept invites knowledge workers to willingly and comprehensively transfer crucial information and data to improve employee onboarding and project process development.

Whether an organization is expanding or contracting, scaling up or downsizing, business continuity, process improvement, performance, and knowledge innovation are the priorities. Organizations must focus on preserving critical and technical knowledge required to conduct business. When KM is part of the organization's culture, performance improves, the competitive advantage accelerates, and competition becomes *coopetition*. Coopetition is cooperating with your competitors, building synergy so that everyone wins. The concept of coopetition will be discussed in detail in chapter 12. With increasingly constrained resources, a knowledge-sharing environment is required—Knowledge Café processes allow for unencumbered access—an open invitation for knowledge workers to unreservedly share their experience, skill, and wisdom—in the most current, highest-quality collaboration space a company has to offer.

You can't manage knowledge—nobody can. What you can do is manage the environment in which knowledge can be created, discovered, captured, shared, distilled, validated, transferred, adopted, adapted, and applied.
—Collison & Parcell (2005)

While we do not have control over our employees' heads, we do have control over the machines' knowledge and their various formats. Most importantly, we control the knowledge transfer environment, the knowledge culture supported by a clear KM strategy and processes. A robust knowledge ecosystem requires organizational nourishment that fosters a knowledge-savvy workforce.

Here is a gentle caution: Your knowledge is not your job security. Your knowledge is your value—it only grows or generates a return when invested in the work and others, and when others invest in you.

In my experience, human beings and organizations don't always gleefully embrace a system of knowledge management. In response to surveys and audience participation at conference presentations, results suggest that employees hoard their intellectual assets. The truth is that more people in the workplace see their knowledge as their job security. This information hoarding and knowledge silo is a significant challenge to implementing a culture of knowledge sharing.

I have carefully selected about a dozen knowledge brokers, creators, and sharers across cultures and nationalities to share their KM experiences in various work and project spaces. I will refer to these inclusions as Case Studies throughout the book—an indirect attribution of concepts to a third, albeit credentialed, party. These are ordinary people you can identify within their KM struggles, challenges, and experiences. I hope these KM stories, along with my analyses, intrigue you.

What are the gaps that prevent us from turning information into knowledge that becomes eternal wisdom? There is a simple, nonthreatening way for initiating and maturing knowledge transfer activities at home, in the workplace, and in the community. In this book, I present to you the Knowledge Café, a baby step toward knowledge management and a process as simple as walking into your favorite café for a cup of tea or coffee with friends to fill the knowledge gaps—and connect the dots between people and knowledge.

Curious yet? Novel hunter? I believe that miracle lies in the unknown. So, be fascinated by and attracted to the unknown—at the café. I am extending a personal invitation to join me inside the Knowledge Café, where we will freely sip, collaborate, converse, and become knowledge caffeinated. So, café conversations are the necessary antecedent to knowledge and wisdom. It connects the dots between people and knowledge. Throughout the ages, conversation, learning, and knowledge exchanges have taken place around saucers—in a café with a cup of tea or coffee without a mandate. The brew at the café creates a knowledge culture. If it's noisy or too quiet at home or work, connect to the café. Sit with me in the Knowledge Café as we sip and collaborate—let the conversation begin!

Enjoy,
BCA

Introduction

A Knowledge Café is a mindset and an environment for engaging, discussing, and exchanging knowledge within a group, whether face-to-face or virtual. It's a knowledge experimentation town square where it's easier to share and reuse knowledge. Café is the environment that supports knowledge circulation and increases its velocity—"breeding" grounds for innovation. The café is in the digital discussion board, enterprise knowledge Wiki library, brown-bag lunch meetings, unstructured serendipitous exchanges, and watercooler conversations. Until now, there has never been a time when there was a need for increased knowledge flow, agility, simplicity, and relevance. Don't you wish there was a space to bring ideas, including your crazy ones, for other caffeinated visitors to test them out? I'm talking about space, curiosity, and attitude for learning where reflective and generative dialogue and discourse are covenanted; debate and diatribe are intentional outside the ground rules. I started the Junior Debating Society in third grade (class 3).

I understand the debate. A debate has its place but is not sustainable. Today's toxic and hostile culture that prefers debate to dialogue calls us for dialogue—in a café.

> The café space and mindset integrate face-to-face or virtual audio meetings with screen-sharing, whiteboarding/brainstorming, group chat for teams/projects, platforms for file sharing, social networking, collaborations, testing crazy ideas, idea generation, agile learning, honest questions, and answers.

In today's world of breathtaking changes, where we drink from a fire hose of information, constant and quick learning of new things, openness to new ideas, and adaptation are not optional but necessary skills. Learn or become irrelevant. But learning is not enough. We want to make sense of what we know. We need that "aha!" moment that happens in a conversational setting that a café provides. Intangible resources or values like knowledge, people, expertise, loyalty, repeated business, and reputation are becoming increasingly valuable. Effective and managed communication is a prerequisite for collaboration, free flow of information, and addictive learning space. Learning agility, versatility, feedback, making meaning of our experience, and collaboration are woven into the fabric of high-performing organizations. The most difficult challenges and hard discussions in our society, like racial conflicts, can be unraveled with understanding, not just knowledge. Understanding has some elements of vulnerabilities. It means walking in peoples' shoes through listening, dialogue, conversation—in a café way. Silence is not the answer. Learning and knowledge exchange should not be cumbersome but should be as simple as walking into a café. Have you desired your global team's input, not just the people sitting in the next cubicle, office, or people you already knew?

We live in a knowledge economy, which depends on the quality, ease of access, findability, discoverability, usability, dependability of information, and conversion velocity to knowledge. Knowledge is the most significant currency in today's project-driven world, yet the current knowledge of an organization or industry may be obsolete in two to five years. Immersing ourselves in new technologies and innovation is like running as fast as possible to stay in the same place without capturing and retaining enduring wisdom that can never be obsolete. The way we acquired and exchanged knowledge yesterday will not suffice today. The greatest ideas are made impotent by the wrong environment and destroyed by the wrong culture.

I'll contend that human interactions are the most significant channels for transferring all human core capabilities like curiosity, imagination, social and emotional intelligence, teaming, empathy, resilience, creativity, sense-making, adaptive thinking, and critical thinking. There is a need for a nonjudgmental learning space where we can voice "crazy ideas," unscripted knowledge, have others think about them, and test them out. That's the "come, let's reason together knowledge space." We all have our prejudices and biases. Many people don't want to say the wrong thing. We need a space where we can honestly bring our prejudices and biases to conversational dialogue, and it's okay to say the wrong things in love, provided it's for knowledge. The absence of a café means everyone retreats, there is silence, and knowledge is stifled. The ignorant and opportunists rule the day.

The knowledge environment and culture are inseparable. What's trending is the environment where knowledge is stewarded. Café-style collaboration platforms enable more casual networking and "whatever you'd like—as long as it's learning appropriate" conversations that spur understanding, connections, relationships, and new knowledge.

COVID-19 has scrambled everything and the way we learn to learn, learn, unlearn, share, and work. And the cry for social justice is reshaping the nature of our conversations and dialogues. Where do we exchange knowledge on exciting lessons learned from the disaster and disruptions, especially from large-scale remote work? Virtual Knowledge Café? How well can a virtual café present an opportunity? Could knowledge users access the data, information, and tools they needed?

Interaction and conversation are on the critical path of every knowledge management (KM) environment. The café is a safe place to exchange knowledge. It's a safe to fail knowledge experimentation.

It's a current, cross-generational, systematic concept designed for a simple conversation to transfer, retain, and manage relevant knowledge. The café is the university of the future. We can only be as good as the environment we create. With Knowledge Café, we'll be able to bust information and knowledge silos. Imagine an environment where conversation is king and where interactive displays, team-building days, huddle rooms, stand-ups, Kanban's Trello boards, Google's office collaborative tools, video conferencing, hot asking, and the like are the language of work.

Retirements, increased job mobility, and information silos create an inevitable "brain drain" and loss of an organization's critical intellectual capital. But, the wisdom of an organization's employees—aka knowledge workers—can potentially endure and curate a competitive edge in the project-driven workplace. In a world of daily disruptions, there is an urgency to capture, transfer, and retain an organization's knowledge workers' accrued knowledge. Without the retention and application of what we know and the learned knowledge of those who came before us, our organizations will be poorly equipped to stay relevant in today's constantly evolving environment of innovation.

Information creates energy only when it is explained or brought into context. Knowledge does not manage itself—it is cultivated and activated by knowledge leaders. People are the creators of the environment where knowledge thrives in a conversational setting. There's no best practice in a terrible environment. Innovation expert and entrepreneur Michael Schrage was right when he said, "Knowledge is not the power. Power is power. The ability to act on knowledge is power. End of story" (Schrage, quoted in Gurteen, 2019). The power of knowledge is activated when it's acted upon! Curiosity is the antecedent to discovering the power of knowledge and the wisdom it becomes. Schrage means that knowledge is power when it is applied.

Human knowledge is required for machine learning, and when we lose this critical business knowledge, we will be on the losing side of the next disruption. Resilience will be necessary to adapt to changing conditions and recover from incidents. The need for continuity of knowledge and operations is an integral part of ensuring a resilient organization. In the days ahead, disruptions, like COVID-19, may be a normal thing. Hence, resilience strategy will be required.

I have utilized the principles of the Knowledge Café since the late nineties. However, my friend, David Gurteen, coined the term "Knowledge Café" in 2002, a versatile conversational process to bring a group of people together to learn from each other and share the experience. We can expand on this concept of Knowledge Café as space and mindset to create a current, multigenerational, systematic environment designed to exchange, retain, and transfer institutional knowledge.

> Knowledge Café is a technique used to surface a group's collective knowledge, to learn from each other, share ideas and insights to gain a deeper understanding of topics, issues, and KM best practices.　　　　　　　　　　　　　　　　—David Gurteen

The Knowledge Café is a collaborative, structured but mostly unstructured vehicle for knowledge transfer. As you would in a café, our minds are ignited and rejuvenated by sharing knowledge freely, and new creative ideas emerge. The Knowledge Café can be in person or virtual, in the office or somewhere else away from home and office. Four walls don't make a café—only people, the knowledge, and ideas they bring to the café. At the café, you can discuss hard-to-solve project issues or resolve a family and community crisis. Rather than presentations and one-way knowledge transfer, in the café, everyone's voice is heard and counts. Small groups discuss a question, topic, or issue and share their ideas with a larger group. The action is at the small-group level.

Knowledge Café creates a simple (agile), theoretical, collaborative space or system by which all generations of knowledge workers can impart and share critical business knowledge and build most in-depth knowledge—lacking in many settings in today's organizations. It's as simple as a corner café—an unstructured and interactive way to capture, share, and bolster knowledge. Knowledge Café advocate Dan Remenyi calls the café "do it yourself knowledge sharing" (Remenyi, 2004). Entering a Knowledge Café stirs our curiosity and allows for a seamless transfer from owned knowledge to shared knowledge.

Knowledge Café is one of several techniques for KM. It is simple, could be both structured and unstructured, is a gateway to other techniques, and interfaces with other KM techniques. The conversation at the café brings all knowledge workers to participate in the small-group discussions of knowledge exchange and transfer.

I want to stir and provoke your curiosity for new knowledge creation, transfer, and innovation. There's a clarion call to capture, transfer, and retain the most-critical knowledge of the organization. If we're going to be relevant, innovate, and become efficient and resilient, we must identify, capture, share, and reanimate knowledge and create new knowledge. Knowledge Café is an organic tool to achieve this. If you have a difficult conversation, if there are silos and uncertainties, if there's a genuine hunger for new knowledge, if you want to cut through the clusters of formalities and espouse free and win-win exchange of ideas and knowledge, just café it! Could you take it to the café?

I intend to join other knowledge enthusiasts and tech industries to bring knowledge management from predominantly in the halls of academia to the center of national discourse with the simplicity and appeal that a café offers.

In this book, I shall use the café as a mindset, a space to create the environment for knowledge exchange, transfer, and management. We shall explore how to design an effective Knowledge Café; how the café interfaces with other KM methods and techniques; what to expect from disruptive technology and tendencies; how to share best practices, communicate with employees, and positively reinforce the knowledge-sharing behaviors and recognition schemes; spark innovation through knowledge exchange; how to create a leadership café; what a thriving knowledge management environment looks like; and finally, the value and fun of knowledge stewardship. In the café-saucer is a rare blend of hindsight, insight, and foresight of knowledge conversations.

Just café it!

1 ■ Knowledge Curiosity

Chapter Objectives

- Human curiosity and the quest for knowledge
- Relate the café experience to the Knowledge Café
- Understand today's information and knowledge landscape
- How does the Knowledge Café help us?

1.1. THE CURIOSITY OF THE CAFÉ-GOER

If you remember everything you learned in a day, you are not learning enough. Hence, we've got to learn agile.

Why do people go to the neighborhood café? Reasons I've heard include free Wi-Fi, caffeine or great beverages, a hit playlist, the arts, boardroom away from the office and home, unstructured, loud or quiet, location everyone agrees to, and so on. At the café, you can share conversation and ideas away from home or office—strategize and share big ideas, plan, draw inspiration, or simply catch up on your social media. Café-goers can caffeinate but also embrace curiosity-driven connections. It's a sharing space to ask and answer questions and exchange knowledge. We want to make sense or meaning of our world, what we know, right? We want that "aha!" moment that doesn't happen in instructions or one-dimensional settings. "Aha!" moments occurs in dialogue, conversation, and a peer-learning knowledge exchange environment. The café is the space for this.

THE RIGHT CONDITION AND ENVIRONMENT THAT ATTRACT PEOPLE TO THE KNOWLEDGE CAFÉ

Everyone will come to the café if the following takes place:

- There's a grand rule that guarantees a dialogue, not a debate, and everyone has an equal voice.
- Everyone agrees to the why, what, when, and where of a café.
- There will be conversations, not a lecture.
- They have crazy ideas well up in their alleys they are dying to share.
- It's not a gathering of perfect ideas and too structured.
- Conversation is king.
- There's a space where people and systems talk *to* each other rather than *at* each other.
- There's a desire for simplicity.
- Curiosity for new learning and knowledge exchange is embraced.
- All have a desire to make sense of what they know.
- Covenant: Belief in knowledge transfer and reciprocity is commonly shared.
- All believe that someone will hear them out.
- When there's a pivot from knowledge to understanding.
- There's empathy rather than sympathy.
- They can leave sympathy behind and reconnoiter empathy.
- There's a willingness to learn agile.

- You see knowledge as a means of production.
- Hunger to steward and revivify knowledge.
- Third place: Café is that space outside home and office where one can collaborate.
- Fun: There's something that compliments a café experience.

Why Curiosity?

The solution is yet to be discovered. There is no predefined outcome. We're open to learning agility and designing something new. The idea of a Knowledge Café stirs our youthful curiosity. Can we take the concept of the neighborhood café and apply it to knowledge management (KM): sharing, exchange, transfer, and leadership?

> It means that the Knowledge Café is a conversational process and a mindset that brings a group of people together to share experiences, test crazy ideas, learn from each other, make new acquaintances, build relationships and make a better sense of a rapidly changing, complex, less predictable world to improve decision making, innovation and the ways in which we work together.

It's fair to say that I have utilized most of the principles of the Knowledge Café extensively since the late nineties, before I met David Gurteen a few years ago. Knowledge Café is the town square for knowledge exchange and stewardship. See the café as your civic knowledge center, market square, city/public square, urban square, or city gate for knowledge sharing and exchanges. Think of piazza, plaza, Utne Reader Salons, and town green to connect, learn, make sense, exchange knowledge, and exhilarate. The café concept is not just about knowledge exchange but making sense of our world, understanding, and making meaning—this is what makes the café different from other forms of conversational gathering and meetings (see table 2). If you have ever attended a brown-bag learning or brainstorming session, lesson learned and after-action events; arrangements like instructor-led, problem-solving, decision-making, status update, information sharing, team-building, and innovation meetings, networking, lunch-n-learn, town hall learning sessions, conferences, workshop and symposium, project stand-up/huddles meetings or gatherings, you probably utilized some of the concepts of the café. I'll explain the difference more in chapter 2.3 and 2.6. There'll be a café framework and step-by-step approach to be discussed in chapter 4.3.

As both a space and mindset, the café is an open knowledge space commonly found in the heart of a traditional knowledge exchange and transfer community. It's high time we brought KM to the town square of the café! Everyone can't afford the country club of KM. Every knowledge is not critical, but every knowledge is relevant. The café recognizes the relevance of every knowledge and idea. It's the café mindset and infrastructure that brings this to reality. In a café, there's a paradigm shift and learning agility—the way and where we learn changes. How we learn, gather to learn, share, and renew knowledge is entirely different and simplified.

WHAT HAPPENS AT A CAFÉ
In the café orbit, we are

- Making sense of the world
- Making meaning of what we know or what we think we know
- Building relationships and understanding
- Creating new knowledge
- Building coherence, maybe even consensus
- Improving dialogue
- Surfacing problems and opportunities
- Breaking down silos
- Engaging in personal development
- Creating new knowledge
- Innovating
- Sense-making, which is its primary purpose or benefit

Little has been written or said about the Knowledge Café. We can expand this concept to create a current, cross-generational, systematic environment designed to transfer, retain, and manage relevant knowledge. Coming to the Knowledge Café also stirs our curiosity.

Greek biographer Plutarch said, "The mind is not a vessel to be filled but a fire to be kindled." The knowledge fire at the café is kindled: new relationships and genuine connections begin, new knowledge is birthed, and innovation springs up. It's a simple and unstructured (can also be structured) environment and a gateway to knowledge management that everyone can identify with.

As said in the preface, knowledge creation and transfer are incomplete without socialization and cross-pollination of knowledge from one state to another—when knowledge workers talk to each other and machines talk to each other and when knowledge constantly changes states.

Nonaka and Takeuchi introduced the SECI model (Nonaka & Takeuchi, 1996), which has become the cornerstone of knowledge creation and transfer theory, and Nonaka (1994) identified four mechanisms for knowledge creation:

1. Socialization: whereby an individual shares tacit (intuitive) knowledge like know-hows, know-whats, and know-whys—those personal knowledge used by knowledge workers to perform their work that often makes sense only in their worlds. Sharing of experiences through observation, imitation, and practice.
2. Combination: whereby one piece of explicit knowledge like knowledge that can be captured in the form of text, tables, diagrams, product specifications is combined with other;
3. Externalization: a process whereby tacit knowledge is made explicit; and
4. Internalization: a process of experiencing knowledge through an explicit source, where explicit knowledge is converted into tacit.

My goal is to stimulate the appetite and curiosity for knowledge culture in all types of organizations. I want to stir curiosity for knowledge stewardship. I want to advocate the institutionalization of a simple café format against cumbersome knowledge management concepts and present a sequel to Gurteen's Knowledge Café.

We Are in a Knowledge Revolution!
A knowledge revolution surrounds us. Today, there are more than 50,000 free online books in every genre. According to the Association of American Publishers' annual report in 2019, publishers of books in all formats made almost $26 billion in revenue in 2018 in the United States, $22.6 billion in printed books, and $2.04 billion in e-books. According to a Pew Research survey, one in every five Americans now listen to audiobooks (Perrin, 2019). There is an estimated 4.66 billion people (Datareportal, 2020) of the global population, more than 60 percent that have access to the Internet—probably one of the most transformative innovations in the last century. In the world today, there are more than 5 billion mobile devices, and over half of these connections are smartphones (Silver, 2019).

Old-style retrieval, capture, and information-sharing tools cannot keep up with the information explosion. The environment for capturing and sharing knowledge is being transformed in extraordinary ways. For example, bookless libraries are stored in the cloud and can be accessed by anyone with an Internet connection. Ever-increasing computer processing speeds, artificial intelligence, virtual reality, and social media create virtual communities and the future's social connectivity.

With all this emerging technology, how do we incorporate the vast amount of information with developing knowledge relevant to our organizations and our lives? If COVID-19 has shown us anything, it's how indispensable technology is to modern life. Serendipitously, digital transformation has fallen on us. There was a poll on Twitter to survey who was instrumental to your company's digital transformation: Your CEO, CIO, CTO, or COVID-19? The majority answered, COVID-19.

Science provides us data, information, technology, and knowledge, but we need wisdom that requires the interaction of social sciences and the application of knowledge and human insight. The curiosity, the quest for greater interaction, conversation, digital media, and face-to-face or virtual knowledge exchange, is more important than ever. Human interactions remain the greatest enabler for transferring all human core capabilities, aptitude and making knowledge transfer a reality. People are still searching for knowledge and wisdom. Human faces around a cup of tea or coffee are irreplaceable. With social distancing, virtual cafés accomplished the same. Connection and exchanging information and knowledge are essential to us as people. The emerging technologies enable these exchanges, both virtual and IRL (in real life).

Knowledge Café is a current, multigenerational, systematic concept designed to transfer, retain, and manage relevant knowledge. Retirements increased job mobility, and information silos create an inevitable "brain drain" and loss of an organization's critical intellectual capital. Without the retention and application of the learned knowledge of those who came before us, our organizations will be poorly equipped to stay relevant in today's constantly evolving environment of innovation.

The curiosity of the café-goer can be satisfied virtually and face-to-face. I hold a monthly virtual global Knowledge Café for project managers, and participants collaborate across the globe. The café can take place in the office space, online, or at an offsite location.

The keys are curiosity and a sustained attitude of learning. So, grab your laptop and a latte. Get comfy as you enjoy the delicacies and modern conveniences of this caffeinated knowledge sharing space. Share knowledge, connect, collaborate, cross-pollinate small and great ideas—and make them a reality, and reanimate knowledge.

1.2. FILLING THE KNOWLEDGE GAPS

Why are we devoting a book to the concept of a space to share and transfer knowledge? What is the relevance in today's world?

Knowledge Is the New Factor of Production

My people are destroyed for lack of knowledge.
—Hosea 4:6 (NASB, 1995)

One could argue that knowledge is the greatest enemy of sickness, disease, ignorance, poverty, and failure. We learned in Economics

101 about three factors of production—land, labor, and capital. Dr. Denise Bedford of Georgetown University and other knowledge thinkers like Baumol, Braunstein, Porat, and Nick Bontis contend that knowledge is an emerging source of wealth and a new primary factor of production—knowledge as capital is the dominant principle in the factor production. Knowledge is the most significant currency in the project economy. Everyone manages a project, program, or operation to solve problems and deliver results, whether at the office or in their personal lives. As a professional project manager, I manage complex and complicated projects with challenging stakeholder relationships. In more accurate words, I often manage projects and stakeholders from hell. My typical day involves someone's pants on fire, and exceptions are my routine! Working in this environment means I need to learn fast, collaborate, preserve the context, or introduce more risk to my projects.

Knowledge is critical to our organizations and us. However, as a project manager, I have witnessed systems that do not talk to each other or share data, and groups and people who don't converse and silo or hoard their knowledge. For me, the concept of a Knowledge Café helped fill the gaps (see figure 1). We are inundated with data and information. We need a context for this information to give it meaning and value to our organizations and us. In the knowledge economy, production and services are based on knowledge-intensive activities that contribute to an accelerated pace of technical and scientific advance and rapid obsolescence. Success depends on the accessibility of knowledge and skilled workers to add context and meaning. As organizations understand the magnitude of a potential loss of valuable intellect and skills in our knowledge economy, the demand for a simple analogy to implement knowledge management will be immediate. As you see in figure 1 on the next page, the Knowledge Café helps satisfy the need to share, reuse, bolster, and create innovation knowledge.

Data are just facts until they are organized and connected; information isn't valuable without context that creates knowledge. Consider brokers or investors reading the stock page of a newspaper (acquiring information), but then turn and talk with their colleagues

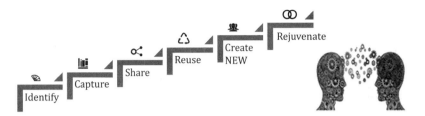

Figure 1: Knowledge is the most important currency in a project economy.

about their stocks (knowledge). Café is the space where this kind of exchange happens. Apply knowledge, and you have long-lasting wisdom. For example, data and information are readily available about the danger of behaviors such as texting and driving. We all have this information, but how often do we put ourselves into the situation to realize the knowledge of these destructive behaviors? We become wise only when we apply our knowledge.

KNOWLEDGE ASSUMPTIONS

Let's test our assumptions about knowledge. Do you agree or disagree with these assumptions?

- No one knows all they know.
- Everyone knows something that no one knows.
- Everyone has shared what they know.
- Some people will not share their knowledge due to constraints.
- Everyone can share their knowledge.
- Everyone can be rewarded for sharing their knowledge.
- My workplace has both good and terrible silos.
- My café's preference can be noisy or quiet.

In my experience of asking these questions at conferences and at work, everyone agrees with these assumptions! Our curiosity toward knowledge, how we steward it, share it, innovate, and reuse it is critical. Will people who are not inclined to share ideas or ask for others' ideas be "found in" or visit a café at all? Are they more likely to grab their coffee and run back to their isolated spaces? The environment will determine.

Lack of a single source of truth for café-goers led me to developing an enterprise wiki knowledge library and a Knowledge Café for all knowledge workers. I was looking for a knowledge-centric environment.

In fact, according to Jez Arroway, about 85 percent of our information, document, and knowledge repository are "ROT (Random, Obsolete, and Trivial); we spend 20% of time searching for something we have in-house, but we were just using the pantry" (Arroway, 2019). What's radically absent is the interoperability of these systems. Today, there are countless effective knowledge-sharing tools out there.

My challenge was an absence of a Knowledge Library site or a complete enterprise search solution—one that gives us a single, personalized place to access all relevant information, insights, and knowledge wherever they live. A solution designed to quickly capture and share ideas by creating simple pages and linking them together, enabling the organization of ideas, knowledge, and documents into some logical and searchable repositories. Wiki knowledge library features could be used for various knowledge-sharing purposes. In my work and experience, there has been a need to get the café participation of multiple subject matter experts contributing content, updating FAQs, sharing new knowledge, and mentoring others in one interactive repository. I see the need to provide a single source of truth for scattered and disparate resources, files, knowledge, and know-how all over company repositories and websites. This is a challenge in both private and public-sector organizations. Version management: I want to see a link to manuals, processes, and regularly updated procedures, pulling the most recent version. Some of our café-goers tell me that they want to keep their SOPs alive, updated regularly, and not bury them in repositories. They want it to be a constant resource for project plans, training new employees, and a single-source lexicon for the project and program terminologies.

Today, as a result of Knowledge Café engagements with diverse knowledge workers and café-goers, we are developing an enterprise Wiki Knowledge Library (Wiki) for our knowledge café-goers, CoPs, and teams—a one-stop-shop for knowledge transfer and exchange.

A key tool for project managers is "lessons learned" from previous projects. However, when lessons learned are kept in repositories—not curated, not indexed, and unsearchable—that knowledge requires an awakening. I recommend living lessons. Every organization keeps a database of all the previously executed projects' information and records, and this information may be stored in a central repository as part of the Organizational Process Assets (OPA). So, OPA may include but is not limited to all the documents, templates, policies, procedures, plans, guidelines, lessons learned, historical data and information, earned value, estimating, risk, and so on. There should be a "living lesson learned." Living lessons learned are those lessons learned that are documented throughout the five processes of the project management and during operations and program implementations. These are converted into existing processes and procedures, utilized during the same project, post-project, and project-postmodern. There has to be a deliberate process of knowledge transfer and management in the organization—and the creation of a knowledge culture, where no one will have to reinvent the wheel! The only reason why we reinvent the wheel is because of ignorance. Ignorance is a choice and an antithesis of Knowledge. Knowledge, if not managed, is lost forever! We all face similar challenges in our projects. What is a new demon to you may be a tired old demon to another person.

To satisfy my hunger for creating and sharing knowledge, I find myself using post-implementation reviews, informal networking, and customer outreach. Using a café environment for sharing and incorporating lessons learned could breathe new life into this process! We can embrace standard project information that is easy to find and access, shareable, and reusable rather than maintaining redundancy and reinventing the wheel.

Is the technology made to connect people, or does it replace people? I found technology becoming the virus injected into a system meant to heal it, but it eventually killed it . . .

My ideal landscape of technology and content enablers includes a fully integrated and centralized project portfolio management (PPM) platform; searchable lessons learned repositories; stories, oral history, and knowledge interviews; database inventory of knowledge assets; systems for tracking of competence, experience, assignments, and specific expertise; indexed online video collections for knowledge application; innovation registers; Yellow Pages or directory of subject matter experts; and other knowledge transfer-related software resources. Wouldn't that be an efficient knowledge system?

These knowledge management gaps and tools fueled my curiosity, activated my adaptive thinking, and swelled my KM creative capabilities.

As I'm writing this book, the city of Tacoma, Washington, has created a digital permitting solution to change how its civic government interacts with its citizens. Tacoma residents now have 24/7 access to digital planning and permitting transactions, with complete visibility into their application status. Besides, the city has reduced labor for internal staff and cut the application processing time. How cool is that! KM simplified customer experience.

We cannot be more potent than our knowledge. Our victories and accomplishments are directly proportional to the depth of our knowledge. One might argue that our success is proportional to how well we can apply our knowledge to execute behaviors. People fail or succumb not because they are unlucky or weak but because of deficiency in knowledge or ignorance or not managing knowledge. When we stop growing in grace and knowledge in all societies or organizations, we become irrelevant; there will be no innovation. It takes knowledge leadership to grasp this.

Knowledge transfer or exchange doesn't work until there's knowledge leadership. I stand the risk of sounding poetic; however, knowledge transfer needs the right space because it is a flowing river. It's iterative, progressive, continuous, deliberate, reciprocating, and rejuvenating. Knowledge is also transient.

OTHER KNOWLEDGE MANAGEMENT CHALLENGES
- An atmosphere of trust and motivation
- Identifying institutional knowledge assets
- Developing and sustaining an agile workforce
- KM in an era of artificial intelligence and human–machine collaborations
- Identifying the risk of knowledge loss and strategies to mitigate loss for high-risk knowledge

- Fostering cross-disciplinary engagement and collaboration
- Practices to engage new knowledge
- Executive sponsorship of KM
- An aging workforce

We will address some of these challenges throughout the book.

1.3. MANAGING PERSONAL KNOWLEDGE

My purpose in writing this book is to stimulate our appetite for knowledge culture in all types of organizations—to stir our curiosity for knowledge and encourage knowledge management as part of all organizations' discourse. First, we must look at how we manage our personal knowledge. Personal or explicit knowledge is both dynamic and challenging to classify. Every learning animal and curious knowledge exchanger comes to the café with their personal knowledge. It increases awareness and increases the likelihood that you'll realize what you don't know and think about spending more time in a "café-like environment."

Knowledge is by its nature personal. Knowledge and knowledge management begins with the individual. Anyone who has ever said or done anything has knowledge. Before discussing organizational knowledge, I must first be curious about managing my personal knowledge. Harvard Business School professor Dr. Dorothy Leonard talks about "deep smarts," the stuff that produces that mysterious quality: good judgment. Deep smarts represent the most in-depth knowledge and understanding possessed by specific experts within an organization (Leonard, 2017). I'll call it accrued knowledge. Do I know what I know, and have I taken advantage of what I know?

What do you do with knowledge? It's the means to an end. It's the capital you use to innovate and solve problems. It's the means that every other means relies upon. You create wealth with knowledge. New knowledge becomes an innovation. We solve problems with knowledge. Knowledge is the beginning of wisdom. It's one of those necessary tools in your wisdom toolkits, like rationality, insight, and intelligence. Even though all of these are contextual, meaning that one can have knowledge in one subject or area and

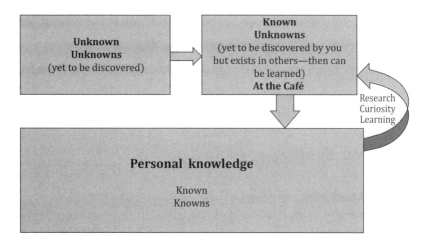

Figure 2: Connecting personal knowledge to the unknowns.

lack knowledge in another area, you could say that someone is wise but lacks insight, rationality, intelligence, and knowledge. Now, wear your curiosity belt, and let's go!

Do you know how much you know? Do you know what you know? Do you know all that you know? Do you know where your knowledge banks are stored and how to access them? When was the last time you updated your ideas, innovation, dreams, and goals? At least, for those who are not self-employed, an updated résumé means that someone is updating their capabilities and achievements. When was the last time you documented what you know? When was the last time you updated your professional résumé? As seen in figure 2, I like to use the concept of known unknowns (things that are known by others—new learnings) versus unknown unknowns (things that no one knows and require curiosity, new learning, research/innovation to solve) to convey how we connect the known and the unknown at the café.

Imagine having in one place all your personal information: medical history, academic, fitness, financial, training, professional, business, and family records; all your lessons learned, accomplishments, successes, and failures at your fingertips. With one code or just one voice command, you could access them from a secure and encrypted place where they have been indexed, curated, analyzed, and saved securely. This would be the ultimate personal KM system. This scenario, however, does raise questions of security and privacy.

To assemble my knowledge assets at one location, I keep a personal knowledge register. I also keep a dream book and personal milestone register, where I record major personal and professional victories and successes. These are my personal KM systems.

Why a personal knowledge register? A personal knowledge register will make one café-ready at home or in your organization. I have accumulated so much knowledge over the years that I cannot recollect everything. My knowledge register fills in the gaps. Retention increases when you document your knowledge in a register, whether handwritten or typed; revision, addition, or rewriting and sharing your knowledge register and notes with family and friends enforces information and knowledge retention. We can separate manageable knowledge from supposed knowledge, preexisting knowledge, or new knowledge in a knowledge register.

According to Pam A. Mueller, Princeton University, and Daniel M. Oppenheimer, the University of California, "the pen is mightier than the keyboard" (2014). They maintain that students who take notes by hand learn more than those who take notes on a laptop. Writing and rewriting increases learning and internalization of learning. Research by Jeffrey D. Wammes and Melissa E. Meade, professors at the University of Waterloo, Ontario, Canada, shows that drawing to-be-learned information or depicting to-be-learned information via visuals enhances memory and boosts performance by encouraging the integration of semantic, visual, and motor aspects of memory (Wammes, Meade, & Fernandes, 2016). Adding graphics or drawings representing concepts, terms, and relationships to your knowledge register helps internalize your knowledge and improves memory and learning.

I document every training I have taken in my knowledge register, every new thing that I have learned, and every project that I have accomplished, including major tasks. I highlight the cost-saving I provided to my organization, efficiencies I helped to enhance. I record the number of people I mentored since one of my goals is to mentor one million knowledge leaders. I record lectures and presentations that

I delivered, the number of hours I volunteered, projects at home that I have accomplished, reviews, lessons I have learned, the mistakes I have made, the significant choices I have made, and their outcomes.

A healthy knowledge culture must understand what it knows (skills, experiences, and expertise of the project team and other stakeholders), and what it needs to know (the known unknowns and unknown-unknown tacit knowledge in the minds of its employees).

> Tacit knowledge is difficult to capture. As seen in figure 2, it dwells in the known unknowns. There are three simple ways to capture tacit knowledge: by creating a culture of knowledge-sharing to change ownership competition mindset, creating an incentive for sharing knowledge, and creating opportunities for sharing—the café responds to all three.

It needs to know where what is known and what it should know reside or are housed and how to make them easily accessible and transferable across projects and the enterprise. The Knowledge Café is the place to update our knowledge.

We use the known and sometimes documented knowledge as a segue to the known unknowns and then to discover the unknown unknowns. As seen in figure 2, with our personal knowledge, what we know, we can discover what others know and explore the unknowns. With what we know, curiosity to learn and research drives us to the café to meet the known and the unknown. All the known and unknown head to the café. We come to the café to share what we registered and learn what others registered. Some of the most popular questions I ask at a café are, "Share some things that stand out in your personal knowledge register. What did you know lately that you wished you'd known 10 years ago?"

Look at it this way: knowledge gains value through use and is of no value if it's not used or reused.

Randy Hopmann, an engineer and former director of district operations at Texas Department of Transportation (TxDOT), told me, "You are not doing a thing if you have not made a mistake." I bring to the fore new things I am supposed to have learned but just bumped into them—books I read, places I visited, valued connections I made in conferences or Knowledge Café events. These have helped me know what I know today. When I update my résumé, I take hold of my knowledge register, and I am always blown away by the things I didn't know that I knew. During my career evaluation, I can use the things that I know to tell the story of what I know and have accomplished. When I go to a job interview, I can explain what I know I have done clearly and what I'm capable of doing. This is how I manage my knowledge—if you don't capture it, you will lose it. The things I know become an inspiration. They activate my curiosity for innovation.

Personal Knowledge Register (PKR)

A knowledge register is more than a personal journal. A personal knowledge journal is also a personal knowledge portfolio. Just like you grow your financial portfolio, you should grow and cultivate your knowledge portfolio. Documentation is an essential process in knowledge transfer. So, journaling is part of PKR. I keep a Victory Register as part of my PKR. Here, I register all memorable knowledge, events, and milestones during the year. As seen in table 1, this is just a snapshot of hundreds of my PKR, without being too personal and detailed. It's a treasure.

When I'm in a café event with others, we cross-pollinate ideas on our accomplishments and failures and demonstrate curiosity for new knowledge, which emerges from existing knowledge. Organizational knowledge management, as complicated as it can be, begins with curiosity and personal knowledge management. It starts with deep thinking, meditation, personal reflection, questions and answers, feedback, and teaching others, sharing what we know.

All these are attributes of personal knowledge management. This speaks to assistant professor of the Degroote Business School professor Nick Bontis's Attitudes and Behaviors category, part of Human Capital, and highly undertreated in the KM literature. When we have these attributes and behaviors, can we say that we know what you know?

What do you do with what you know? How do you steward it? How do you make what you know accessible to you? Do you leave

Table 1. Personal Knowledge Register (PKR)

Activity	Goals, Dreams, and Aspirations	Results
My Growth Plan: Growth Milestone Every 5 Years		

1. Learn at least three new creative ideas every day. That's how you get to one new viable concept quarterly—or maybe more.
  a. Attended webinars on the following topics: artificial intelligence, stakeholder engagement, project management, knowledge management, financial management, leadership development, innovation, and problem-solving
  b. Read a book
  c. Learn one new concept or a problem-solving strategy
  d. Meet and learn from at least one of my mentors every month
2. Impact at least one person every week
  a. Increase the number of new mentees by x percent
  b. Focus on family
3. Social media outreach
4. Write a book
5. Develop a new presentation
6. Volunteer in a nonprofit
7. Obtain at least one terminal degree, diploma, license, or certification ever 5 years		

Training and Projects		
Research and develop project management training and workshop materials	Benchmark or follow PMI guidelines, NCHRP Scan research, 52-member AASHTO, and TRB Knowledge Management community, KM industry standards, knowledge fairs, and café and brainstorming outcomes for SMEs and researchers	Completed January 2020; modified materials based on class feedback

Table 1. (*continued*)

Date: **Knowledge:** Financial Markets **New Knowledge:** Trained on stock trading and invested; tested my attitude to risk—level of my risk aversion. **Risk/Fear Overcame:** Financial investment fear; you can gain a lot or lose everything. **Relevance to Career**: Risk management **Regrets:** Not doing this earlier	• Grow portfolio by 50 in 2020 • Options and Futures trading • Assigned a percentage of my savings and investment to the stock market	Opportunity in the stock market. **Wow!** One needs knowledge, patience, and the right strategy to win in this space. Realized that one could participate in the stock market with little or a lot of money.
Date: **Knowledge:** Enterprise Project Management **New Knowledge:** Designed an Enterprise Project Management Dev Program **Risk/Fear Overcame:** • A new challenge worth taking • Learned how to integrate these into the toolbox of my CoP effectively	Train 60 project managers of PMs by July 2016 with PMP certification Follow PMI guidelines Institutionalize PM in the agency Secure career pathway for all PMs in the agency	Trained 60 project managers 24 certified in the first 6 months and more than 100 by 2020 Received a Certificate of Achievement for outstanding honorable performance for high standards of excellence by TxDOT Executive Director, 2016 **Wow!** • The enthusiasm this sparked was terrific.

(*continued*)

Table 1. (*continued*)

• I initially thought that more people were smarter and more seasoned to take on this project, feeling inadequate. • I'm now a "possibiliterian" **Relevance to Career:** KM career **Regrets:** Not doing this earlier; how far these tools will meet the needs of the CoPs		• Dozens of PMs on the waiting list with zero marketing efforts for the program. • Several participants have advanced their careers after participating in this program; each letter of promotion and new position I receive from participants makes my day (one person had 45% increase from a new offer after certification)
Knowledge: Collaboration and conducting a meeting with WebEx, Zoom, and Jabber **New Knowledge:** Explored collaborative functions of these tools **Risk/Fear Overcame:** New challenge **Relevance to Career:** KM career **Regrets:** Not doing this earlier	Conducted several leadership meetings with these tools	Part of my KM technology enablers

Table 1. (*continued*)

New Ideas, Inspirations, Places, and WOW Moments Write all new ideas and inspirations in this register.		
• Identified, researched, and developed Knowledge Café as a KM tool • Secured a book deal with Berrett-Koehler Publishers after presenting at the PMI Global Conference in Los Angeles • Presented on project management and knowledge management in 16 cities, learned new cultures, made new friends, broadened my networks • Developed a workshop on Help! Managing Projects and Stakeholders from Hell • Held 5 leadership cafés in Austin	10 Knowledge Café events in the year, targeting different solutions and professions Curating, indexing, storing, and making lessons learned and knowledge interviews/storytelling, accessible, searchable, and findable across the enterprise	Met thrice in the first quarter and scheduled gatherings for the next quarter Gather friends or coworkers in a new location monthly for a Knowledge Café Knowledge Café solves family problems, convening innovators, leaders, PMs, SMEs, compassion and NGOs, the interface of government, business, and faith communities, etc.

(*continued*)

Table 1. (*continued*)

Serendipities: Great Discoveries, Tricks, Innovative Ideas		
Date:	Savings $	Savings $
Knowledge: Financial wellness **New Knowledge:** Saving from buying quantities; Stumbled onto two discount stores in Austin; Disciple of family monthly budget **Risk/Fear Overcame:** New challenge **Relevance to Career**: Financial responsibilities and wellness **Regrets:** Not doing this earlier	• Initiated the Hope Water project for poor communities in my home country • Learned the best way to buy a car • Learned the best way to make international shipment • Learned the best way to send money abroad	**Wow!** • Attended David Ramsey's Financial University class • Saved $25 on one item from a discount store • You cannot grow bigger than you give • Learned how to set up a home office with multiple monitors, and furniture • Learned how to set up the trampoline with kids; the bonding with my teenage kids

it to chance? You are truly responsible for managing your knowledge. You should know what you need to advance in your career. Know whom to connect with. Everyone cannot contribute to your knowledge and growth.

Life is like sitting in a café where you choose your own seat. You don't wait for someone to choose for you. Similarly, if you expect your boss to manage your knowledge for you, you will be in for a long wait.

HOW TO CHOOSE YOUR SEAT IN A CAFÉ
- Decide what you want—quiet or hot spot?
- Choose your café friends the same as your other friends
- Evaluate your knowledge
- Take a bold step

- Be intentional and proactive
- Walk through the cluster
- Locate your seat
- Occupy your seat
- Don't feel guilty for making your choice or applying your knowledge; this is wisdom

These are some of the essential features of a productive Knowledge Café. I've seen many really "wasted café" spaces—both virtual and physical—because there was no set of shared assumptions and beliefs about what would happen there and why you would "go there." Know why you are going to the café. The café is for knowledge.

Take this opportunity to develop a knowledge register of your own (see table 1). Organize them, rank them, prioritize them, make them memorable, make them findable, and make them searchable in your mind. You are the only one who can identify what you need to know that is relevant for your growth and advancement. Take responsibility for managing what you know and how you apply what you know to your life. Is it beneficial to conduct a "SWOT" analysis (Strengths, Weaknesses, Opportunity, Threats) of your knowledge register? With SWOT, one would know where they stand about their knowledge assets. Strengths are your personal mission-critical knowledge, something you can share, and the knowledge that makes you unique. Weaknesses are something where gaps exist in your knowledge base, and you need some input from your peers. Opportunity is where you can relate particular knowledge assets to your career growth, and the threat is where some knowledge can possibly harm or have ill effects on the community. For instance, in wireless technology, saving passwords is convenient but may be inviting more cyberattacks and identity thefts.

1.4. PEOPLE FIRST, THEN PROCESS OR TECHNOLOGY

If you have the guts to help people find their way and excel at what they do, wouldn't you like to have a coffee with them? If you have the time to write a six-page process description, wouldn't you have a need for 30 minutes to know more about the person you are helping? If you accompany someone through the process of whittling down complications while sharing what you know, wouldn't you expect a thread of endearment? There's no replacement for a personal touch.

So, don't throw technology at people. It's an enabler and a stakeholder.

Knowledge management rests on three enablers: people, process, and information/technology, and some may argue that the fourth leg is content. I'm puzzled because the predominant discussions about KM convey complicated processes and technology. The history of this three-legged stool is traceable back to the 1990s Ackoff model. KM was in progress for 30 years before we had affordable technology. It just helped us to popularize it. Now that it is a commonplace, it is reverting into the background. Technology is *only* an enabler, and it can also be a *disabler*! People become lost in a sea of complexity. Again, ignoring the knowledge transfer preferences of the knowledge creators and users is very rampant. What is missing are people and a mindset of simplicity—a simple and easy-to-use knowledge base and social collaboration space. How can you know the intellectual capital—the knowledge locked up in people's minds and hearts—without knowing the people themselves? How can you know or learn from people without some relationship?

We genuinely look for relational as opposed to transactional learning. You don't want to learn from or share knowledge with people you dislike. Café conversation and relationships are more natural and realistic than the mechanical transaction methods where people exchange knowledge because they feel there's an obligation. How can there be a relationship with both virtual and face-to-face connections? One tenet of the Agile Manifesto is face-to-face conversations. How can there be a connection unless the process is simplified and there's a place to meet? With the lessons from COVID-19, collaboration possibilities are limitless. Oprah Winfrey, in her Harvard commencement speech in 2013, said,

And even though this is the college where Facebook was born, my hope is that you would try to go out and have more face-to-face conversations with people you may disagree with. That you'll have the courage to look them in the eye and hear their point of view. And help make sure that the speed and distance and anonymity of our world doesn't cause us to lose our ability to stand in somebody else's shoes and recognize all that we share as a people. This is imperative for you as an individual and for our success as a nation.

Most life problems can only be solved in a face-to-face format. A café mindset makes this possible.

There has to be some way that this darkness can be banished with light. It begins at the café. The café conversation is a panacea.

At the heart of people (the knowledge users and creators) lies the spirituality of knowledge. It occurs to me that we have missed the livewire or spirituality of knowledge, which is the people connection.

The real world has taught me that you don't just manage projects; you lead people and integrate processes to achieve results. If you only manage projects, you can't see the forest for the trees. Alexander Laufer, author and director of the Consortium for Project Leadership at the University of Wisconsin–Madison, contends, "The key is that projects must be led, not just managed. We need both leadership and management, but right now, the prevailing paradigm is that projects are managed—that planning and control can solve all the problems. My studies have shown me again and again that the best projects are, first of all, led and managed or led to be manageable. I found the traditional project management methodology was missing a formal 'knowledge' component—and need more of the people-leadership element" (Cohen, 2009). The "directing manager" should not turn the café into an old-style classroom and stop all that sharing before it begins. Café is currently taking place in several classrooms today.

Professional practitioners are the exclusive custodians of their own business knowledge. They need to recognize the benefits of sharing their knowledge. It's debatable who owns the project or work knowledge, but you don't own what you don't know. Best practices for organizations require an environment where knowledge sharing not only exists but is nourished and rewarded. Rather than "them versus us," see knowledge as jointly owned. My most innovative results occur when I exchange expertise, pollinate ideas, and aggressively share knowledge with all the project's stakeholders. When knowledge is openly shared, it ignites new information. New information reliably begets innovation.

How do you know your organization's critical knowledge, or, when, and how to share? Once the organization's critical intellectual capital is identified, it needs to be captured, acquired, interpreted, analyzed, transformed, curated, and made available, findable for future stakeholders. Forums must be developed where knowledge workers can interact to share and broker their experience, resulting in new knowledge and innovation. I'll discuss communities of practice in chapter 12.

I became disenchanted with the information silos that occur without some sort of knowledge sharing. We have several lessons-learned repositories, and *nothing* is learned! The right environment and the right mindset are critical for knowledge exchange to be possible. Knowledge must be contextualized or it's nothing. I perpetually felt as if I was inefficiently reinventing the wheel each time I led a project—it was like chasing rainbows! Do we have a need for knowledge leadership? Yes. Knowledge leadership cafés provide oversight and governance to a knowledge system.

I have witnessed "brain drain" on my projects due to retirements, increased job mobility, and information silos. I was terrified by the number of valuable experts aging out of my professional environment. For instance, the surveyors and geomatics scientists' community of practice at the Texas Department of Transportation (TxDOT) participate in knowledge exchanges, fairs, and cafés because an average surveyor is 65 years old. TxDOT is the 12,000-employee flagship government agency in the United States. Even though the public face of the agency is generally associated with the construction and maintenance of the state's immense state highway system—it has under its jurisdiction, 80,455 centerline miles and nearly 55,000 bridges. The agency is also responsible for overseeing aviation, rail, and public transportation systems in the state (TxDOT, 2019). With the looming apocalypse of brain drain, we must alter how we teach, learn, retain, and transfer knowledge from person to person and to systems. A wealth of knowledge was exiting my workplace. How can this exodus of knowledge be mitigated?

ANALYSIS OF THE AMERICAN WORKFORCE TODAY

For the first time in history, five different cohorts make up the American workforce:

The Silent Generation: Born between 1925 and 1946
Baby Boomers: Born between 1946 and 1964
Generation X: Born between 1965 and 1980
Generation Y/Millennials: Born between 1980 and 1995
Generation Z/Centennials: Born after 1996

Each generation is distinct in the way it assimilates information and explains it to become knowledge. By 2029, 76 million of these employees—specifically the baby boomers—will retire from the workforce at about 11,000 per day. An unsettling reality is that by 2030, an estimated 20 percent of Americans will be 65 or older (US Census Bureau, 2014). As these workers age out of the workforce, organizations are experiencing a loss of critical business knowledge, skills, and experience. In most larger organizations, hundreds of project and program managers are duplicating their efforts. Without managing business knowledge, there isn't a method of capitalizing on previous projects' intellectual capital. Work continues at warp speed from project to project without effective knowledge transfer and future business deficits. How can the numerous pockets of knowledge management activities be identified, explained, and recorded? Technology and machines have exploded, with intranets for storing captured knowledge. Do we have the right environment for knowledge sharing? Experts have developed many processes. Where is the standardization of this process? Are these enabling knowledge sharing? You can take a horse to the water, but you cannot force it to drink. The environment is the most significant opportunity enabler or threat for any grand concept, vision, or strategy.

In one of my cultural change projects at TxDOT in 2015, I identified, developed, and led 43 certified project management professionals

(PMPs) to mentor dozens of other PMPs. Every participant in the two pilot projects I managed has a seasoned certified project manager as a mentor, who was a mentor and a coach who created café space for the prospective mentees to ask questions and for the free transfer of project knowledge. I also identified pockets of knowledge management activities in our organization, such as communities of practice, job shadowing, social media activation, team collaboration, data and information management, post-project interviews, team building boot camps, and so on.

With the help of subject matter experts (SMEs) with long institutional knowledge in areas like IT, HR, Communications, Research, Strategy and Innovation, Library and Information Management, Data Science, and so on, we scanned and ranked our organization's KM elements. We identified dozens of elements based on their relevance and value they add toward knowledge identification, capture, sharing, reuse, and rejuvenation. This scan was a guide and roadmap when we developed an enterprise KM strategy.

In all this commotion, it became evident to me that something was missing. Where was the rallying point? As my project progressed in terms of time, resources, and sophistication, I saw the need for a "KM clearinghouse." From a macro and managerial standpoint, there was a demand for a systematic way to procure information from subject matter experts. It was time to aggressively steer the cross-enterprise knowledge workers toward a knowledge society.

There needs to be a conceptual "home base" for KM, and finding it should be as simple as running into a corner café. The café construct establishes the foundation to identify, capture, curate, share, and reuse vital business information and critical intellectual capital. Establish a café space for knowledge enthusiasts to gather, review, discuss, establish strategies and tools for knowledge, to share best practices, gather and address information on successful and innovative project practice, and explore resources for communities of practice. Knowledge Café is a serendipitous and organically grown invention. In my experience, the healthier KM ecosystems foster an interactive space of various interests and diverse patrons. The Knowledge Café brings different, but not necessarily random strangers into one location. The Knowledge Café is straight to the point and will be attractive to millennials responsible for keeping this knowledge transfer movement rolling forward.

I aspired to invite practitioners to a simple conversation space—a Knowledge Café—to brainstorm, investigate, aggregate, and optimize the multiple available knowledge levels. Café-goers are knowledge creators and users who are enthusiastic about knowledge creation, sharing, and velocity. When you have only information and process, knowledge management becomes mechanical and cosmetic. We need to interject a real relational café mindset with organizational learning. People. Relationship. Café. Knowledge.

I've learned more in the Knowledge Café setting throughout my career than in a traditional classroom or boring meetings. In hindsight, the best and the most significant people I've met were through volunteer opportunities—in a café kind of setting. I've harvested the best ideas from such café experiences and turned them into reality. Within the café environment, I let go of my greatest fears and met the best of friends. Learning happens in engaging environments. Information environments tend to be isolated, ingesting environments but not necessarily for deep understanding. And the best part is that we go beyond information at the café to explaining, sharing experiences, deep thinking—this is knowledge.

Knowledge Café is a gateway or introduction to knowledge management. It's that relational mindset for the superiority of tools and space; it accelerates and scales casual conversations over those that focus on documents, artifacts, and cumbersome formality.

Call a knowledge fair and café to begin a knowledge management conversation! A knowledge fair showcases organizational knowledge assets and practices. It is an alternative to traditional presentations and is a more interactive experience. Because there is no one size fits all, I prefer to combine a Knowledge Café with a knowledge fair to add some level of formality. This combination gave me the liberty or leverage to escalate the outcome of a Knowledge Café to leadership café—the outcomes are considered fine-tuned for management policy, institutionalization, and KM implementation. I'll discuss leadership café in chapter 11.

1.5. CASE STUDY: GENERATIONAL CHANGES—THERESA LUEBCKE

This case study by Theresa Luebcke is an indirect attribution of concepts to a third, albeit credentialed party. For context, the Project Management Institute (PMI) is the largest global professional organization for the professional project manager (PMP), one of the credentials offered by PMI. Certified PMPs manage projects in almost all industries, and PMP certification is recognized in every country of the world. PMI has more than 300 chapters with 10 regions. Theresa Luebcke, PMP, was the PMI Region 6 Mentor for 26 chapters in the south-central United States. You can agree with her when she talks about the experience and the efficacy of knowledge transfer. She thinks that you are a better leader, smarter, and even irreplaceable when you share your knowledge and allow knowledge transfer to thrive, and not the other way around. Amen!

Here's Theresa's story:

I began my work in mid-1985 as a supplier to a major manufacturing facility in the Midwest. I quickly learned the "old-timers" (those with 20+ years' experience with the manufacturing company, or the "baby boomers") were reluctant to "share" their knowledge. The mindset, at the time, was: ". . . if I share what I know, someone is going to take my job! If I keep my knowledge to myself, they (the company) cannot afford to get rid of me!" I saw a similar mindset in those who transitioned to the supplier (they had spent many years with the manufacturing company but became employees of the supplier company). They felt a person in management should have worked and therefore know every aspect of the business they were managing. They should not rely on someone they managed (or their "report") to "know" more than they did! I experienced this thinking held true until some of these folks reached retirement age, and new blood began to fill these positions. There was no café or knowledge exchange culture in these environments.

In both situations—employees who remained with the company and those who left to work for the supplier—I did not feel there was a "formal" process to transfer knowledge or an expectation to do so. I saw the knowledge transfer become commonplace with the influx of newer employees wanting to move up (or move on), so they were more apt to share their knowledge with others, so they were not so "irreplaceable."

I like listening to experienced project managers and knowledge brokers like Theresa. No one is irreplaceable, but you become your organization's most critical asset if you are a knowledge broker who shares knowledge. Share your knowledge or become irrelevant!

1.6. CURIOSITY: IDEAS, TIPS, AND TRICKS

I've learned many tips and tricks over the years. I gladly share my ideas with you.

Personal and professional KM systems like Evernote, Google Keep, OneNote, and Google Drive can be used to track your personal knowledge. Enterprise access tools such as SharePoint also offer personal KM features. Some other knowledge capture tools for agile or waterfall teams are easy to use, available on your mobile phone, and can transcribe your notes. Examples are a voice recorder, Agile for Scrum, VersionOne, Jira Software, Audacity, Active Collab, Atlassian Jira + Agile, Cogi, and Otter.ai. The café is not the gathering of people who have stewarded some knowledge and want to know-how. Café is like a show-and-tell of your mental knowledge repository. The personal knowledge register in chapter 1.3 is an enabler. When you use these tools for personal knowledge inventory, you can also bring them to the café and share it with others.

Personal KM involves demonstrations, documentation, teaching others what you know, and social interactions. When you interact with others, it helps you to improve retention levels and capture the big picture. All of us can share what we know. Nobody will know what you know until you share it; both you and others learn better when knowledge is shared. It is when you share what you know that what you know is tested. What do you really know? Personal knowledge is your power, and you can never be smarter than what you know. So, how wise are you? Wisdom is applied knowledge—knowledge is of no value until it's applied. Check what you know and how you use it. People are wise not because they know everything, but because they know what they know and activate it properly. When you know what you know, you will be a wise person.

Learning is supposed to imply knowledge—otherwise, it's just information exposure. We use knowledge to manage projects, relationships, businesses, and innovations but do little or nothing to manage the knowledge itself. How many times have we made a mistake and made the same mistake repeatedly and do not learn from it? I can recollect being a victim of repeating my mistakes, occasionally, which is very sad. Managing my knowledge helps me not to go down the doggy trail of mistakes to really learn.

> Café is about great questions, but don't answer your own questions.

I'd rather be known as a learner than a teacher. It's terrible to teach what you've not learned, and every great teacher is first a fantastic learner. I believe that every leader is a learner. Learners ask questions. When we stop learning, we start dying. We learn to share. We share to learn. Learn or become irrelevant. The best type of learning is conversational—that is where Knowledge Café comes in. Café is dialogue instead of debate, questions and answers. Leadership and management expert John Maxwell even wrote an entire book on the significance of questions in conversation, titled *Good Leaders Ask Great Questions*. He thinks that great questions are important because they unlock and open doors that would otherwise remain closed and are the most effective means of connecting people. The most effective way to connect with others is by asking questions, allowing us to build better ideas and give us a different perspective (Maxwell, 2014).

Café is cross-fertilization of the idea, curiosity for new knowledge, and the most important: making sense of what we know. Ask questions.

Is our brain wired to remember and avoid our last mistake because we'd rather subconsciously believe that it never happened? This is debatable. Memories have a structural component, but there are numerous other functions to the brain, such as perception and planning. Many components have little to do with memory (glia cells, myelin). Memory begins when we respond to outside stimuli and reinforcement compounds to rewire our brain. KM techniques like lessons learned or after-action reviews enable us to remember the last mistake and not make it again, learn and unlearn our past. A Knowledge Café can be organized specifically for this purpose.

There is a mad rush for new learning, new ideas, innovations, and new knowledge. How many people reflect, search, and learn from their mistakes? How many people have taken inventory of what they know? Build on it, sharpen it, and watch and see new knowledge and innovation erupt!

Is it possible to forget what we know? Absolutely. It is possible for us to forget what we know, and it's possible to forget that we forgot. We can know what we forgot. This will happen if we activate our curiosity, cultivate our knowledge, steward what we know, and rekindle our knowledge. It is not how much we learned that matters. It is not how much we think we know, either. What matters is how much we know that we know and what we do with it. You can know one thing, and how you manage it triggers innovation and creativity. You can also learn a ton and feel good about it and not innovate because knowledge alone is not equivalent to innovation. Still, when the knowledge is managed, it produces new knowledge. The new knowledge leads to innovation, just like new research can lead to innovation and further research.

TIPS

- When your systems talk at each other rather than with or to each other, it's a terrible way to manage project knowledge! KM is when systems talk with each other, and there are knowledge exchange conversations.
- Systems should be able to talk to each other; connect them.
- I used to have an employee who always shouted and talked at you when you had a normal discussion. I took our

meetings to the café. Our discussion changed. We began to talk to each other because of the environment. If you have a contentious relationship, try sorting it out in a café. Everyone may learn to grow up.

- When a gap or something is missing, look for it.
- Don't accept a knowledge gap. The status quo is not good enough. Connect the dots.
- You cannot find the gaps until you have analyzed your situation.
- Do you know why we have very few wise people? Could it be because we don't apply our knowledge, the source of wisdom?
- If your solution is not working for you, look for best practice.
- A solution should work for what it's designed for.
- Curiosities drive us to ask questions.
- When you break out of the boundaries of the known paradigm, find new knowledge and innovation.

2 ∎ What Is a Knowledge Café?

Chapter Objectives

- Explore the definition of the café
- Analyze why people go to the café
- Investigate the origin of café
- Identify siloed information and knowledge
- Explore how to bust knowledge and information silos
- Explain how to rejuvenate the knowledge of a project team

2.1. WHAT [THE HECK] IS A KNOWLEDGE CAFÉ?

> I remember that—you know, I didn't receive a formal education.
> I was educated in the Montevideo café, in the cafés of Montevi-
> deo. There, I received my first lessons in the art of telling stories,
> storytelling.
>
> —Eduardo Galeano

Uruguayan journalist Eduardo Galeano said that he was educated
in the café, not in the classroom, library, or conference. Today, most
of my friends are bringing café to their classrooms, workshops, and
conferences. My intention is not to diminish their indisputable
knowledge powers, but knowledge exchange miracles have been happening at the café since time immemorial. Truth be said, many
classrooms are becoming powerful cafés today. I want to choose my
seat, not be seated by others. All of us know something others don't
know. Let's hug halfway in the mug at the café. Let's café our knowledge and knowledge-share in our café.

What Is the Origin of a Café?

Author Adam Gopnik, in his review of Shachar Pinsker's book, *A
Rich Brew: How Cafés Created Modern Jewish Culture* (New York
University), said that cafés "were essential social institutions of political modernity—caffeinated pathways out of clan society and into
a cosmopolitan world. European cafés were 'thirdspaces,' neither entirely public nor entirely private, where revolutionary discourse
flourished" (Gopnik, 2018). Gopnik argued that "the theory, associated with the eminent German sociologist and philosopher Jürgen
Habermas, is that the coffeehouses and salons of the seventeenth and
eighteenth centuries, in part, were foundations of the liberal Enlightenment—a caffeinated pathway out of clan society into cosmopolitan society. Democracy was not made in the streets but among the
saucers" in the cafés. Difficult risk identification and analysis, difficult conversations, friendships, tête-à-tête, and comradery were
formed in café-like environments.

Figure 3: Knowledge Café is the melting pot for learning agility and resilience in a pandemic and post-pandemic era.

Café is a social space, intentionally created outside the state's direct control, work, home, conventional classroom, learning settings, boardrooms, or meeting places, for conversation, collaboration, and coffee or tea. It is the Shachar Pinsker's "thirdspace," where civil societies leave the first place (home) and second place (work) and start to flourish in unexpected ways.

Café as a social institution means many things to many people. To some, it's an escape from the noise or quietness at the home of work. As seen in figure 3, it's a melting pot for knowledge-curious project managers and knowledge workers. To others, it's a theater of flirtation and romance or connection with a similar caffeinated person. While to some it is a central meeting place where your cup's price or the choice of your tea doesn't matter; the smell of food, the art, and simplicity makes all the difference.

So, what [the heck] is a Knowledge Café?

Knowledge management guru and conversational leadership father David Gurteen has been a forerunner of the Knowledge Café through his online blook, *Conversational Leadership*. If you want to know what already exists in terms of knowledge, walk around the café and check out the floorplan before sitting down. Take a break from the business of the day. Walk along some other creative minds in a café. According to May Wong (2014), walking can boost creative output by 60 percent. Enter the space where what the organization knows and what it should know intersects. As you determine the best spot to sit, let's clarify the meaning of the term *knowledge*.

A Knowledge Café is the conceptual "home base" for knowledge management (KM) conversation. It's as simple as a corner café—an unstructured, sometimes structured, and interactive ecosystem for generating ideas, sharing, communicating, and rejuvenating knowledge. It is a straightforward way to begin the conversation about KM. It's the meeting point between knowledge workers and knowledge exchange. Here every knowledge worker has a voice, and no one is judged for their contributions at the café—it's a "judgment-free" or "knowledge safe space." We learn—agile, fast, collaborate, reflect, ask, and answer difficult questions at the café. As Adam Mitchinson and Robert Morris (2014) contended in their research, our focus must shift from the traditional way of learning to finding and developing individuals who are continually able to give up skills, perspectives, and ideas that are no longer relevant and learn new ones that are, challenge status quo, and do it again.

Complementary to the Knowledge Café is a knowledge fair. It is a knowledge event that showcases diverse information, learning styles, knowledge methods and management, and best practice in an organization. Here, knowledge users display what they know, how they capture, share, store, and where what they know resides. Knowledge fairs can be topic-specific or general. Knowledge fairs are put together out of curiosity to know what we know and who knows what.

When I put together my first knowledge fair and café several years ago, there were little to no works of literature on the café practice.

More so, there are divergent opinions on how to realize it. I combined my knowledge fair with a Knowledge Café for one simple reason of bringing communities of practice, knowledge management enthusiasts, learners, innovators, knowledge brokers, mentors, and mentees together to showcase knowledge exchange or management methods, tools and techniques, activities, information management practices, silos-busting best practices, and KM technology enablers used by different users across the enterprise.

Yes, the café can be spontaneous or planned, small or large—the critical feature is the exchange and the volatility of knowledge flows.

I don't believe in the one-size-fits-all approach for anything. Knowledge fair is an alternative to the traditional presentation-style gathering—speakers are optional. A knowledge fair gives attendees options to explore areas of knowledge and information of interest, what others are doing, how they manage knowledge, results, challenges, and to personally engage knowledge brokers (experts) and those who have best practice. There may be demonstrations and booths displaying information or knowledge management elements and best practices for attendees.

Like other types of fairs, there is a lot of interaction that may not be available in other settings. Attendees network and build teams to expand their knowledge, practices, and value realization. So, if you need to know how much your organization knows and understands and how much they share, call a knowledge fair. A knowledge fair alone is like "booths" and storefronts—but storefronts that are open and inviting; too many fairs are still "push" rather than that network kind of flow.

You may add a café to your knowledge fair too. It could be your knowledge town-hall meeting to tell-and-show your intellectual capital, those with institutional knowledge, where the knowledge and information are, best practice, build knowledge teams, communities of practice, mentors and mentees, and spark off the fire of an enterprise knowledge management.

Café is both physical space, virtual space, and a mindset.

Knowledge Café is a knowledge exchange tool or method, just like communities of practice, succession planning, leadership development, lessons learned, data and information management, mentoring, and so on. However, you can begin the conversation about any of these techniques at the café. I will explore the café and other KM techniques interface in chapter 10 when discussing methods and knowledge management tools. It can be virtual or face-to-face. You can learn, share, and exchange knowledge on every imaginable issue ranging from KM, business, risk, relational, family, improvement, best practices, new ideas, innovation, and more. I will explore how to organize a knowledge fair and café in chapter 4.

CONNECTION BETWEEN KNOWLEDGE AND EXPERIENCE

There is an inextricable connection between knowledge and experience. Knowledge is the information and skills acquired through experience or education. Experience is the knowledge or skill acquired by a period of practical experience of something (Wilson, 2015). Knowledge—the most important currency in a project and knowledge economy—is often confused with data and information. My favorite definition of knowledge is the fact or condition of knowing something with familiarity gained through experience or association. Experience is the key!

- Knowledge will transcend information, all day, every day.
- Knowledge is believed, true, and reliable. However, not all knowledge is true and reliable. Knowledge is what a person knows—a person may know or believe something that is not factual.
- Accurate and comprehensive data that is organized becomes information, and when explained to becomes knowledge, that is the indisputable business foundation for solid decision making.
- Knowledge is the relevant and actionable facts, information, and skills we acquire through experience, association, or education, including a theoretical or practical understanding of the how, when, and why of what we do.

What Is the World Café, and How Does It Relate to the Knowledge Café?

> It's never enough just to tell people about some new insight. Rather, you have to get them to experience it in a way that evokes its power and possibility. Instead of pouring knowledge into people's heads, you need to help them grind a new set of eyeglasses so they can see the world in a new way.
> —John Seeley Brown (Brown & Duguid, 1996)

A similar concept to the Knowledge Café is the World Café—when you search online for "knowledge café," you may also get results for "World Café." I love it. The concepts are similar, but not the same. World Café uses seven design principles and a simple method "for engaging people in conversations that matter, offering an effective antidote to the fast-paced fragmentation and lack of connection in today's world. Based on the understanding that conversation is the core process that drives personal, business, and organizational life, the World Café is more than a method, a process, or technique— it's a way of thinking and being together sourced in a philosophy of conversational leadership." The World Café is a more "structured conversational process for knowledge sharing. Groups of people discuss a topic at several tables, with individuals switching tables periodically and getting introduced to the previous discussion at their new table by a table host" (www.theworldcafe.com).

The Knowledge Café I'm espousing is a KM technique, a mindset, and a space; held at the location and time agreed by participants, it has ground rules and conversational covenant for knowledge workers to make sense of what they know and identify the "aha!" moment of what they know. The Knowledge Café can be both structured and unstructured.

Knowledge is contextual. Wisdom is contextual. Knowledge Café is also contextual. Knowledge Café is different from World Café because it could be both structured and unstructured, and the purpose is for knowledge exchange, transfer, and reinvigoration (see table 2). You can use the café for a variety of reasons and purposes to exchange ideas and revivify knowledge—it may be project-specific.

Still, you can have a café to answer questions related to family, friendship, or business.

Knowledge Café is also a knowledge management technique—a systematic approach for managing organizational knowledge. Why? When you steward knowledge by capturing, sharing, circulating, or exchanging it, you manage knowledge. It involves identifying, understanding, and using knowledge to achieve organizational objectives and innovating. It brings a group's collective knowledge to the surface. It stimulates collective intelligence to promote learning between group members. The conceptual café creates an ecosystem that gains a deeper understanding of topics, issues, and KM best practices. Collaboration is a vehicle for the creation of new knowledge. Knowledge Café is the enabler.

Café can be used for a variety of scenarios that I'll show you in this book. No matter where you are in your KM journey; initiation of strategies or call to action; developing an enterprise strategy; designing and implementing KM capabilities; or evolving, maturing, and sustaining, café conversation is the mindset and space for engagement. The simplicity of the café model against the traditional and intimidating restaurant format of KM makes it easier for me to use this technique at home, with my board members, teams at the office, or for an enterprise search for new knowledge and solutions. I use the café model to engage knowledge creators and users to explore any issue or topic like the place of security in DevOps to find healing to pain caused by change at work or home, confronting complex problems that need new knowledge and innovation for solutions. As said earlier, what we do is to manage the environment for knowledge to flourish.

Why manage the environment? Because management is an industrial economy concept, and it facilitates and invests in the knowledge economy concept.

Collison and Parcell (2005) express how complicated it is to manage knowledge and the importance of creating the right environment that enables knowledge workers to capture, understand, store, share, and stimulate knowledge. Working in a knowledge society should be as natural as entering any corner café, taking a quick scan of the room, and finding the perfect spot to set up your coffee and computer. This is the ideal space to share experience and build incremental knowledge. Do not force daily stand-ups or obligatory status meetings into this area—while those are project-centered tools and techniques and have important roles, they don't belong in the café.

2.2. HOW TO MEET AT THE KNOWLEDGE CAFÉ AND THE FACILITATOR

Richard Thalheimer, the founder of Sharper Image, once asserted, "It is better to look uninformed than to be uninformed. Curb your ego & keep asking questions" (Close & Close, 2018). Two things that come to mind in a cafe environment are questions and the liberty to connect your ideas with others'. But it may devolve to other kinds of meetings without ground rules.

Ground Rules of the Café

Ground rules provide clarity and rules of engagement. It sets the expectation of the conversation, so there are no surprises. If you don't have ground rules, everyone creates theirs because nature abhors a vacuum. Would you want to play a game where there are no rules, or you make the rules as you go? I hope not. That will suffice for a debate, not a dialogue. There will be fears, insecurities, and people who don't like to be vulnerable unless they agree to protect everyone.

Peter Drucker once said, "My greatest strength as a consultant is to be ignorant and ask a few questions" (Lozep, 2020). Café is about questions; we use ground rules to create the environment to make sense of the answers. Ground rules provide a set of guidelines that help shepherd meaningful conversation and dialogue, have evocative meetings or better-facilitated sessions. Ground rules are meant to be self-governing, and everyone has a stake in the game. I'm not talking until there's a ground rule.

David Gurteen of Conversational Leadership and David Creel-man of Creelman Research came up with the Conversation Covenant, which I consider the baseline for all difficult and meaningful conversations. They define a conversation covenant as "an agreement between two or more persons to abide by a set of rules when engaging in conversation. The rules help knowledge workers and project teams work in harmony to create a psychologically safer space for seemingly impossible conversations" (Gurteen, 2020). The following ground rules for a café are a marriage of David Gurteen's café ground rules and mine.

GROUND RULES

1. Promote dialogue, not debates or argument
2. Create a conversation covenant
3. Voice your "crazy ideas" and let others test it
4. Safe to fail
5. Driven by powerful questions based on the theme and purpose
6. Encourage open and creative conversation
7. Preserve conversational flow
8. Everyone has a voice—everyone participates in the process
9. Value diversity of perspective—identifies options, possibilities, pros & cons
10. Draw out broad participation through small-group conversation format
11. Elicit deeper understanding of issues
12. Lively facilitation
13. Develop and evolve thinking on specific business issues
14. Eliminate fear

I shall provide elaboration on the ground rules in chapter 4. Besides, I have listed the café ground rules and described why you want to have a Knowledge Café environment and some benefits. Now, how does a Knowledge Café work? What's the role of a facilitator? Anyone can facilitate a café, but for the purpose of an enterprise KM, I recommend the following qualities for a café facilitator.

Qualities of a Café Facilitator(s)

1. The café must have a facilitator(s) who is/are enthusiastic about knowledge sharing and are passionate.

2. The most important attribute of a café facilitator is that it's not about him/herself.

3. The facilitator is skillful in encouraging conversation and dialogue, not a debater; he or she respects other people's opinions.

4. The facilitator secures the stakeholders' buy-in, creates the environment, and organizes the café.

5. The café is more successful if the facilitator is a project manager—not because I'm a project manager—or have the attributes of a project manager, but it is not required; a leader who can secure the buy-in of both management and rank-and-file employees can also be successful.

6. The facilitator could be someone with experience in any of the following knowledge-transfer tools and techniques: information and library science, taxonomy creation, content and document management, the development and maintenance of knowledge portals and business intelligence delivery systems, outreach, business process improvement, training, data management, and knowledge architecture.

7. The facilitator may have the ability to integrate areas of knowledge with expertise in areas such as data, library and information management, communications, learning and development, workforce planning, organizational development, human resources, and strategy. However, the most important qualifications are open-mindedness, common interest, shared values, reciprocity, learning curiosity, and the like.

8. The facilitator could also be a strategist, persuader, measurer, consensus builder, knowledge-sharer, and learner. They should be organizationally savvy and have change management skills.

Café is not just a casual and unserious event. It's a severe knowledge-sharing event, even though it can be casual too. I have had executives and senior leadership individuals participate in my cafés. Do you have the enthusiasm, skills, and drive to facilitate a Knowledge Café? If you have ever conducted a meeting or a brainstorming session without sending everyone to sleep, you can run a Knowledge Café. Give new strength to the knowledge of the project team by calling a café meeting. Discuss this with your team. You'll be amazed at what you come up with. The café framework and step-by-step approach are discussed in chapter 4.3.

Based on my experience with numerous KM brainstorming and knowledge-sharing sessions, there are practical, reliable ways to nourish a Knowledge Café society and enliven knowledge users and creators. If you open the café, stakeholders will come! See chapter 2.3 and 2.6 for practical steps on how to lead a café. The following café recommendations for knowledge sharing may look like Wenger and Lave's 10 ways to build and nourish communities of practice (CoPs), but they are not. I'll discuss extensively how CoP interfaces with the café. CoPs can use a café space and mindset to engage in conversation, learning, and sharing knowledge and ideas.

CAFÉ KNOWLEDGE SHARING RECOMMENDATIONS
- First, make a café a safe space for the exchange of crazy ideas and relevant knowledge.
- Create and agree on a simple KM Framework/Approach covering the "rules of engagement" and "the documentation and recording" of knowledge.
- Encourage knowledge sharing by establishing and enforcing a time/location for the café process.
- Organize regular lunch-and-learn sessions to raise KM awareness and sustain the knowledge workplace.
- Invite stakeholders from other departments/regions/ divisions to listen to calls and conferences.
- Inform every stakeholder of the knowledge policy change and brainstorming opportunities.

- Actively reach out and collaborate with professional colleagues.
- You may conduct cross-functional training.
- Practice follow-up documentation after knowledge exchange with fellow workers.
- Plan corporate social activities: Toastmasters, sponsored lunches, off-site team building, and other activities that foster personal interaction during work hours.
- Offer incentives, both personal and professional, to come to the café.

Involve your leadership and secure vital management adoption of the Knowledge Café mindset. Engage leadership to help you develop department/organization/regional communication and share across the enterprise. Establish a knowledge leadership café (Café 2.0) framework. This is the middle ground between simplicity and formalization of a KM program. I'll discuss this later in chapter 11.

Café is the environment for CoPs, as you can see in chapter 10. In a project, the project manager is responsible for the overall café project success. However, everyone—and I mean everyone in the café—is accountable and responsible for surfacing ideas to improve the processes used to create the café deliverables.

PROJECT MANAGER'S ROLE IN A CAFÉ
Within the Knowledge Café context, the project manager should play his or her role and exercise the following recommended duties if knowledge transfer is part of your organization's strategy:

- Get a sponsor and set expectations
- Formally adopt Café 2.0 (Leadership Café)
- Facilitate charter development: objectives, plan, proposal, business case, success criteria
- Identify champions and stakeholders
- You may develop a café project plan
- Manage deliverables according to the plan
- Acquire, identify, and onboard planning team

ation must build and espouse an ecosystem in which all workplace
stakeholders are invited to share their experience, skill, and wisdom
unreservedly. Full disclosure: I hate boring meetings. Unfortunately,
I spend more than 90 percent of my work time communicating—a
good chunk of it is in meetings. I even have meetings to plan for a
meeting. Many meetings are redundant and a waste of time, especially when you have a terrible meeting manager or host. If you replace boring meetings with a café, I'm in!

The café is not just another meeting or meetup—you meet up at
the café to be caffeinated with knowledge. As stated earlier, it is an
unstructured, collaborative space to exchange, share, transfer, and
renew knowledge. It has some attributes of other types of meetings,
as shown in the comparison in table 2, but it is not your typical meeting or conference. It's often a one-way knowledge exchange at a
conference, but the café is a two-way exchange.

You can use the café for a variety of purposes: to exchange ideas
and reawaken knowledge, to find a solution for your projects and
programs, to connect and get to know each other, to break out of
the noise or quietness of the house or office, to share best practices,
to bring everyone to the same knowledge baseline, to identify knowledge assets, to create new knowledge, to resolve matters that are

Table 2. How the Café Stacks with Other Communication Gatherings

	Knowledge Café	Knowledge Fair	Traditional Meeting/Conference	Meetup	Stand-up/Daily Scrum
Purpose	Knowledge exchange, making sense, "aha!" moment, rejuvenation	Display of KM practices	Agenda dictates	Find and build community	Synchronize activities and plan
Ground Rules	Yes	No	It depends	No	It depends
Small group	Yes	No	It depends	Yes	Yes
KM technique	Yes; a technique for any of the meeting types	Yes; KM technique to highlight KM best practices	No; any of the meeting types	No	No
Audience	Knowledge workers, common interest, anyone	Knowledge workers, anyone	Anyone	Common interest group	Project team
Relationship with others	Can be used in multiple settings	Can be used in knowledge display settings	Can be used in multiple settings	Used for this purpose alone	Used for project purpose alone

(continued)

Table 2. *(continued)*

	Knowledge Café	Knowledge Fair	Traditional Meeting/ Conference	Meetup	Stand-up/Daily Scrum
Structure	Question-driven; little or no presentations networking	Display of KM best practices; presentations; café add-ons	Presentations, discussions	Presentations, discussion, networking	Short stand-up meeting
Format	Face-to-face or virtual	Face-to-face	Face-to-face or virtual	Face-to-face or virtual	Face-to-face or virtual
Facilitator/host	Facilitator	Facilitator	Depends on meeting	Host	Dev Team
Location/Time	Agreed by all	Organizer	Organizer	Organizer	Organizer
Characteristics	Could be structured and unstructured and open	Displays	Needs clear agenda to be effective	Designed for networking	Taskboard
Excitement level	High	Medium	It depends, Low	It depends, High	Low

hard to discourse, and so on. For example, The National Aeronautics and Space Administration (NASA) established the Exploration Systems Mission Directorate (ESMD) in the 2004 time frame to manage a new portfolio of programs and projects aimed at lunar return. They used a series of Knowledge Cafés to identify risk issues and how to mitigate those risks. Here are some of the takeaways from their May 2010 Café: Knowledge Mapping Techniques, Knowledge Frameworks, Capture Methods, Transfer Methods, Knowledge-Based Products, Roles of Security and Records Management, Organization and Planning Issues, and Risk Management Integration (NASA ESMD Knowledge Café, 2010).

SIX TYPES OF MEETINGS

MeetingSift identifies six general types of meetings. The Knowledge Café format can be used for any of them ("The Six Most Common Types of Meetings," n.d.)!

1. Status Update
2. Information Sharing
3. Decision Making
4. Problem Solving
5. Innovation
6. Team Building

Here is a comparison of some of the types of communication gatherings. When you think of a café, consider peer instruction with traditional lecturing. Questions, answers, dialogue, and conversation are prominent in a café.

Peer Instruction versus a Café

Peer instruction, an evidence-based, interactive teaching method popularized by Eric Mazur (1997) captures some of the essences of the café. Many scholars like Mazur agree that it's not about the instructor's facilitation in front of the class or a presenter at the conference or workshop. It's about the students or the café attendees and their minds. You don't learn by listening; you learn by doing, by conversing.

PEER INSTRUCTION

In peer instruction,

- the instructor poses questions based on students' responses to their preclass reading; in a café, the facilitator poses a question for knowledge dialogue
- students reflect on the question, just like in a cafe
- students commit to an individual answer; in a café, everyone has a voice
- the instructor reviews student responses; at the café, everyone learns from the responses
- students discuss their thinking and answers with their peers; in a café, everyone discusses their thinking and solutions/answers with café attendees
- students then commit again to an individual answer; in a café, it's not just the personalized answers but for new knowledge that is a take-home
- the instructor again reviews responses and decides whether more explanation is needed before moving on to the next concept; the café facilitator moves to another question, table summary, or open mic (mike).

2.4. WHAT MAKES KNOWLEDGE WORKERS COME TO A KNOWLEDGE CAFÉ?

Some serendipitous cafés are open 24/7. If someone has an idea they want to share at 3 a.m., they can go to the café. Thanks to virtual cafés.

Welcome to the café! What makes knowledge creators and sharers come to the café? Curiosity. You must be curious enough to generate the curiosity of others. If knowledge must be shared and transferred, a drive-through café concept may not be appropriate. A sit-down, sip-your-coffee café may be the right environment.

Jean-Luc Abelin, director, Knowledge Management Group, Lafarge, said at the KMWorld 2015 conference that we have two significant KM challenges facing international companies. The first is to prove that a KM platform of management is vital to top management. "We have to convince all the top management level that it will be critical for the company. We have to find all the topics and all the solutions to convince them to put money on the table and authorize us to deploy that kind of platform." The second challenge is to convince people to share: "When I say share, I mean both givers and takers" (Abelin, 2015).

Management sets the tone of an organization's knowledge culture, but knowledge leadership café sets the tone and determines the knowledge users and creators to be invited to the café. It all depends on the manager and the organization, and the level of the manager. Strong personalities at the unit level can override espoused organizational cultures.

Knowledge leadership café is the framework for formalizing KM systems with a nimble and agile mindset. I'll discuss the leadership café later in chapter 11. Consider project managers, archivists, historians, trainers, knowledge managers, public information officers, data scientists, and librarians. The truth is that everyone who uses and creates knowledge can be invited to the café.

Research by the Project Management Institute shows that 95 percent of organizations effective at knowledge transfer have identified someone in the organization who is ultimately responsible for it, compared to only 54 percent of organizations that don't do knowledge transfer well (Project Management Institute, 2015). Who is responsible for KM in your organization? What or where is the rallying point for knowledge exchange? This relates to knowing how knowledge flows in the organization now. Once we know that, we can then use that information to encourage the persistent or spontaneous creation of Knowledge Cafés. At organizations like the World Bank, when they have a new VP, they walk them through the workflow map. You need to know what your knowledge flow is in the organization to leverage the café.

So, what would bring knowledge workers to the Knowledge Café? Let's take inspiration from a survey of 1,370 individual café outlets by Australian Café Pulse (Top five things your customers really want in a café, n.d.) for the top reasons respondents chose their favorite café . . . literally. If you'll pardon the metaphor, we might consider parallels with people's experience of actual coffee shops. Let's relate each one to the Knowledge Café.

Coffee Strength and Taste

How do you like your coffee brewed: mild, medium, or strong? What flavor of coffee inspires you? Identify the strength and taste or most mission-critical knowledge in the minds of employees to attract café-goers. The strength, taste, and packaging of café deliverables determine the environment it creates. Café conveners must be willing to bring taste, power, and depth to the café with organizational, leadership, and facilitation skills. People may not come again to your café unless it's exciting and powerful.

Quality of the Café

If we are going to have an environment for knowledge sharing, relevance and the quality of the café must be paramount. Product quality is based on the quality of the customer requirements. In a café, do you know what drinks the customer buys most? Adding bells and whistles don't work when it's not what the customer wants or needs. First, it would be helpful to have a list of café features, kind of like a Yelp review. What are the things we look for when selecting a café? Quality of the exchange. The product of the café is a piece of new knowledge or relearned knowledge or unlearned knowledge, other output, or outcomes of the café.

Location

A strategic location is important for a café to be successful. Do you know where your organization's mission-critical knowledge is stored and who is the most knowledgeable about it? Not all knowledge is critical, so it is important to identify the most vital knowledge and where it resides in your organization. What are your knowledge gaps? What is the quality of that knowledge? Who knows where the mission-critical knowledge is? Ensure the strategic objectives align with your organizational strategies, just like a strategic location can make or break a café.

Pleasant Ambiance

The senses are fundamental—the first impression matters. The impression of what we see and feel contributes to whether customers or café-goers will come back. If knowledge is a valuable asset to your organization, create an environment where people want to participate and return. Put knowledge management in its place in terms of strategic priority in your organization.

Quick Service

The café must be smart, efficient, and exciting. This is not your typical training, conference, or workshop. It's not a drive-through learning experience—we listen and think in the cafe. A café shouldn't compete with traditional restaurants where you have to take a full-course meal. Café service should be quick and fun! Because there's no preconceived idea, you are not inundating café attendees with big ideas and new programs. If there are some big ideas, it's coming from the café attendees. Remember that KM is like eating an elephant—one bite at a time.

Price

Price is always king. If a product or idea is excellent, but the price tag is unreasonable, no one buys it. The price must match the value it delivers. Price is relevant to the customer and the owner. There are two different kinds of investments and two different reasons to participate. The price for the consumer cannot be considered in isolation of the cost to the investor. If an organization sees its knowledge assets as a competitive advantage, a tool for innovation, it must invest in managing that knowledge, just like any other organization's strategic initiative. I developed a strong business case for my executive sponsor to see how much tangible and intangible benefit, cost-benefit analysis, including the cost of doing nothing vis-à-vis the organization's value knowledge management.

Staff/Barista Attitude

What is the role of "staff" in a café? Usually, they don't engage in knowledge exchange—they just serve the coffee and tea and provide the right fun and exchange environment. They provide the stimulus. What is the equivalent stimulus in a Knowledge Café? Consider the facilitators of a café, creating a welcoming atmosphere, asking the right questions, providing service, and facilitating fun. In a café, the attitude, competence, and friendliness of the staff matters. For a project or program to be successful, staff must be engaged—the face of the KM program matters and impacts the enterprise's buy-in. The skills of the Knowledge Café's facilitator contribute to the success, and personal relationships are the heart of the café. Strong executive sponsorship and buy-in of significant stakeholders are crucial to success. Don't waste your time and effort on an enterprise KM program without it.

Brand of Coffee

I can get a good cup of coffee walking into Starbucks, but I don't sit unless there is a really fascinating bunch of folks there. If you need solitude and quietness, a café is probably the wrong place for that. At the café, you may have a favorite coffee whose brand you recognize and respect. Just as with your favorite coffee brand, if you want to make KM and Knowledge Café an enterprise program, create a brand that people will recognize. People participate in your café based on the strength of your branding. You've got to sell it. In my organization to brand KM, I told enthusiasts and practitioners that we were creating a knowledge culture and having fun making it. Branding of a KM program must fit with the culture and environment of the organization. What works for one organization may not work for another. Choose your branding well. Align and brand your KM program with your organizational strategy and branding. Align and brand your KM program with your organizational strategy and branding. It should align with customer expectations, product type, organizational structure, strategic advantages, and environmental trends.

Ethically Sourced

We go to the café to receive and give. Café-goers "stay or engage" because other café-goers have similar values and beliefs. There's a gentlemen's agreement for mutual exchange. Are ethics and integrity true to your brand and organization's offerings? I am grateful for the perspective and lessons learned from organizations I have been involved with, such as Project Management Institute (PMI), National Academy of Science, Engineering, and Medicine's Transportation Research Board (TRB) Information and Knowledge Management Committee, AASHTO Committee on Knowledge Management, WSDOT, VDOT, the café strategy team at TxDOT, and Knowledge Management Community of Austin and central Texas, which I co-founded. Always under-promise and overdeliver. Did I say, overdeliver? Do not overdeliver beyond the scope of the project. Gold Plating—adding functionalities beyond what is covered by the requirements—is unethical and not allowed by the Project Management Code of Conduct. Have a clear scope statement or statement of work and proper scope management plan. Have a change management plan, which helps you manage the change process and ensures control and discipline in scope, budget, schedule, communication, and resources.

Coffee Roasted Locally

Note the most effective café and KM program is the one that adapts to the local environment and organizational culture. Do not cut and paste another organization's café or KM style. Make it local. Make it yours. Customize your program.

2.5. CASE STUDY: OPEN, VULNERABLE, AND EAGER TO SHARE—TONYA HOFMANN

In 2018, I had opportunities to speak at several conferences and workshops, including local, regional, and global Project Management

Institute conferences. I've been speaking for a long time because I have challenges I need to share with others I believe are experts in this art and can expand my knowledge. In 2018, I spoke on "Managing Projects and Stakeholders from Hell" at the Executive Women's conference in Texas. At this meeting, I was introduced to Tonya Hofmann, a café-goer who was also a speaker, and her husband. Tonya is the CEO and founder of the Public Speakers Association and Wowdible Phone Application. In August 2018, we held a Knowledge Café. At this café, I wanted Tonya, who I consider to be a speaking expert, to help me. I wanted to learn from her. She asked me, "How can I help you, Benjamin?" At the back of my mind, I was the person that needed more knowledge but here was my approach: "Hey, Tonya, can I pay for your lunch?" (I pay for lunches for knowledge transfer.) "And, by the way, I'm the president of the PMI Austin Chapter; I'm responsible for getting speakers to our Community Spotlight. I'd like to know how I can help you and learn from you too."

I demonstrated a sincere intention to help her in her endeavors. She eventually became one of the panelists during our very successful October 2018 Community Spotlight. The rest is now history, as I've learned so much from her, and we have shared knowledge during several café settings and meetups. PMI Austin's Community Spotlight is a café-style interactive event and attracts more attendees than any other monthly dinner event. Customer satisfaction was about 97 percent because of the sharing and knowledge exchange participants gain. Attendees to my café events testify that café-style knowledge exchange is preferable and more valuable than other types of learning and developments for professionals.

Here's Tonya's story:

As a café-goer, I run into a lot of professionals who believe that what they know ought somehow to be exclusive to themselves; that if they teach others what they know, it might somehow take away from their knowledge or their potential revenue. But top speakers and trainers do not reach their level of success by keeping knowledge to themselves. In a knowledge economy, there's a free flow of knowledge. Knowledge is cherished, stewarded, and exchanged. They understand that the transfer of knowledge is how to raise others and, in turn, promote themselves. In simple terms, it is the fear of loss instead of the belief in gain that separates the haves from the have nots.

Fear of losing keeps so many people from really growing. We have all learned what we know from someone else. We may have a unique twist or a different way of looking at things, but the belief that knowledge is ours exclusively is just plain selfish. On the contrary, those who go out and shout it to the world are the real winners. Those who never blink an eye at sharing knowledge or how it will benefit someone else will create real momentum in the knowledge transfer space.

Some years ago, I worked with Matt (Matt is not his real name). He told me that his mentor advised him to learn something that interested him and was unique and to keep the knowledge to himself and share it with no one. And then there was a change in technology, and knowledge of the program that Matt could not keep up. Those who hoarded knowledge became irrelevant. Matt had to play catch-up as other knowledge workers, who were not closed in, moved ahead of him. The moral of the story is that those who keep everything to themselves and horde their knowledge will witness their peers flying past them in success, acknowledgment, and wealth! The fact that they don't talk freely about what they know stifles their progress.

When I meet someone new, I ask them a question about what they know. People typically respond in one of two ways. The first is to give open information on what they know, what I should know, how they can help me, and what to avoid. I immediately feel that this is someone I can do business and or build a relationship with long-term. The second type of person is guarded, may want to charge me immediately for some piece of knowledge they have, and may even ask for an NDA before sitting down with me! This type of person I do not have time for or want to build a relationship. I immediately feel the fear in them. Ask yourself, who wants to do business or be friends with someone who is always making you feel like you are trying to steal from them or hurt them? Or, simply put, who wants to be cast as untrustworthy? There is a reason why they say in sales that people not only have to like you, but they must trust you as well. This is a prerequisite to doing a successful business. I see it over and over again that the people who move fast, make the most money, and create long-term relationships are the people who are open, vulnerable, and eager to share. I look for the hug and handshake, not the sign on the bottom-line people. These are the people who want to help, even before I feel like they want something in return. This is the way I live my life and build my business, and I believe I am a lot richer for it in both money and friendships!

People "Arrive at" a Café through Many Routes—Bringing Them to the Café Is Just One Strategy

If you are going to create a knowledge transfer community or bring people to a café, there must be trust and reciprocity, as the case study reveals. Poverty-minded people and environments muffle knowledge transfer and revitalization. Tonya said that the "fear of losing keeps so many people from really growing." Some people cannot share unless they are guaranteed what they'll receive in return. This mindset needs to be broken. Someone with a poverty mindset can park his Lamborghini, stand in line for a free burger, and ask you to pitch in for gas for giving you a ride. Knowledge leadership and an attitude of prosperity are necessary for success. Tonya's case study reveals that "those who keep everything to themselves and hoard their knowledge see people flying past them in success, acknowledgment and wealth!" It's giving and sharing your way to an abundance of knowledge that guides a knowledge leader. Those who share will never be poor. If you are a user of experience, you must be a creator of knowledge and be troubled when knowledge is hoarded.

Pay It Forward—Don't Make a Profit, Make a Point

Profit is interpreted differently in the knowledge economy. It takes the form of more knowledge, more valuable knowledge, and more business value. It's not a money concept in the 21st century. The problem with many knowledge creators and users is that they want to make a profit rather than make a difference. The publisher Berrett-Koehler recently held a global conference called People-First Economy. Several organizational leaders that believed in people first—and social responsibility—were featured. There has never been a time in human history when many organizations are clamoring for the realism of making a difference. This is sharing, making a point, and not necessarily milking profit. Please understand me. Companies need to make a profit. Their mission drives excellent organizations, and they, in turn, make a profit. But it should be making a point—changing lives, impacting lives, fulfilling its mission, and then, profit becomes natural.

After that conference, I contacted Shawn Doyle, a connection through LinkedIn, who has authored 24 best-selling books. I asked him how much it would cost me to learn from his wisdom—deep smarts. His office scheduled a call for us to talk. We talked for 40 minutes at no cost. Others of his caliber might quickly charge someone per minute to share their knowledge. This is an example of investment in relational capital.

I talked to my executive editor about sharing some portions of my book through articles and social media postings and if it violates my contracts. She said, "Ben, those who give away stuff seem to be the most successful writers." Yea! When you raise others, you grow yourself. When you teach others, you prepare yourself. I want to mentor one million leaders; in the process, I'm helping myself.

What you know is for the world, not just for you.

2.6. PRACTICE CAFÉ: IDEAS, TIPS, AND TRICKS

In a workspace with multiple generations and an aging workforce, knowledge and knowledge management are critical strategic resources.

Silos can impact communication, productivity, and growth—bust silos between groups, systems, and knowledge sharing to develop organizational efficiencies and resilience.

TIPS ON WHY WE HAVE A CAFÉ

Here are my ideas about why to have a Knowledge Café:

- We need a face-to-face or all-hands approach to KM.
- Small groups give everyone a voice; the action is in the small groups.
- Conversation stirs new knowledge.
- Identify the knowledge, knowledge sharing enablers, tools, techniques, and best practices.
- A café can be a gateway entry into organizational knowledge management.
- When we stop learning, we start dying. According to *Harvard Business Review*, we should largely be recruiting based upon an ability to learn rather than any preexisting qualifications. In the *New York Times*, Eric Schmidt contends that a significant pillar in Google's recruitment strategy is to hire "learning animals."
- A café is a space to identify different approaches and best practices for knowledge sharing away from home and office distractions.
- New knowledge is birthed. As you cross-pollinate and broker ideas at the café, new knowledge emerges—hence, innovation.
- No one "talks at" the knowledge workers, but everyone brings experiences, skills, and knowledge to the table; this is true if you have a "manager" involved, and the ground rules tell us that everyone's voice is equal.
- Rejuvenation. At the café, curiosities are stirred.
- Agility. Knowledge Café is unstructured and could be structured, unlike other similar concepts. Everyone's opinion counts.
- Wisdom. The ultimate purpose of knowledge is wisdom— the application of knowledge—the comprehensive

enhancement of our cognition—the highest level of superior understanding. The wisdom teacher, Dr. Mike Murdock, said that knowledge is what you know; wisdom is what you do. Knowledge must be applied to gain wisdom. Bust silos through conversations; dialogue at the Knowledge Café releases the knowledge.

WHAT IS NEEDED TO HOST A KNOWLEDGE CAFÉ

Here is some practical advice on what is needed to host a café if it's a broader KM organizational strategy.

- Have a skilled facilitator who is enthusiastic about knowledge management and can organize the café and engage others.
- Secure stakeholders' buy-in and management support, including an executive sponsor: Conversation is bottom-up, inside out, and outside in. Rarely is it top-down. This is the "talking at" kind of conversation. I talk, and you listen.
- It would help to clarify different roles in a café. Just like the various actors in a real café, you have the facilitator or organizer who is like the staff/barista, café attendants.
- Engage leadership to help you develop department/ organization/regional communication and share across the enterprise.

HOW TO NOURISH AND REKINDLE KNOWLEDGE USERS

Based on my experience with numerous KM brainstorming sessions, here are some practical, reliable ways to nourish a Knowledge Café society and rekindle knowledge users and creators.

- Encourage knowledge sharing by establishing and enforcing a time/location for the café process.
- Organize regular lunch-and-learn sessions to raise KM awareness and sustain the knowledge workplace.
- Invite stakeholders from other departments/regions/ divisions to listen to calls and conferences.
- Inform every stakeholder of the knowledge policy change and brainstorming opportunities.

- Actively reach out and collaborate with professional colleagues.
- Conduct cross-functional training.
- Practice follow-up documentation after knowledge exchange with fellow workers.
- Plan corporate social activities: Toastmasters, sponsored lunches, off-site team building, and other activities that foster personal interaction during work hours.

3 ■ Caffeinated Knowledge: What Is Knowledge Management?

Chapter Objectives

- Define knowledge management
- Identify its origin and literature surrounding KM
- Define silos and how to bust them
- How to embrace knowledge transfer

3.1. WHAT IS KNOWLEDGE MANAGEMENT?

In the preceding chapters, I've shown you how a Knowledge Café can be a gateway to knowledge management. But what is knowledge management?

HOW PEOPLE DEFINE KNOWLEDGE MANAGEMENT

When I hold a Knowledge Café or knowledge leadership café (by invitation only), I ask attendees to define KM in one word or phrase. Here are some of the definitions I've received.

- Archives
- Capture, share, knowledge
- Collaboration
- Transparency
- Communication
- Community of practice
- Database Platform
- Depth Disseminate Growth
- Diligence Organization
- Documentation
- Education Preservation
- Empowering, Visionary, Plan
- Essential Key to Continued Success
- Essential to Sustaining Personnel development
- Guiding Training Shepherding
- Important, Necessary
- Informal and Unstructured
- Information
- Intelligent Research Verify

- Intentional
- Interesting
- Interesting Needed Useful
- Leadership, Mentoring, Coaching
- Learning and Leadership Development
- Lesson Learned
- Lessons Learning
- Leverage
- Mentoring
- Necessary
- Needed
- Open Communication
- Organization Documentation Leadership
- Power Legacy Retention
- Power Positive Necessary
- Power to Improve Efficiency
- Powerful
- Preservation Insurance
- Retention of Information
- Security Efficiency Stability
- Share

- Share Information Efficiency
- Shared Communication
- Shared Resource Risk Retention
- Sharing
- Sharing Efficient
- Sharing Expertise Best Practices
- Sharing Knowledge
- Sharing, Best Practices, Efficiency
- Sharing, Caring, Preparing
- Sharing, Collaboration, Training
- Sharing, Mentoring, Legacy
- Sharing, Open, Transformational
- Sharing, Progressive, Valuable
- Sharing, Robust, Tacit
- Succession planning
- Success
- Success Crucial Important
- Time-saving

- Training
- Transfer
- Transparent Value Share
- Valuable Lacking Misunderstood
- Value Consistent Depth

As you can see from this list, there is no universal understanding of knowledge management—it is a massive concept. Defining it in one sentence is like the conclusion of the proverbial six blind men who visited an Indian Rajah's palace and encountered an elephant, as masterfully described in Lillian Quigley's children's book. The first blind man put out his hand, touched the elephant's smooth side, and concluded it was like a wall. The second blind man touched the round trunk and defined it as a snake. The third blind man put out his hand and touched the elephant's tall leg and said, "Oh, it's like a tree." The next blind man touched its thin tail and defined it as a rope. Get it? Everyone describes the elephant from their vantage point.

I have seen dozens of KM definitions; however, there's no single or agreed-upon definition of KM across the business, epistemology, social sciences, and psychology. In fact, author and professor John P. Girard gathered a collection of more than 100 KM definitions (Girard & Girard, 2015). If a concept like KM has so many definitions, it presupposes that it doesn't have a definition at all. As important as KM is across multiple professional organizations, one would think that there should have been a Knowledge Management Book of Knowledge. During one of the workgroup revisions for PMI's *PMBOK® Guide,* sixth edition (2017) (Project Management Body of Knowledge), I made a case for including KM. I was told that the KM concept is too broad, and that is accurate. I called a major employer who posted a job for knowledge management director in 2019 and realized that they were looking for a training director. Training is just a little piece of KM.

Here are some of the definitions I've come across in my KM research—plus some definitions of my own.

"Knowledge Management is the process of capturing, distributing, and effectively using knowledge." (Davenport, 1994). This classic one-line definition of knowledge management offered by Tom Davenport in 1994 is a succinct, single-line definition.

Knowledge is the "brain" of the human capital of an organization. According to Investopedia (2020), human capital is classified as the economic value of a worker's experience and skills, including assets such as education, training, intelligence, skills, health, and other things employers value, such as loyalty and punctuality. Human capital is an intangible asset, not listed on a company's balance sheet.

KM is a systematic approach for identifying, understanding, and using knowledge to achieve organizational objectives and innovations.

The Project Management Book of Knowledge (PMBOK) defines knowledge management: "It's all about making sure the skills, experiences, and expertise of the project team and other stakeholders are used before, during, and after the project" (*PMBOK® Guide*, sixth edition, 2017, p. 100).

> The means by which an organization builds, sustains, and leverages the know-how and experience of its employees and partners to deliver its projects and services and manage the systems for which they are responsible.
>
> —National Cooperative Highway Research Program (NCHRP, 2014)

Shyan Kirat Rai contends that, "Knowledge management is a discipline that promotes an integrated approach to identifying, retrieving, evaluating, and sharing an enterprise's tacit and explicit knowledge assets to meet mission objectives. The objective is to connect those who know with those who need to know (know-why, know-what, know-who, and know-how) by leveraging knowledge transfers from one-to-many across the enterprise."

Knowledge management is collecting, building, capturing, acquiring, leveraging, elicitation, organization, distillation, codification, sharing, and transfer of both tacit and explicit knowledge. It is creating new knowledge and relishing the experience! That's right!

If there's no fun in knowledge exchange, it's like eating a fine delicacy on a full stomach.

What do speed, the advancement of science and technology, and innovation do to knowledge? A more technology-focused definition is that KM is a systematic way or solution that integrates with a variety of video and record management systems, captures institutional knowledge in heads of employees, and ingests digital evidence to a central repository where it is transcribed, indexed, and tagged; subsequently, enabling easy management, quick search, and retrieval, person-person-exchange, secure sharing while maintaining chain of custody and other legal requirements. Café is a part of the "knowledge use" architecture design. It works well because of human interaction at the center of the café.

Is knowledge capital? At what rate does it depreciate? If knowledge is capital, why is it not treated as such? In economics and sociology, capital goods are physical and nonfinancial inputs used to produce economic value. These include raw materials, facilities, machinery, and tools used in the production of goods and services. While money is used to purchase products and services, capital is more durable and is used to generate wealth through investment. I could make a case that knowledge is intellectual capital whose output is innovation.

There is a consensus among many intellectual capital researchers about knowledge capital or intellectual capital. Knowledge capital has been discussed extensively by many intellectual capital researchers, including Bill LaFayette, Wayne Curtis, Denise Bedford, and Seem Iyer in their book *Knowledge Economies and Knowledge Work*. In the book, they described intellectual capital and human capital (tacit knowledge, skills, and competencies, attitudes, and behaviors), structural capital (explicit knowledge-information, procedural knowledge, and organizational culture), and relational capital (networks and network relationships, and reputational knowledge) (Lafayette et al., 2019, p. 90). The authors contend that human intellectual capital focuses on individuals' knowledge, while structural capital focuses on knowledge within the group or community, or organization. I can say that we have KM when we articulate and recognize the interfaces, intersection, and relevance of the intellectual structural, human, and relational capital within the group. Café is the intersection of these elements, so intellectual capital.

Can we have definitions that capture people, processes, technology, and simplicity? What about developing one source of truth for enterprise information, connection, and collaboration? In other words, a simple café-like process that knocks down the silos to create new knowledge for innovation. Any KM definition that omits innovation runs afoul of the true meaning and output of KM. New knowledge is the precursor to or bedrock of innovation.

> Some of the greatest challenges facing organizations today are as follows: knowledge identification, capturing, acquiring, organizing and communicating, sharing, and retention.

> Knowledge Management is defined as a discipline focused on integrating people and processes enabled by tools throughout the information lifecycle in order to create a shared understanding and increase organizational performance and decision-making.
> —U.S. Department of Defense

All these definitions of KM capture different elements of the subject matter, but a few gaps exist. This brings me to my definition of knowledge management:

> Knowledge management is an intentional mechanism and ecosystem for identifying, capturing, and sharing/exchanging mission-critical institutional knowledge assets, including the ones in the head and hands of employees and machines, creating new knowledge and having fun in the process.

Intentional: KM is a proactive and intentional act of organizational strategy.

Mechanism: KM is a vehicle for delivering a knowledge culture.

Ecosystem: KM is a community of interacting organisms and their physical environment: a complex network or interconnected system.

Identifying: Part of KM is a knowledge audit. It's an inventory of an organization's knowledge capabilities—an effort to understand, investigate, and qualitatively and quantitatively analyze its knowledge health, where it stands in terms of knowledge identification, repository, reuse, and transfer capabilities.

An enterprise knowledge management program must include many components to be successful.

Knowledge Capture. Capturing means collection, building, eliciting, the codification of both tacit and explicit knowledge; knowledge capturing is through knowledge interviews, last lecture, after-action review, lessons learned; knowledge (exit) interviews, storytelling, oral history, dynamic online questions and answers, forums, monitored crowdsourced platforms, and Wiki contributions.

Knowledge Sharing and Exchange. Knowledge transfer, distillation, collaboration, enhanced, and intelligent findability and discoverability

Institutional Knowledge Assets. Institutional knowledge assets refers to two of the organization's knowledge bases.

Organizational Knowledgebase. Databases, documents, guide, policies and procedures, software, patents, consultants, and customers' knowledge base

Workforce Knowledgebase. The totality of all intellectual capital: information, ideas, learning, understanding, memory, insight, cognitive and technical skills, and capabilities.

Tacit Knowledge. The knowledge that is only in the heads or minds of employees and is hard to codify. This is the totality of everything you have learned and known throughout your life, including skills and competencies.

Knowledge Audit. Systematic and scientific examination and evaluation of explicit and implicit knowledge resources in a company, including what knowledge exists, where it is, how it is being created, and who owns it (Hylton, 2002a, 2002b, as cited in Yip et al., 2015). A knowledge audit is knowing what you know, what you don't know, what you should know, and what you should unlearn—and then prioritizing it all.

A knowledge audit is an overall evaluation of what is held inside and what is allowed out of a knowledge resource (i.e., the knowledge worker), regarding the organization's system, process, project, or product. It's a gap analysis of where the mission-critical knowledge assets reside and how they interact with the organization's mission-critical and non-mission-critical functions. It is within the conceptual café that the audit process executes.

KNOWING WHEN YOU NEED A KNOWLEDGE AUDIT

Here is another way you can identify when you need a knowledge audit, according to Karl Wiig (1993a).

- Information glut or scarcity
- Lack of awareness of information elsewhere in the organization
- Inability to keep abreast of relevant information
- Significant "reinventing" the wheel
- An everyday use of out-of-date information
- Not knowing where to go for expertise in a specific area

A KM audit identifies and captures the individual's intellectual capital, the organization's knowledge (especially, hard-won expertise), and the external knowledge that impacts the organizational knowledge, sharing, reusing, creating, and rejuvenating knowledge.

In a research paper published by the *African Journal of Management*, Azizollah Jafari and Nafiseh Payani (2013) proposed four areas of efficient knowledge audit methods:

1. Identifying and accessing organizational knowledge
2. Identifying the organization's experts and specialists in various fields
3. Prioritizing an organization's knowledge fields for knowledge state improvement
4. Identifying potential points to share knowledge among experts, departments, and organizational units

"Lessons Learning" in Place of "Lessons Learned"
Knowledge gained is best when it is iterative and immediately re-used—a living, dynamic activity. KM is systematically making sure that knowledge—skills, experiences, and expertise—are not only a post-project effort but occur before and during the project. In a KM environment, lessons learned are knowledge gained by unlocking the project team's and stakeholders' experience and expertise. Lessons learned become living activities—they are reused before, during, and after the project. It's worth mentioning that 91 percent of project managers believe lessons learned reviews or after-action reviews on projects were necessary. Only 13 percent said their organizations performed them on all projects, and only 8 percent thought the primary objective of the reviews was to understand the benefits that would accrue to the organization (Ernst & Young, 2007, as cited in Marlin, 2008).

In many instances, the concept of lessons learned is a big joke. Some attendees in my café think it should be done away with and be replaced with "lessons learning"—a more actively used process. From my experience, those lessons learned documents are just for show or a check-off box. They never get referenced or used as input during newer projects. Whether it's people thinking they already know everything, or if they're too overwhelmed at project start to look into past lessons learned, or whether lessons learned seem antiquated, I think people are missing the usefulness. Author Chris DiBella said, "I'm actually working on a project to elevate 'lessons learning' and how I basically want to get rid of lessons learned and make it more of a Lessons Learned Implementation" (C. DiBella, pers. comm.). This should be the direction: lessons learned should be reconsidered in light of lessons learned implementation—where they become an integral part of any new project that gets launched. I will shed more light on lesson learning in chapter 10. In knowledge transfer, lessons learned are lessons learning. Here, we use lessons learned before the project begins, during the project, and after the project, and lessons become part of the process and a new way of doing things.

Creating Curiosity and Having Fun Sharing Knowledge
Knowledge management may create additional work but shouldn't be burdensome; this defeats the purpose of KM. Adding to an organization's knowledge base should excite workers and create value without burning out knowledge workers. Going to the café to share knowledge is simple and effective.

Where does knowledge come from?

Robert Audi (2003) distinguishes what he calls the "four standard basic sources" by which we acquire knowledge or justified belief: perception, memory, consciousness, and reason. A basic source yields knowledge or justified belief without positive dependence on another source.

We acquire knowledge through ourselves or others. Examples of knowledge acquired through self: experiences; reasoning: logical, inductive, deductive; instinct; learning; personal perception; convictions; personal growth; intuition: illumination, preparation, incubation, and verification; analytical thinking; failures and successes; faith or personal belief; trial and error; dreams; and unlearning. Through others and outside influences: mentors; other knowledge creators and sharers; reading; tradition; research; authority and SMEs; categorical syllogism; scientific approach; meditation; naturalistic inquiry; lessons learned from others and projects; inspirations; and training and development. Credit for some of the sources of knowledge: Dr. Raffeedali. E, Assistant Professor, MANUU, CTE, Srinagar.

3.2. PAST AND CURRENT KNOWLEDGE MANAGEMENT

Knowledge management emerged in the 1980s and was influenced by cognitive science, business theory, social sciences, information sciences, and artificial intelligence (AI). According to KMWorld, the term "Knowledge Management" was first used by McKinsey in 1987 for an internal study on their information handling and utilization. In this scenario, KM went public at a Boston conference in 1993, organized by Ernst & Young.

However, Bob Buckman, one of the early pioneers of KM, attributed the label knowledge management to the creation of C. Jackson Grayson, who was the founder and head of American Productivity & Quality Center (APQC) when they put on the first major conference on knowledge that was held in Houston in the 1990s. The second knowledge conference was put on by McKinsey and Brook Manville. Gurteen argued that at the subsequent conference by APQC, the term "knowledge management" was created to describe what they were doing or trying to do.

The author T. J. Beckman (1999) contends that knowledge management was coined for the first time in 1986 by Karl M. Wiig, the chair and CEO of the Knowledge Research Institute and professor of KM at The Hong Kong Polytechnic University. They authored one of the first books on KM, *Knowledge Management Foundations*, published in 1993.

INTELLECTUAL ROOTS OF KM

Many authors have discussed the roots and origins of KM. See, for example, Karl M. Wiig (1993b and 1997), Harlan Cleveland (1985), Herbert A. Simon (1976), and Peter M. Senge (1990). Wiig in *Knowledge Management: An Emerging Discipline Rooted in a Long History* (2000), identified these intellectual roots of KM in this way:

- Religion and Philosophy (e.g., epistemology) to understand the role and nature of knowledge and the permission of individuals "to think for themselves."
- Psychology to understand the role of knowledge in human behavior.
- Economics and social sciences to understand the role of knowledge in society.
- Business Theory to understand work and its organization.
- Rationalization of Work (Taylorism)
- Total Quality Management and Management Sciences to improve effectiveness.
- Psychology, Cognitive Sciences, Artificial Intelligence (AI), and Learning Organization to learn faster than the competition and provide a foundation for making people more effective.

According to Encyclopaedia Britannica (2020), "From the earliest times, in Egypt and Babylon, training in craft skills was organized to maintain an adequate number of craftsmen. The Code of Hammurabi of Babylon, which dates from the 18th century BCE, required artisans to teach their crafts, transfer, and share their knowledge to the next generation. . . . By the 13th century, a similar practice had emerged in Western Europe in the form of craft guilds. It was a system suited to the domestic industry, with the master working in his own premises alongside his assistants. This created something of an artificial family relationship, in that the articles of apprenticeship took the place of kinship."

The Knowledge Café concept nurtures a reciprocal knowledge-sharing interaction typical of craft guilds and articles of apprenticeship.

From childhood, we learn the know-how and how-to of everything. We often know more from what we see or do than what we hear. What we tell our children and what we do are both consciously and unconsciously knowledge sharing. Our actions must match our words for our children to learn what is right and wrong. Knowledge sharing has proven to be the most effective way of transferring knowledge and molding values for individuals and organizations. For example, in surgical residency programs, there is the powerful traditional teaching method of "see one, do one, teach one." Apprenticeship, mentoring, coaching, cross-training, see one, do one, teach one, and sharing knowledge have remained the ways of transferring knowledge from one individual to another from one generation to another. The café environment is a space to begin this kind of discussion.

According to the World Development Report (World Bank, 1998), "Knowledge is needed to transform the resources we have into things we need, and to raise standards of living, improve health conditions, provide better education and preserve the environment, and to do this in the most optimum way possible. All these value addition activities require knowledge."

While some of these KM definitions and endeavors are still relevant today, it's fair to say that some of them are non-implementable or not sustainable.

Workplace knowledge management has a long history that has evolved to include on-the-job discussions and training, formal apprenticeships, discussion forums, reason behind corporate libraries, professional training, lessons learned, and mentoring programs (Liu, n.d.).

Knowledge Café is the bridge between the past and the future of knowledge management. We must adopt knowledge management in order to address the imminent loss of workers and their knowledge. The café seems to be the environment that mitigates information hoarding. The mindset of knowledge hoarding engenders a siloed workplace and prevents the organization's cross-functional flow of information. Information hoarding effectively impedes progress. By bringing knowledge workers into the café, you are effectively unclipping their wings. There is an urgent need for a Knowledge Café handbook that makes the study understandable by all industry levels—the white papers and academic texts must be curated and conveyed in a colloquial voice.

Café-style learning is the university of the future. COVID-19 has made the impossible possible, and many who were not only apathetic but hostile to alternative work strategies like teleworking have come to embrace it. That is the working method of the future and the now knowledge economy. Café mindset will be the attitude toward knowledge acquisition, exchange, and transfer of the future.

When I became the president of the Project Management Institute Austin Chapter, we worked to bring 15 of my predecessors to the board transitions and strategic meeting in October 2017. I discovered that past presidents and board members couldn't wait to disappear into thin air as soon as they finished their terms. No one even saw their brake lights! These leaders had performed great exploits and killed many demons. However, I chose not to retrace their footsteps by killing the same monsters. We brought all significant knowledge brokers and leaders to the café for simple but deep knowledge conversations and to make use of their knowledge and wisdom.

Project Management Institute (PMI) defines "knowledge transfer" as "the methodical replication of the expertise, wisdom, insight, and tacit knowledge of crucial professionals into the heads and hands of their coworkers" (Project Management Institute, 2015). Consistent and habitual knowledge sharing prevents organizations from doing unnecessary work while cultivating innovation. PMI's research reveals that most effective organizations at knowledge management improve project outcomes by nearly 35 percent. The duality of leveraging experience and promoting innovation is vital. Organizations will advance from the effective use of their collective knowledge—old and new.

In a KM ecosystem, every employee becomes a purposeful advocate of knowledge free flow throughout the organization. Knowledge becomes obsolete quickly, bad news for those reluctant to share. New knowledge, new discoveries, new technologies, and new circumstances will always make irrelevant knowledge that is not shared. Furthermore, the knowledge that you do not share will eventually be replaced by a machine (World Economic Forum, Forrester, Gartner, Accenture, Hay Group, 2020 Workforce).

Every year, *KMWorld* publishes a list of the top 100 KM companies (see Wells, 2019, for last year's article). These are the organizations that turn data and information into actionable insight that has real business value. Some of these KM companies include HP, IBM, Google, Accenture, Xerox, and Oracle, to name a few. Look at their knowledge management approaches for best practice.

Based on my research, the United States Army and NASA are probably the best knowledge management models in the public sector. Both have a KM Office and chief KM officer for their units and organizations. Over the years, I have worked with these knowledge management veterans. Retired army officers are some of KM's best champions—based on their convictions of the value, relevance, and application in the military.

Knowledge management is gaining enormous traction in the public sector. The American Association of State Highway and Transportation Officials (AASHTO) is a nonprofit, nonpartisan association representing highway and transportation departments in the 50 states, the District of Columbia, and Puerto Rico. In 2018, AASHTO established the Committee on Knowledge Management to provide a forum for collaboration among 52 member-departments for the exchange of information, industry-standard practices, experiences, and emerging approaches and concepts related to knowledge management (AASHTO, 2018). I was part of the committee's designing taskforce. Because of the urgency of knowledge management, eight years ago, the Transportation Research Board (TRB) established a KM Task Force, now information and knowledge management committee, to support its diverse national transportation researchers, including 13,000 researchers and transportation officials that attend its annual meetings.

The Project Management Book of Knowledge (PMBOK) officially added "manage project knowledge" as one of the critical processes for managing a successful project in its sixth version in 2018. The authors recognized the essential loss of project knowledge due to knowledge silos among practitioners and aging professionals. Knowledge management is a necessary tool to address the loss of institutional knowledge. Organizations need it to build bench strength and improve organizational resilience. A KM culture is essential for the creation of new knowledge to meet the challenges of disruptive technologies. Knowledge management should be woven into the tapestry of every organization's architecture.

3.3. KNOWLEDGE FAIR AND CAFÉ: BUSTING SILOS

You cannot have great ideas in a vacuum. New ideas don't emerge from the filing cabinet. Databases and data lakes and repositories are not birthplaces of innovation. Silo is not the middle name of social networking. There are no great ideas inside the head of a hoarder. If you are willing to accommodate any idea, new ideas will be in your residence; there are great ideas in the middle of the noise. Café helps to unleash new ideas and innovation.

Most mission-critical knowledge is held captive in the minds of the organization's workforce. Sharing knowledge is one of the most significant challenges facing organizations today. Organizations have failed to realize the potential benefits of bridging the knowledge-sharing gap. Many knowledge workers, including project managers and especially in the public sector, consider the information gained from professional experience as their job security. According to Hall and Sapsed (2005), employees in project based organizations struggle with issues regarding knowledge sharing. Employees' "hoard" their knowledge to protect their specializations and positions. Knowledge workers are often penalized rather than rewarded for sharing their knowledge.

It's fair to say, though, that there are costs associated with KM, just as there are costs related to any cultural change. Leadership, time, commitment, and resources are among the costs.

So, what is the secret sauce for a conversation and thoroughly integrated knowledge management system or program? There needs to be an unstructured and straightforward way to begin the discussion—a "youthification" approach that gives every knowledge worker a voice. I consider a café approach a home run among dozens of KM techniques.

What Are the Dangers and Disruptions Caused by Information and Knowledge Silos?

Natural silos occur because groups within the organization are defined by location, job function, process area, or other factors. I get it. These natural barriers create independent group cultures.

However, there are also problematic silos when teams, knowledge creators, or project managers within an organization are stranded on knowledge islands. They are not sharing valuable or critical work-related information that impacts other team members, project managers, relevant stakeholders, and the organization as a whole. Silos impede effective collaboration, disrupt feedback, and limit opportunities for maximum productivity, efficiency, and success. Silos impugn the ability to harness the collective will—knowledge of the community.

According to award-winning columnist and journalist Gillian Tett, the word "silo" does not just refer to a physical structure or organization (such as a department). It can also be a state of mind and occur in social groups. "Silos breed tribalism. But they exist in our minds and social groups too" (Tett, 2015). Silos arise because social groups and organizations have conventions about how to classify the world.

Silos are not all bad, but several silos within a team may be selfish and inward-looking, where information and knowledge are hoarded, and there is no space to create new and improved knowledge. Siloed teams can suffer from information obesity. Silos are the antithesis of eating our own dog food. Do we do what we preach, and do we see silos? In the Annual Employee Engagement survey at my organization, the 12,000-employee Texas Department of Transportation, 65 percent of all respondents extremely agreed that there are silos within our agency, even within divisions and sections and teams. It is an organization's responsibility to create a café "safe space" to bust the silos. Today, several KM and silo-busting programs are reversing this trend.

Another example of silos is bottlenecks in a process that relies on one person rather than using several individuals' expertise to ensure the best results and diversity of thought and knowledge. Several community members or individuals' expertise is summoned in communities of practice (CoPs) to ensure that best outcomes and diversity of views and knowledge are utilized to produce the best solution. The assembling of CoPs must be organic and not mandated to be most effective. In our gig economy, building a KM base within communities helps to keep the workforce agile and effective despite turnover. Identifying and connecting knowledge workers in my community help us learn, help, share, and grow.

Stakeholders are often siloed in respective project teams and spend little or no time practicing knowledge management: identifying, capturing, sharing, rejuvenating, creating, and innovating critical organizational knowledge. There's no time to ask questions about knowledge on a project, how to steward or manage it, and make it easily useable, accessible, and relevant to all end users. In silo-busting lunch-and-learn sessions I have facilitated, some attendees complain that their challenge is not the lack of willingness to share their knowledge but the lack of time. They indicated that taking time for appropriate knowledge transfer felt like abandoning their primary duties. Organizations are typically wired in a way that leaves insufficient time for KM. The café is the silo-buster!

Where Do You Start to Build and Nurture a Knowledge-Sharing Culture That Busts Silos?

I've thrown several ideas at the wall hoping that one will stick in terms of creating organizational momentum for a knowledge economy. I'm continually meeting hundreds of practitioners and CoPs across the United States who all seem to come up against the same demon of knowledge loss. I'll tell you why I think Knowledge Café is the panacea.

Knowledge exchange opportunities increase stakeholder engagement. Café can be an incentive for employee engagement. In 2017, 88 percent of businesses sought to improve employee engagement in the workplace (Kronos Incorporated and Future Workplace®, 2017). An engaging milieu or engagement will increase the likelihood of knowledge sharing. People are less likely to share their knowledge in an environment that is not knowledge sharing-friendly or when they are disengaged. There is a binary choice for engaging employees—structured or traditional ways of an engagement or a nontraditional coffee bar setting that I call café-way. A café environment has an open hand, without preconceived outcomes that open the dialogue for engagement. In the absence of engagement, there is disengagement. An employee spends an average of 4.2 years at a job (U.S. Bureau of Labor Statistics, 2020). Engagement during that time is important to capture, acquire, organize, communicate, and share knowledge. Besides, it can take 33 percent of an employee's annual salary to replace a departing employee (Otto, 2017).

Capturing knowledge must be a strategic and proactive effort! Capturing employees' tacit knowledge must occur long before their departure from an organization from retirement, transfer, or job change. Departing employees will not take a knowledge capture exercise seriously after they have submitted their two weeks' notice. The organization's knowledge capture must be regularly implemented and reinforced to nourish a healthy knowledge culture.

It makes me wonder about the future of the workplace and KM. Given the current fast-paced work environment across industries and in all roles, there's insufficient time for data gathering, analysis, and reporting. Research by organizations such as Deloitte/Bersin and McKinsey & Company shows that the future of work is being shaped by automation, robotics, and artificial intelligence, along with workforce talent, skills, and knowledge. KM will play a prominent role in the future of work, and the café makes it easier for this conversation to begin.

Bust silos by encouraging knowledge sharing and collaboration at the Knowledge Café. Diffuse silos by tracking and diverting the escalation path, and diffuse silo tension with professionalism.

3.4. CASE STUDIES: ORGANIZATIONS ARE MISSING OUT FOR NOT EMBRACING KNOWLEDGE TRANSFER— DR. NIDHI GUPTA

The following case study is from Dr. Nidhi Gupta, a trained dentist, and certified project manager. She understands the relevance of people, technology, and process in delivering dentistry and projects.

Introduction and Journey of Knowledge Management in My Career
I have been serving the public sector, the city of Austin, and the state of Texas for almost 10 years. I have realized that the public sector abounds in enormous amounts of data, and if this data is channelized and absorbed correctly, it can be put to great use for Texas citizens. The Health and Human Services Commission (HHSC) has the mission to improve Texans' health, safety, and well-being by offering reliable, effective, and timely support for services through good stewardship of public resources. Though knowledge management is one of the most talked-about subjects in the current era as it relates to benefits in policymaking and service delivery, it is also the most neglected practice when it comes to practical implementation— the human face-to-face interaction and knowledge exchange is sacrificed at the altar of technology.

Organization and Formal Knowledge Transfer Programs

As a public-sector consultant for Texas Health and Human Services Commission (HHSC), I see data that have been accumulated over the years that need to be studied, comprehended, and analyzed to reach some informed decisions. Though the agency uses several tools to disseminate knowledge, there are no formal procedures to strictly enforce knowledge transmission. There are increased efforts, especially with the execution of Senate Bill 200, to aggregate the knowledge centers and centralize the knowledge portals to attain effective decision-making and increase transparency and cost-effective reporting. All the program divisions, business areas, and IT are intricately working to accomplish this effort.

Investment in Knowledge Management

Currently, Texas's state government relies heavily on data marts and data warehouses for data storage repository systems, but unfortunately, these systems vastly operate in isolation. As per the Senate Bill 200, 84th Legislature Regular Session, Health and Human Services is mandated to reorganize the information and data structure agency-wide to provide effective and robust analytics for the data currently residing across diverse source systems and information portals. Further, agencies are requested to define and streamline the data across different program areas and divisions to gather performance measures and create an informed dashboard and effective reporting system to benefit the Texans through data-driven decision-making initiatives. The long-term plan is to automate the knowledge repository, so the data-driven points can run the desired analytics and yield appealing decisions quickly, efficiently, and seamlessly.

Challenges Encountered While Transferring or Sharing Knowledge

Several challenges are faced during knowledge transfer. As the cross-division information and valuable data reside across several siloed source systems, it is virtually difficult to acquire the data, readily access the information, or comprehend and derive any useful analysis. As the federal and state rules and guiding policies change, the underlying information structures and policy guidelines also undergo substantial amendments, thereby putting a lot of onus on legacy information portals to update the information as deemed necessary. As the SMEs across each division and program area are scattered sporadically across the agency, it is challenging to identify the right resource group to assimilate the desired information. In a large agency such as HHSC, it is particularly challenging to identify and approach the correct knowledge groups and get their buy-in on the subject. The SMEs knowledgeable about the program sectors have no common avenue to share, collaborate, and contain the information. The information across divisions stays segregated, with no means to derive consistency and delineate standard business process definitions. Information across the systems resides in legacy systems that are incompatible with other systems and the latest technology trends available in the market. Due to this discrepancy, information and knowledge portals work in silos with no interaction agency-wide.

Issues Encountered When Knowledge Systems
and People Don't Communicate
When there are multiple systems across the agency, and the systems do not mutually interact, the information resides in isolation. The agency cannot benefit from the broad, and in-depth perspectives that the consolidated and unified system can offer. Such knowledge-sharing tools that work in isolation significantly impact the transparency, communications, and coordination within the system and hamper the aligning system activity with the agency priorities. Our organization currently uses these enterprise content management systems and elements: SharePoint, ProjectWise, OnBase, ontology, taxonomy, metadata, information architecture, and so on. There are PMRS (Project Management Repository System), ontology JIRA, and HP ALM as the chief tools to serve as repositories for project-related artifacts and documents in other organizations. At the same time, program-related information and clinical data reside in individual data source systems. For instant messaging, the agency uses Skype business to facilitate daily communications. As we develop

systems to talk to each other, teams across the enterprise should café to understand the best practice for identifying, stewarding, and exchanging institutional knowledge.

Currently, the information gathering with personnel across diverse state setups, facilities, and divisions takes a significant amount of time. It may take even a couple of days to weeks to gather any preliminary data set depending on access issues to the knowledge information portals.

Significance of Sharing Knowledge

Sharing information is very vital to achieve successful outcomes and yield an effective collaborative work environment. Once the teams share their knowledge, there can be a significant improvement in the work operations, and staff can contribute equally and productively to achieve desired outcomes. Additionally, the workforce feels motivated, and Knowledge Café and sharing can help in innovations among the team members. Further, in the absence of any resource, the work will not be impacted, and the operations can move seamlessly. Thus, knowledge sharing can prevent the loss of critical know-how.

Is Knowledge Transfer a Challenge or Fun?

At times, our program divisions are actively involved in knowledge transfer. It encompasses engaging the subject matter experts and business area owners to participate in active brainstorming and Joint Application Development (JAD) sessions to deliver their share of information. However, most of the time, exchanging and transferring information is a challenge due to the difficulties involved in physically engaging the SMEs and bringing them on the same platform. People may show some reluctance in exchanging their knowledge set to safeguard their job security. Information residing in isolated systems with no mutual interaction between the system poses a massive threat to uniform and seamless knowledge dispersal.

Painful Results from Lack of Knowledge Transfer

Due to a lack of proper knowledge transfer, I have encountered impediments in ineffective knowledge dispersal and assimilation.

There have been episodes when the project team has undergone frequent churn due to indecisive and unproductive occurrences because the knowledge gathered is redundant, has gaps, or is conflicting. This has led to adverse impacts on the project as this has resulted in further rework, inferior product, ambiguity, lack of precision, and delayed schedule. Incomplete and inadequate knowledge transfer has created a vague picture in stakeholders' minds. The executive leadership has received skewed metrics on the project progress, accomplishments, and the next steps.

Conclusion
Knowledge sharing and dissemination are vital steps in an organization's success. It involves little discipline to set up preliminary efforts and procedures to implement the knowledge-sharing program. Once established, the organization can benefit instrumentally.

About Dr. Nidhi Gupta
Dr. Nidhi Gupta works for the largest state agency in Texas, HHSC. Everyone seems to have similar challenges when it comes to exchanging and managing knowledge. KM is about systems talking to systems, and people becoming caffeinated with knowledge at the café exchange. Most organizations, especially in the public sector, are still trying to put their arms around the concept of knowledge management. A simple knowledge fair and café will explore where an organization is, what it knows, how they share, and why they should exchange knowledge.

4 ■ Designing Effective Knowledge Cafés

Chapter Objectives

- Understand why intentionality is important
- Discuss the where, when, and how of conducting a café and fair
- Understand the importance of developing the right café questions
- Demonstrate various ways of communicating at the café
- Explore examples from case studies
- Café enablers
- Identify helpful resources

4.1. THE INTENTIONALITY OF KNOWLEDGE MANAGEMENT (JOKE MANAGEMENT)

I have never found myself in a café by accident. It was purposive and predetermined. Knowledge management must be intentional to be successful. It must be a strategy of the organization. Like a project, it doesn't manage itself—it must be managed. Implementing KM means creating a conducive environment to capture, transfer, share, and create new knowledge (innovation) possible. Make it a culture!

Knowledge exchange and transfer (KET) are important components of knowledge management that encompass knowledge sharing. To reap maximum benefits for an organization, knowledge of KET must be intentional. According to the Project Management Institute, 2015, The Pulse of the Profession, "Knowledge Transfer is the methodical replication of the expertise, wisdom, insight, and tacit knowledge of key professionals into the heads and hands of their coworkers." KM is methodical and intentional.

Knowledge is the most important asset of an organization. The ability to preserve organizational knowledge determines profitability, sustainability, competitiveness, and the ability to grow. No organization can afford to lose its knowledge base. According to the World Economic Forum, 95 percent of CEOs claim that knowledge management is a critical factor in an organization's success; and 80 percent of companies mentioned in *Fortune* magazine have staff explicitly assigned to KM (Kampioni & Ciolfitto, 2015).

Innovation is the child of new knowledge created through the process of KM. According to Pasher and Ronen (2011), innovation has three components: reusing existing organizational knowledge, creativity or invention, and exploitation to create value. A balance between these elements ensures that the knowledge is not wasted, that the organization renews, and that innovation has a business rationale. To be truly innovative, a product, service, or company has to be unique, it has to be valuable, and it has to be worthy of exchange (Stevenson & Kaafarani, 2011).

However, the sad reality is that the most critical organizational knowledge is confined in individuals' minds; individuals lock up knowledge in the form of data and information in case of studies, files, and documents. Knowing what we know is challenging enough, and even more problematic is for everyone to share the knowledge freely. Osterloh and Frey (2000) posit that sharing specialized knowledge is the greatest challenge facing organizations today. Consider the five generations of knowledge workers working together in the project management space today. Are we going to leave knowledge transfer to chance or assume that knowledge creators are sharing?

A healthy knowledge culture leads to a knowledge society and must be a systematic and disciplined endeavor. How do you create a knowledge-sharing culture? A KM program must be calculated, well planned, executed, and perceived as an organizational strategy to be successful.

What a company or an individual knows today will not suffice for tomorrow. Burn, Marshall, and Burnett (2002) were right when they said, "Knowledge is dynamic since what is new and innovative today may well be the core for tomorrow."

QUESTIONS ABOUT INTENTIONALITY
- Many organizational leaders reading this book already understand the importance of a knowledge economy, but are they intentional about knowledge management?
- How much of the organization's budget is steered toward KM?
- Has a knowledge audit been conducted?
- Do you have a climate where KM thrives?
- Are employees incentivized for sharing knowledge?
- What is your engagement plan for the mass baby boomer exodus in the next decade?
- Are you intentional?
- Are you planning?
- Is there a proactive knowledge transference system plan in place?

Many things in life happen naturally: During volcanic eruptions, ash picks up so much friction that the build-up of static electricity causes lightning. Moroccan goats naturally learn to climb trees in order to better snack on their tasty argan fruit. Canada's Spotted

Lake has a summer style—dessert roses, a special form of the mineral gypsum, developed in dry sandy places that occasionally flood and look like polka dots. On the other hand, knowledge and projects don't organically happen; they are managed. We need the skills, experiences, and expertise of every stakeholder to manage projects and operations successfully. All project management begins with the knowledge in people—knowledge assets—the totality of an organization's intellectual capital. There's often the question of who owns the knowledge. Only after this intellectual capital is identified, leveraged, and shared is the question of ownership valid.

Another major setback of knowledge management is that the discipline is loaded with jargon and may sometimes sound too academic for the average knowledge creator and user. There are multiple definitions of concepts and not a singular body of knowledge. I agree several practitioners think that the problem is that we have too many consultants who see this practice as a quick opportunity to make some money—they rarely do the foundation work to understand what the theory is or integrate their work back into the discipline's body of knowledge. There are several standard efforts that have attempted to standardize terms, but the challenge is always that the theorists rarely engage in those efforts and the practitioners only know what they have done. The best approach is to say KM is an ample practice with many perspectives. Each perspective has some truth and value, but we need to learn to see it from that perspective. Just as there are facets to every medical definition, so are their facets to every KM definition (Denise Bedford, personal communication, April 2020).

For the first time in my lifetime, five generations of project managers and knowledge workers are found in the same project space, and every generation speaks its own knowledge language. There is the "hey, write me a letter," the "let's get together," "send me an email," "txtme," and "let's TikTok."

No one gate-crashes into the café. I always know when to go to the café, whom to meet at the café, and which café to attend, including the beverage of my choice at the café. It's intentional. Everyone says that they are managing knowledge, but intentionality is conspicuously absent. To many, KM is like a New Year's resolution. You know what I'm talking about—New Year's resolutions are forgotten in the second month of the year and remembered again at the beginning of the next year. It's like saying that you are managing a project without requirements, no defined scope and objectives, and as for deliverables, you are not sure of your project's outcome.

This isn't knowledge management; it's called "joke management." There is this fun story of an award ceremony in heaven (this is a joke that has gone through quality assurance). An announcement was made to recognize a man that fulfilled his mission on earth as husband and dad. There was an unusual silence until one man raised his hand. When he was called to the stage, he was asked to share the secret of his success—how he beat everyone and exceeded all expectations as a husband and a dad. His response: "I don't know what you are talking about. My wife asked me to raise my hand." There you go! Intentionality matters.

The worst thing that can happen to a person, family, or organization is the absence of faithfulness, steadfast love, and knowledge. Knowledge is the chief among them because you will understand steadfast love and faithfulness if you possess the knowledge. I believe that there's spirituality in a lot of things. That is why we have feelings, dreams, passion, and love. But, spirituality without grace, love, compassion, and knowledge will be very shallow. If you need to grow in any business area or spirituality, you'll need to grow in grace and knowledge. The quiescent knowledge not shared and given new strength to is useless to everyone.

4.2. KNOWLEDGE CAFÉ AND FAIR TO THE RESCUE

Café = dialogue—(writing + lecture)

The café is about conversations, knowledge sharing, and making sense of what we know, not necessarily about writing, presentations, and lectures. Some of the innovative ideas I've gotten in my life emerged during a conversation—at the café.

The conventional way of learning is through mediums like instructions (lecturing), videos, and reading (books). At the café, there's no lecturing. Instead, there's dialogue and what Harvard University physics professor Eric Mazur calls Peer Instruction for Active Learning. David Gurteen called it "flipped teaching," which reverses, or "flips," traditional in-class lectures and homework. Students watch the teacher's prerecorded lecture at home, and in-class time is used for students to test their skills, apply their knowledge, and interact through hands-on projects, discussions, and exercises. Knowledge management implementation involves a monumental paradigm shift in any professional environment. That's why I recommend having a Personal Knowledge Register prior to a Knowledge Café. See chapters 2.3 and 2.6, and there'll be a café framework and step-by-step approach in chapter 4.3.

> Education in a sense, is a two-step process. One step is the transfer of information, and we have many ways of transferring information. One is books, the other is video, and . . . by lecture. . . . However, the crucial part of education is for the student to make sense of that information, to have the aha moments–oh, I get it. So, you can apply the knowledge embedded in the information in a new context.
>
> —Eric Mazur

Making sense of what we learned only happens when we have the breathing space to think, question, converse, dialogue, and exchange knowledge. That is when the "aha!" moment happens; it's the café.

Entering a Knowledge Café, movement from owned-knowledge to shared-knowledge is seamless. There is an informal integration of knowledge from fellow patrons, aka knowledge workers, and the appetite for learning increases. The analogy of the typical siloed workplace can be described as a white-linen restaurant experience in which patrons expect insulation from fellow patrons. I'll call it knowledge social distancing. Expectations of conversations are muted and private. Talk between tables is considered impolite.

On the other hand, in a café, crosstalk improves the experience! The café concept implies an interactive ecosystem convergent of various interests and players in the knowledge management orbit. It is a one-stop shop for connection, collaboration, and conversation.

The café concept supports an appropriate, nonthreatening environment where knowledge is shared and exchanged. Once an organization's mindset embraces knowledge management, there is fun to be had in the process. Inevitably, I see the incidence of workplace burnout decrease. Everyone benefits in the café!

Another potential benefit of the Knowledge Café is more excellent employee retention. A national survey by Kronos Incorporated and Future Workplace (2017) of 614 human resources leaders took a candid look at how burnout drives turnover. It was amazing that 87 percent of respondents claimed improved retention is a high/critical priority (Kronos Incorporated and Future Workplace, 2017). In my research, 95 percent of the leaders admit that employee burnout is sabotaging workforce retention and felt there was no apparent solution on the horizon. What could be more comfortable than a welcoming and stress-free environment?

Hmm, does this sound like a corner café? Café is a low-churn space where knowledge transfer, exchange, and retention thrive. Knowledge management done right is the corporate landscape that prevents burnout.

As described in the previous chapter, Knowledge Café is a knowledge management (KM) technique used to surface a group's collective knowledge, learn from each other, share ideas and insights, and gain a deeper understanding of topics and KM best practices. Knowledge fair (fair) is an event that showcases organizational knowledge assets and best practices. Knowledge fair is an alternative to traditional presentations when more interactive experiences are desirable.

Knowledge Café can occur anywhere—virtually or face-to-face. I have supplemented these less formal settings with a knowledge fair using a café-style approach. At knowledge fair events, we showcase our organizational knowledge assets and knowledge exchange best practices to surface the agency's collective knowledge, learn from industry experts and each other, strengthen our communities of practice

(CoPs), and share ideas and insights. We gain a deeper understanding of knowledge management topics, issues, and knowledge transfer best practices at the fair. This interactive experience helps us to break information and knowledge silos and improve efficiencies and resilience.

Knowledge fair is an alternative to traditional presentations and is a more interactive experience. Because one size does not fit all, I prefer to combine a Knowledge Café with a knowledge fair to add some level of formality. This combination gave me the liberty or leverage to escalate a Knowledge Café to a leadership café—the outcomes are considered fine-tuned for management policy, institutionalization, and KM implementation. I will discuss the leadership fair in chapter 11.

Knowledge fair and café help address the pain points of an us versus them mentality, fear, multiple locations, and a demanding culture that discourages discussion. Call a knowledge fair and café to begin a knowledge management conversation!

EXAMPLES OF THE CAFÉ QUESTIONS

Over the years, I have used a knowledge fair and café to convert all types of professionals to knowledge managers. I have convened knowledge workers, mentors, and CoP leaders to a Knowledge Café that is nonthreatening, with no preconceived outcomes, driven by powerful questions such as:

- What are knowledge management techniques and tools at work in your workspace? Do they work?
- What are the barriers to knowledge sharing in your professional environment(s) and how do you overcome them?
- How can you move from "owned knowledge" to "shared knowledge"?
- What are knowledge management collaborative and tools at work in your workspace or in your community of practice?
- How can you start and sustain a community of practice?

4.3. DESIGNING A KNOWLEDGE FAIR AND CAFÉ: BEST PRACTICES, WHERE, WHEN, AND HOW

In organizations where I have managed project knowledge, I usually organize knowledge fairs and café. I believe that all organizations are not the same, and what works for one environment may fall apart in another setting. So, my café is a combo café and goes beyond the recommendations by David Gurteen or Dan Ramenyi.

GURTEEN'S CAFÉ GUIDE

The café usually runs for 1½–2 hours depending on how much time is available, but never less than one hour. The only hard and fast rule is that most of the time is spent in conversation—it is not about one person presenting to the group. The value of the café is in the conversation itself and the learning that each individual takes away. Here is a typical Gurteen café session format.

1. The facilitator or host may give a presentation on what Knowledge Cafés are about and the role of conversation in business life (about 5 minutes)
2. One hour with a few conversational exercises, unless participants are already familiar with the concept of the café
3. The facilitator welcomes people to the café (about 5 minutes)
4. The facilitator spends 10–15 minutes outlining the subject or theme of the café and poses a single open-ended question. For example, if the theme is knowledge sharing, then the question for the group might be, "What are the barriers to knowledge sharing in an organization, and how do you overcome them?"
5. The group breaks into small groups of 3 or 4 (no more than 5) and discusses the questions for about 45 minutes, then comes back together as a whole group for the final 45 minutes, when the individual groups share their thoughts. If the café is a one-question café, it's appropriate for small table discussants to rotate from their tables every 15 minutes.

6. Optionally, in the small group sessions, people change tables every 15 minutes to broaden the number of people they get to interact with and thus the differing perspectives of the group

7. Usually, no attempt is made to capture the conversation, as doing so tends to destroy the conversation. In some circumstances, it makes sense to capture things from the café depending on its purpose, and there are ways of doing this that minimally interfere with the dynamics of the conversation.

ENHANCED PROCEDURES FOR A CAFÉ EVENT

To enhance the café as described by Gurteen, I recommend these procedures. You need to plan and have an objective and expectation that will be measured against the outcome of a café or fair event. At the café, everyone's voice counts, fear is eliminated, and the environment preserves the conversational flow.

1. Walking into the café is like walking into any networking event. You get to know other knowledge-curious animals. Warning: Most people are not conversational whizzes. You have to make them talk.

2. Virtual café is a challenge since you have to log into different sessions and come back for plenary sessions.

3. Have a communication and training strategy; identify champions, experts, super users, or early adopters in the business who face similar knowledge and information challenges.

4. Choose a timekeeper and notetaker.

5. Choose your table. The café is better at tables. Allowing about 4–6 people at a table gives everyone at a table an opportunity to contribute. Everyone at the café should be able to share their knowledge. It helps to announce that people should choose a table after the first set of networking. I like to give attendees the first 15 minutes for networking or using icebreakers. I encour-

age attendees from the same office to sit at different tables.

6. Participants can choose to sit, stand, or even sit on the floor. This is okay if everyone is comfortable and especially if this is an unstructured café.

7. Break the café into sessions or parts. When I have a 2-hour café, I break it down to three 45-minute sections or parts, according to the expectations or objectives of the café.

8. Café discussions are mostly held at the small table meeting, even though there are opportunities for general discussions after short table café exchanges. I've had several virtual cafés as a result of COVID-19. I used the chat section to encourage responses and made sure that everyone contributed in a café.

9. Collect notes and summaries from the tables: There is a designated notetaker for each table. Summaries of the discussions from the tables are collected at the end of each question discussed for everyone to be enriched from all small-group discussions.

10. Share best practice in terms of how to communicate with employees and reinforce the knowledge-sharing behaviors.

11. Compile knowledge-exchange notes, and new knowledge that emerges from fair and café are distributed through push and pull communication methods. These notes and summaries from the table are useful for the entire knowledge community, especially those who couldn't participate. I usually send out these notes to the whole of the knowledge community and post them on the Knowledge Café site (Wiki site) for the community. Café is knowledge crowdsourcing.

POSSIBLE GOALS OF A CAFÉ

Specific goals for the Knowledge Café and fair events I have hosted:

- Identify knowledge-sharing techniques, methods, and best practices from teams, divisions, and offices: Here, the purpose of your fair and café is to scan the organization to know how others are exchanging knowledge and the methods or techniques they are using.

- Show techniques that are working and the setbacks: The purpose of your café event may be to know what's working and what's not working in the context of knowledge exchange and knowledge management, setbacks, best practices, solutions, and so on.
- Connect knowledge communities or communities of practice to other communities: While you can have a café for one or all of these purposes, you can also have a café and/or fair to connect different knowledge communities to interact with each other for the single purpose of knowledge exchange or creating an environment of KM.
- Connect knowledge users to resources: Another important reason for a café may be to connect knowledge users to resources. It may be to provide knowledge technology enablers, tools, and resources to knowledge communities.
- Identify information/knowledge silos and how to break them: An excellent café event may be to identify silos and how to break them.
- Show an enterprise knowledge diversity, collateral, culture, tools and techniques, and knowledge champions.

GENERAL FRAMEWORK FOR A CAFÉ

Ground rules for guidance—a framework: Here are some rules you may follow when organizing a café. This is important as the café is not a typical meeting. Minds are being connected to the transformational exchange of knowledge. Typical characteristics of a knowledge fair and café include:

- Conversation covenant
- Voice your "crazy idea" and let others test it
- Driven by powerful questions based on the team and purpose
- Promotes dialogue, not debates or argument

- Encourages open and creative conversation
- Preserve conversational flow
- Everyone has a voice—everyone participates in the process
- Values diversity of perspective—identifies options, possibilities, pros and cons
- Draws out broad participation through small-group conversation format
- Elicits deeper understanding of issues
- Lively facilitation
- Develops and evolves thinking on specific business issues
- Eliminates fear
- No preconceived outcomes
- No coercion
- Allows consensus to emerge
- Reciprocity
- A pledge to apply what we learned
- Fun

SOME DOS AND DON'TS AT THE CAFÉ

These will prevent you from going off a cliff in a café and juice up the café experience. Some of us are already sick of another meeting.

- Avoid conference presentation-style format (presentation is in the conversation)
- Avoid one-way knowledge exchange (café is two-way)
- No social distancing in a café, unless local officials require social distancing
- Convenient venue for participants
- The café can be face-to-face or virtual
- It's okay to be vulnerable; develop trust
- Attendees choose to attend and not necessarily "voluntold"
- Team-building games, jokes, snacks, and lots of laughter
- Have a theme for each café; this provides guidance for café questions (I have several sample questions at the end of this chapter)

POSSIBLE KM ACTIVITIES AND DISCUSSIONS

Some of the KM activities and discussion that participants have brought to the café:

- Tools for Enterprise Content Management used as standard systems of record such as MS Delve, SharePoint, ProjectWise, and OnBase
- Knowledge interview activities and how knowledge is captured from experts
- Social learning and communities, collaborative platforms used for knowledge exchange such as LinkedIn, Kudos for knowledge advocates, Slack, Microsoft Team, Wikis, and social media
- Storytelling knowledge practices (some organizations such as Alberta DOT and IBM have Storyteller positions on staff)
- Best Practice Office activities (process improvement, project management, etc.)
- Knowledge capturing templates, CoP charters, communication plans, strategies, etc.

At TxDOT, during our KM development, we identified 50+ communities of practice, developed a knowledge interview program, and held regular Knowledge Café events that have attracted participation of 90 percent of knowledge managers from its 59 divisions and districts. The reason for the first knowledge fairs and cafés we had was to bring these CoPs together for knowledge exchange.

REASONS FOR OUR FIRST CAFÉ

Some of the reasons for our first fair and café:

- Bring the groups' collective knowledge to the surface; to learn from each other, share ideas and insights, and understand topics, issues, and knowledge management (KM) best practices across the enterprise. "Knowledge Cafés are best convened where there are many stakeholders and opinions, and there are no right or wrong answers" (David Gurteen).
- Understand industry trends, such as the American Association of State Transportation Officials (AASHTO) and

the TRB's Information and Knowledge Management Committee. TRB is one of the seven major program divisions of the National Academies of Science, Engineering, and Medicine (NASEM). We look beyond the public-sector KM space to the private sector with several KM associations and organizations.

- Meet other communities of practice (CoPs) across the organization practicing KM; we identified and began to mature more than 50 CoPs.
- Share best practices and collaborate to build bench strength for organizational resilience and effectiveness.
- Learn and access resources, tools, and techniques for knowledge sharing in our professional communities (CoPs), divisions and districts, or sections.
- Identify existing knowledge sharing and retention activities and grow in KM.
- Innovate, create new knowledge, and stop the brain drain!
- Discuss how others are collaborating and staying ahead of the game in a café!
- Meet up for reverse mentoring. Former GE CEO Jack Welch championed the concept in the late 1990s, asking GE executives to pair with people in the organization to learn how to use the then-emerging Internet. The truth is that iron sharpens iron. When two knowledge managers are doing something similar, and come to the café, they learn from each other. They sharpen each other. The novice or younger person learns from the older person and vice versa.

In a café, there is far more freedom for knowledge workers to express their opinions. The ground rules tell everyone that there's no right or wrong answer. Everyone has a place at the table.

Employee Coercion Is Not Allowed in a Café
Every knowledge worker at the knowledge fair and café events buzz with electricity. About 93 percent of the attendees expressed an interest in attending the next café; we measured customer satisfaction

at 93 percent. The café was instrumental to the birth of other techniques like the knowledge interview, mentoring, incorporating technology into KM's people component, and developing an enterprise KM strategy.

Besides office or business settings, Knowledge Café and fairs can be used for a variety of other great purposes. I have had a Knowledge Café with my kids, family, clan, board, and teams outside the office. I designed a café for finding a middle ground between developers and operations on security (DevSecOps). I've also used the café format to find solutions, break information silos, identify best practices for projects and programs, deal with difficult stakeholders, relationship and team building, share innovative ideas, and so on.

Example: Café to Understand Enterprise Knowledge

As a strategic project manager, when I wanted to scan our organization to understand various elements of KM, I knew that I needed to café with some knowledge brokers from specific segments of our organization—in particular, Human Resources, Information Management, Communications, Library, and Information Science, strategy, and so on. These stakeholders have institutional knowledge and wisdom, and they understand the knowledge exchange process, information, technology, and content that enable KM. This kind of café is very focused—we want to identify and rank KM elements that are active in our organization.

POSSIBLE QUESTIONS AT A SIMPLE CAFÉ

This kind of simple investigative café will be used to answer questions such as:

- What is your role in the organization?
- What is happening in your area?
- How are we sharing information and knowledge?
- What are some KM best practices?
- How can we increase the velocity of knowledge exchange?
- What systems are talking at each other instead of to each other?
- Where are the silos?

- How do we bust silos?
- What are the best practices for busting dangerous silos and preserving the good ones?
- What information is findable and accessible? Note: We access knowledge but search for information.

Café for Developing an Enterprise KM Strategy

You can have a knowledge fair and café just for fun or for the case of knowledge exchange and knowledge connection. However, you may want to go beyond that to galvanize the whole enterprise for an environment and culture where knowledge exchange and transfer are predominant. If you're going to develop an enterprise strategy for KM, there are several things you'll need to do. A café can be handy for bringing specific knowledge leaders and business units with institutional knowledge to access and rank the knowledge management elements or activities already in existence in your organization. These elements will help develop an enterprise KM strategy and organize a café, but you don't have to follow them meticulously since every organization and setting are different.

POSSIBLE ACTIONS FOR AN ENTERPRISE STRATEGY

1. Identify goals and objectives.
   a. Scan the organization for elements of KM to rank the elements and activities.
   b. Identify KM practices and activities to carry out the strategy.
   c. Identify resource needs and enablers.
   d. Develop metrics and evaluation methods.
2. Interface with relevant stakeholders to plan the café.
   a. Decide if you'll need or require elaborate props or facilities.
   b. Set a date and select a convenient venue.
   c. Set targets for invitees. Traditionally, invite 20–30 open-minded café-goers who have common or shared interests. I've hosted about 100 curious participants in a café.
   d. Develop an agenda for the café (break it down into parts of sections).

e. Develop questions for discussion during the café. The questions will provide answers for the KM activities and practices and be of the attendees' common interest.

f. Rank the questions from zero to 5: zero means the KM element does not exist; one means the element is randomly applied; five means the element is fully integrated and deployed across the enterprise.

3. Practical actions, or what to do at the café.

a. Give attendees a few minutes to interact and briefly introduce the purpose of the café. The café is broken down into sessions based on the question we generated.

b. Provide badges and create a way for attendees to reach each other post café—exchanging emails and other contact information is helpful.

c. Introduce participants. In a large meeting of more than 30 people, it's more beneficial for participants to introduce themselves at the table to save time. I have had a café of 67 attendees and allowed everyone to introduce themselves by mentioning their names and the business units they represent. It lasted for about 7 minutes. Because this is a simple café event, there's no need for a short presentation from anyone. We showed a quick 90-second or two-minute video and had a message on the subject matter, told a joke, and had an ice breaker.

d. Be sure there is a continuous supply of hot or cold drinks—coffee and teas. You may keep the lights and music on. Jokes are the coffee for a virtual café. But, you don't have to serve drinks or snacks at the café.

e. Introduce the objective or purpose of the case at the beginning.

f. Acquaint attendees with the café ground rules, give them a question to discuss, and send them to the small group exchanges. Have a timekeeper.

g. Read the question(s) to be discussed at the group or tables. Repeat this until you've responded to the question that provides solutions or answers to the objective of the café.

Encourage everyone to share and participate in small groups.

h. Get all the tables back to the plenary session to harvest new ideas that emerged from small groups.

i. Call the groups together. Take summaries from the small table teams.

j. Collect the written summaries or ask the scribes to email you the summaries.

k. After all the café exchanges, provide some consensus to the attendees. What is the outcome of the café? What's next? I usually administer a live survey to my café attendees to know what they'll like to do next and if they want to attend another café. I've had more than 93 percent of attendees enjoying another fair and café.

4. After the café, provide summaries to the attendees and those who couldn't make it and the next line of action. Synthesize the deliberation and use them for KM policy. For the above café, the rankings and the identified KM elements' analysis will provide guidance for crafting an enterprise KM strategy.

5. Create more appetite for another café.

6. Update your Personal Knowledge Register.

7. Implement the next steps. For example, develop a budget, a detailed plan for subsequent initiatives, a list of milestones, and a communication plan. You can have another café with critical stakeholders to develop these.

BEGINNERS STEPS FOR KM INSTITUTIONALIZATION

If you believe in the concept of managing knowledge and want to lead the effort for institutionalizing KM in your organization, here are some of the steps you'll want to take.

1. Understand KM and explore some of its techniques or elements like knowledge fair and café.

2. Hold a knowledge fair and café.

3. Meet a potential sponsor or champion. When efforts are made to transform a workplace to that of a knowledge

management environment, it is best accomplished with the support of an executive advocate within the culture and to secure the buy-in of large, vital stakeholders in your organization. Without an endorsement from upper management or a sponsor, it is nearly impossible to affect culture-wide change.

A solid KM approach can only be developed without mandate or management compulsion. Dr. Moses Adoko, the chief knowledge officer of NASA Goddard Space Flight Center, calls it a federated approach (Adoko, 2019a, 2019b). Every division or department in your organization is unique and should tailor KM practice to its environment. The café is the launching pad for a group's thinking and not a prescriptive dictate. It is a meeting around questions or hot issues where every participant's opinion is welcomed. A Knowledge Café can create a space to achieve reverse mentoring.

4.4. THE IMPORTANCE OF CAFÉ DISCUSSION QUESTIONS

The Knowledge Café is replacing complexity with simplicity. It's not only about sharing, but it's also about identifying, capturing, analyzing, and creating knowledge and rejuvenating. Café questions are designed to stir up amazing answers. An answer can never be greater than the questions. So, questions must be on issues that are of mutual interest to participants. As knowledge carriers, creators, and users gather at the café, expect the answers to create new knowledge. Expect assumptions to be challenged. Expect obsolete knowledge to be replaced and new knowledge to exhilarate participants. Implementing a Knowledge Café pushes a cultural paradigm to a knowledge ecosystem.

RECOMMENDATIONS FOR CREATING A CAFÉ SPACE

Talk to a colleague who shares the same concerns with you about knowledge and information sharing across the enterprise. Ask some of these questions:

- How do you feel about sharing your knowledge? Empowered, hesitant, or feeling duped?

- Where do you see knowledge management activities, such as knowledge sharing and transfer, in our organization?
- How easy is it to find the information you need to do your job?
- How can we connect with other professionals who encounter similar project challenges so we can learn from each other?
- Do you sometimes wish you could share your experience with younger professionals or engage in reverse-mentoring, where younger professionals share what they know with much older ones? How do you make this happen?
- What can we do so we are smarter and don't reinvent the wheel in projects and programs?
- Discuss how a knowledge-sharing workplace will provide a space to build bench strength for organizational efficiency and resilience.
- How can we use a knowledge-sharing atmosphere to create a space for increased learning, collaborations, and help our organization gain a competitive advantage?
- What mission-critical knowledge are we at risk of losing? What should our prevention strategy be?
- How does our organization know what its knowledge workers know or the need to have a knowledge audit? How do we know what we know and what we need to know?
- How do we develop a knowledge map of where different skills, experience, expertise, and abilities are stored in the organization, and why should we know?
- What has our organization done to capture its intellectual capital for sharing, knowledge resurgence, and creating new knowledge?
- How do you feel when you know that you'll be leaving the organization or your department with all your experience and expertise?
- Do you think we could've done better by capturing and sharing that knowledge?

- Who will be a great sponsor or champion to facilitate a Knowledge Café?
- Who do you think will be a grand champion or sponsor of an enterprise KM?
- How and when can we start the knowledge management discussion, to know what's already existing at a café-styled meeting?
- A top-down approach will not work. How can we make the Knowledge Café organic?
- List all the knowledge workers you think will be beneficiaries of a café.
- Everyone is busy; how do we make knowledge transfer as painless as possible?
- We don't want to build another "monster" program. How do we make this as simple as possible?
- How do we measure and show success?
- When can we have our first Knowledge Café?

POSSIBLE CAFÉ QUESTIONS

Use the above questions or similar questions to start discussions at your café. I recommend that café questions be open-ended questions. Yes-or-no questions can be on a survey. The beauty of a café is that it is a café of dialogue, not a debate.

When you are contemplating an organizational café or KM program, ask yourself and other vital stakeholders these questions:

- When you share your knowledge, does it make you feel empowered? Duped?
- Where do you see knowledge management activities (like knowledge sharing and knowledge transfer) occurring in the organization?
- What is the organization's strategy for knowledge management?
- What do you consider to be the priority for an implemented KM program?
- What are the generational challenges in our organizational knowledge exchange?

- How do we share taboo info?
- What are the roadblocks to free-flowing information and knowledge?
- How do you maintain or ensure reusable content?
- Where is the balance between security and collaborative work?
- What is our succession planning strategy?
- How do we become a learning organization?
- How do we prevent loss or brain drain?
- Do you have tension between transparency and knowledge sharing?
- How do you improve organizational efficiency and resilience?
- If we prove to you that an investment in KM provides measurable added value (400 percent ROI), will you invest in it?
- If KM increases efficiency, improves performance, and establishes a competitive advantage, will the business case requirement(s) be met?
- What are the consequences of knowledge loss and reasons to implement a KM program?
- Where is the existence of knowledge silos, and could a KM program be a response to busting it?
- How do we balance KM's people, process, content, and technology components while providing project leadership/governance for each category?
- Will you support the staff connecting with other professionals who are encountering similar project challenges for the purpose of learning from each other?
- Do you wish that you could share your learned wisdom with younger and less experienced professionals?
- Is it smarter to share acquired knowledge or develop new processes for projects and programs?
- Do you believe that a knowledge-sharing workplace will build bench strength for organizational efficiency and resilience?

- Do you believe that knowledge management is an effective strategy to mitigate the loss of project knowledge?
- Do you think there is a need to have a knowledge audit?
- Will it be of interest to see where the best ideas, the best technologies, and our organization's best expertise reside?
- Do we have a knowledge map?
- How would you deal with the drastic exodus metric (11,000/day) for knowledge workers due to retirement or job mobility?
- Could you start a knowledge management discussion at your senior level to better understand what the organization is willing to do to cultivate a knowledge society?
- Who [else] are the organization's key players, champions, and possible invitees to an enterprise café?

Call for a café today. In 2019, I presented in a national workshop representing dozens of public- and private-sector organizations; 75 percent of attendees did not have a formal KM program. Attendees were drawn from the public sectors, including 50 U.S. state departments of transportation, research and educational institutions, and the private sector. Many may be waiting for the perfect conditions before they start. You will never have an ideal condition. Start.

4.5. COMMUNICATION AT THE CAFÉ AND COLLABORATION ENABLERS

The role of the project manager is 90 percent communication. The communication at the café is marked with curiosity, openness, knowledge connections, and reciprocal knowledge exchange. The purpose of the café is to break open conversation and enable project and organization success. It's about communication and appreciating our individual and collective tribal knowledge.

Language and communications in a café are the very necessary ingredients for an environment that unleashes KET. Proper communication and language make possible effective social interaction and influence how people conceive concepts and objects and respond to interactive social learning and knowledge exchange.

At its best, a Knowledge Café adheres to several conversational principles that help create a relaxed, informal environment conducive to open dialogue and learning. It is non-adversarial and nonthreatening. The Knowledge Café is a place where KM (knowledge capture, acquiring, organizing, communicating, sharing, and transfer) is discussed and brainstormed. Furthermore, techniques are explored and expanded upon so that CoPs and others can implement what is learned. The learning that individuals take away, and the conversation in the café itself, is the most critical value of the café. It unleashes the power of collective intelligence; it whets the appetite. Take it to the café.

SOME COLLABORATION TOOLS

What enables collaboration? The best café is face-to-face. However, there is an array of alternatives. Some of these are free. No matter the tools, the most essential part of the café are the people.

- Video conferencing: Zoom, WebEx, GoToMeeting, Microsoft Teams, Skype, Flowdock, Slack, Google Hangout, HipChat, Flock, Brief, Facebook Workplace, Chanty
- Creating together tools: Igloo, Google Docs, Quip, Codingteam
- Project and tasks: ProofHub, Redbooth, Wimi, Monday .com, Asana, Dapulse, Milanote, Trello (Kanban board)
- Others: Dropbox, Evernote, MindMeister, Bannersnacks, Adobe XD, GitHub, Office Online, Bit.ai, Hightail, Google Drive, Salesmate, Freshconnect, Acquire

I once asked David Gurteen what he thought about my version of the café. Here's the version I presented to him.

Knowledge Café is a collaborative space and a mindset, an unstructured knowledge-transfer vehicle—learning, my way, sharing, my way, our minds are ignited and reawakened, we leave with new knowledge. The Knowledge Café can be held in a space in the office or at an outside location, or it could be held virtually on a video meeting platform.

Here's David's response:

"The Knowledge Café is not only a collaborative space but also a mindset. It can be adapted for many different purposes. One application is as a lightly structured knowledge-transfer vehicle where each participant learns from others in their own way. The Knowledge Café can be held in a space in the office or at an outside location or held virtually on a video meeting platform such as Zoom, WebEx, and Teams. It is the antithesis of a presentation style of knowledge-sharing. In a Knowledge Café, everyone has a voice and every voice counts."

So, the café is a collaborative space for connected minds. Author Steven Johnson in his TED Talk on "where good ideas come from," concluded that "chance favors the connected mind." Innovations and inventions are a product of networks and connections rather than a matter of serendipity or presentation at conferences. The thrust of the café is connection, communication, and conversation. This is one of the most extraordinary times in the knowledge revolution. The boundaries for learning and knowledge acquisitions are being ripped off. Most innovation comes from nearby innovation when an idea behind a cup of coffee interfaces with another idea behind a cup of coffee.

The café is a mindset, and communication is boundless. For instance, according to NCHRP 20-68A, in 2014, "Accenture has over 1,500 online CoPs on its Knowledge Exchange portal, where people come together in virtual groups spanning geographic and organizational boundaries to collaborate with each other, connect with peers and experts, and access the latest thinking on a specific topic or practice area." The café mindset can be adapted for many different purposes. One application is a lightly structured knowledge-transfer vehicle where each participant learns from others in their way.

Knowledge Café is the antithesis of a presentation style of knowledge sharing. Café happens where and when there's a need for a café, where there's a need for improved idea communication, conversation, learning, and knowledge exchange.

During the 2020 shutdown due to the COVID-19 pandemic, everyone was left with one option for learning and knowledge exchange—virtual meetings and learning were the order of the day.

That will be the future of learning and knowledge exchange and transfer as a physical location will no longer hold knowledge workers hostage. Libraries across the world are conforming to the dictates of this café disruption and communications.

CAFÉ IN THE MIDST OF DISRUPTIONS

- Connects employees, professionals, and knowledge workers
- Simplifies complexities
- Improves interpersonal relationships
- Breaks down organizational silos
- Improves trust
- Enables new idea generation, innovation, and knowledge sharing
- Develops communities of practice
- Increases transfer engagement

There's always preparation before a meaningful café experience. Where observation is concerned, chance favors only the prepared mind, according to French biologist Louis Pasteur.

Trapezoid communication is significant at the café.

In geometry, a trapezoid is a four-sided figure with two sides that are parallel. Discussion at small tables is better with 4–6 participants. The cool thing about a trapezoid is that it's neither a rectangle, square, circle, nor triangle, but an equilateral triangle with the tip chopped off so that it's made up of two parallel lines on top and bottom. Communication at the café is not like a democratic setting where everyone's knowledge is equal. Every contribution is welcome, but the café team determines what carries the day. Trapezoid communication means that there are bases and heights, and all heights are not equal but may be similar. However, everyone is not at the same level of knowledge. Everyone brings a uniqueness, a perspective, adeptness, and heights, and the basis for the café is knowledge exchange. Every knowledge worker contributes to the size of the café. The parallelism at the café suggested alignment (with a knowledge culture) and collateralization (a pledge to share) and equidistance (meeting people where they are) of ideas and thoughts for KET and resurgence. Everyone wants to give and receive.

Tables 3 and 4 show typical menus (agendas) for one of my knowledge fair and café events. It was designed for two-way communication. These are recommendations, not prescriptions.

Table 3. Café Agenda

Theme: Knowledge Café: Building a Community of Practice for a Knowledge Management Culture. The Knowledge Café is divided into four segments.

Part I
- Introduction and key innovative ideas worth learning
- Overview of KM and CoPs: CoP, CoP1, CoP2, and CoP3
- Testimonials from pilot CoPs
- Q & A

Part II
- Questions: What are knowledge management, techniques, and tools at work in your workspace? What are the existing knowledge mapping techniques?
- Brainstorming and deliberations in groups
- Summary from each table

Part III
- Questions: Creating a knowledge culture—what are the barriers to knowledge sharing in an organization, and how do you overcome them?
- Brainstorming and deliberations in groups
- Summary from each table

Part IV
- Questions: How do you start a community of practice? What are the knowledge frameworks, capture methods, and transfer methods and challenges? Identify.
- Brainstorming and deliberations in groups
- Summary from each table
- General summary, closing, and what's next

Table 4. Café Agenda

Theme: Capturing and finding information and knowledge to do your work during the pandemic. The Knowledge Café is divided into four segments for a typical 2.5-hour café.

Part I: The most critical aspect of this part is the warm and rousing welcome (purpose of the café and café ground rule, small table discussion, and summaries)

- Welcome (2 min.)
- A short video on a 3-year digitization project that was completed in 3 weeks because of COVID-19 (2 min.)
- Interactive survey (4 min.). Often, I send this interactive survey to attendees to capture their opinion on several issues like yes-or-no answer questions relevant to the theme, and satisfaction and ways to improve KM and café events.
- Introduction (3 min.). Note: when I have more than 30 in a café, openings are better at the small tables. Depending on the context, we decide how much of an introduction we need from the attendee. If it's a relational café, we spend more time here to know each other.
- Purpose of the café and café ground rule (2 min.). Note: the purpose of the café is often communicated to the attendees before they attend.
- Overview of the last café (2 min.)
- 5 min. presentation on the role of digitization in a knowledge-centric organization (5 min.). Note: the purpose of the café is for interaction and two-way communication; therefore, one-way communication is discouraged.
- Instruction for table conversation and breakout session (2 min.)

Café 1: Teleworking and remote working present new challenges related to sharing knowledge, interacting, and collaborating. How are you adapting KM to the Digital Enterprise? How are you getting the information you need to manage your projects, programs, and operations, and how do you enhance the process and enrich knowledge users' experience? (30 min.). Note: attendees can switch tables after the first 15 minutes.

- **Summaries** and notes from the tables of 3–7 attendees (5 min.)
- Testimonials from experts. Note: this is necessary when there are teams that are ahead of the game that can share lessons they are learning (3 min.)
- Break: 10 min.

(*continued*)

Table 4. (*continued*)

Part II

- Icebreaker Q &A (4 min.)
- Instruction for table conversation and breakout session (2 min.)

Café 2: Nowadays, face-to-face collaborations are rare. Are you losing the human element of KM? What are you doing to get the same level of cooperation and human-machine collaboration on your project? (20 min.)

- Summaries and notes from the tables of 3–7 attendees (5 min.)
- Testimonials from experts. Note: this is necessary when there are teams that are ahead of the game that can share lessons they are learning (3 min.)
- Q&A (3 min.)

Part III

- Icebreaker (2 min.)
- Instruction for table conversation and breakout session (2 min.)

Café 3: What practical thing have you done to capture and steward your organizational knowledge? Share your experience with Knowledge Interview and Wiki Knowledge Library and how to connect captured knowledge, findability, and discoverability (15 min.).

- Summaries and notes from the tables of 3–7 attendees (5 min.)
- Testimonials from experts. Note: this is necessary when there are teams that are ahead of the game that can share lessons they are learning (3 min.)
- Q&A (4 min.)

Part IV

- What have we learned and unlearned today? (2 min.)
- What can be implemented today (2 min.)
- Final survey (2 min.)
- What's next? (2 min.)
- Wiki, CoP, and other KM meetings and resources (2 min.)
- General summary, closing (2 min.)

Additional questions: How best are you capturing critical knowledge, and how are you increasing the findability and discoverability of this information and knowledge? How do you make captured knowledge available to those who need it and when they need it?

Each of the café events focuses on a particular aspect of the KM program, such as knowledge audit and mapping techniques, knowledge frameworks, capture methods, transfer methods, roles of security and records management, technology enablers, organizational and planning issues, risk management integration, and KM elements/tools/techniques.

4.6. CASE STUDY: SWEEPING AT FOUR-YEAR-OLD, DISRUPTIONS AND KNOWLEDGE-TRANSFER PREFERENCE—AMARA ANYACHO

Background: I have a smart 14-year-old daughter, Amara. We usually have what we call daddy–daughter day. This is like a café meeting with no formality at all. In one of my café-life conversations with my daughter, I asked her, "Honey, how do you like to share and transfer knowledge?" She pondered my question and then answered, "Dad, you mean my best way to learn stuff (learning preference)?" I responded, "Learning is part of knowledge acquisition." She went on to explain to me that her preference is to watch short videos and/or instructions. Here's her café story.

> I like learning from other people but not in a way that could upset you or make you angry. When I learn from someone, my preference is to watch a YouTube video or read directions. I don't like people speaking over my shoulders. I don't learn well in an environment where someone is correcting me and looking over my shoulder. I had one memory when I was 4 years old; my dad was teaching me how to sweep. He showed me how to do it; once I took the broom and started sweeping, he just grabbed the broom to show me the correct way to sweep and kept correcting me all the way. Every stroke I took on the floor would get corrected by Dad. I hated it! I would much rather watch a video on something because you wouldn't have someone looking over your shoulder. I like simply following instructions. All my friends are the same way; we would much rather easily follow instructions than get angry over someone not letting you do what you should do.

Amara also pointed out that the transferee or receiver can control the knowledge transferer's emotion—you can turn off or pause the video and come back to it, but if the knowledge transferer is in front of you . . . Without a doubt, one of the missing links in knowledge transfer is not considering the knowledge user's and creator's preferences or even learning predilections. For project managers, we develop a communication management plan as part of the overarching project management plan. Here, the project manager identifies all stakeholders' communication preferences, communication methods, and channels to make sure that stakeholders are communicated to based on their communication preferences. Why is it that the knowledge creators' and users' knowledge-transfer preferences are rarely considered in many KM environments?

There's no one-size-fits-all in knowledge transfer. I advocate for a knowledge-transfer plan (KTP), which will be dealt with in another setting. KTP will identify all the knowledge creators and users and their preferences in sharing and transferring knowledge. Like the communication management plan, the purpose of the KTP is to clearly define the project, program, or team's knowledge transfer and communication requirements. We will further identify how information, and most importantly, know-how experiences (or deep smarts) will be circulated. The KTP will define the flow of the team and enterprise knowledge transfer. It will also identify any generational, technological, or other internal or external constraints, which affect the free flow of knowledge transfer and free flow of knowledge among the team or enterprise.

Although it has been several years, I recall my first day as an adjunct instructor at ITT Technical Institute in Austin, Texas. As I was presenting the first segment of the introduction to my Marketing Management class, I realized that 80 percent of these young future leaders were all on their cell phones. I thought they were tempting me. I pursed and asked why everyone was on their phones. They responded that it was normal for them and that they were still engaged in the class. For me, that was absurd. I gave them a quick quiz to ascertain their level of engagement. Believe it or not, they passed the quiz and demonstrated that they were following the class instructions. There are generational and knowledge-transfer preference differences here. Why is it that when I call my kids downstairs, they don't usually answer, but send them a text message and they respond in a split second? Could this be the new knowledge-transfer preference? When I was in college, I usually sat in the front row of the class and noted every word that came out of the professor's mouth. Multitasking in learning or knowledge transfer was not in my vocabulary.

The knowledge-transfer preference of the knowledge creators and users determines complexities, density, and café style in terms of simplicity knowledge-transfer engagement. Knowledge leadership means identifying what knowledge transfer choice works for the individual, team, and the entire organization.

Knowledge workers depend on accessibility, findability, and succession of information and knowledge in the knowledge economy.

THINGS TO KNOW ABOUT KNOWLEDGE
AND CAFÉ TECHNIQUES

Here are some things to know about knowledge fair and café as a KM technique:

- A clearinghouse for knowledge workers like CoPs
- A digital and physical collaborative platform (informal) that helps knowledge workers, especially, to identify opportunities for collaboration
- A melting point (place) where valuable information and knowledge activities can be discovered, discussed, and dissimilated
- A space to gather, review, discuss, and establish strategies and tools for communities of practice and other KM techniques
- Forum to gather information on successful and innovative KM best practices
- A place to learn about knowledge management and encourage the adoption of sound knowledge management practices
- Provides a forum for dialogues regarding KM options and methods

- Encourage participation in communities of practice
- Share CoP resources and learn from each other
- Build knowledge management capabilities
- Facilitate integration/implementation of knowledge management into an organization's knowledge culture
- Create a platform for establishing standards for KM
- Produce materials and resources to support KM best practice adoption
- Establish qualitative and quantitative metrics to track integration and the impact of KM practices
- Disseminate industry best practices and case studies
- Produce materials and resources to market and support knowledge management adoption
- Create a communication/outreach plan to implement the outreach effort
- Assess knowledge management capabilities in member agencies and identify opportunities to strengthen practice
- Prepare an annual report on knowledge management metrics and results

5 ■ Knowledge Workers at the Café Revolution

Chapter Objectives

- Understand the roles of the knowledge workers at the café
- Discover what creates apathy to knowledge exchange and why the spirit of sharing creates the proper environment for knowledge management
- See why the spirit of sharing and giving is a predominant culture at the café

5.1. KNOWLEDGE WORKERS AT THE CAFÉ

In the digital age, you need to make knowledge workers out of every employee possible.

—Bill Gates

> Knowledge workers are neither farmers nor labor nor business;
> they are employees of organizations.
>
> —Peter Drucker

Knowledge workers are the creators and users of knowledge. Every employee and everyone who uses knowledge to do their work is a knowledge worker. While there are a variety of reasons to converge at a physical café, the purpose is to engage in knowledge exchange. Every knowledge worker depends on the free flow of information to do his or her work. Let's café. It means let's begin the discussion. Let's talk about it. Let's share what we know. Let's brainstorm. Let's get caffeinated. Let's analyze what we have around a saucer. Let's bring all this information into context. Can we bring the human element into it? Can we apply the knowledge we have acquired for discussion-making? The minder of the café is synonymous with sharing.

Several years ago, I managed a project and needed to organize project assets, processes, and policies; I searched the intranet of lessons learned repositories. I realized that every team had its repository for lessons learned and new knowledge from the café. I then searched our organization's intranet for a project template. Believe it or not, the result was fantastic, probably more than 10,000 results of everything but a project charter! Sometimes, it's like we are all swimming in a directionless swamp or pond. This is a perfect definition of what knowledge management should not be to the knowledge worker. We need an intentional and clear-flowing river that has a direction and clarity of perception. Could it be that we had documented knowledge scattered across many repositories without managing the knowledge within the documents? It was not tagged, curated, filtered, rated, prioritized, synthesized, or combined into new documents such as guidance, best practices, or Wiki content.

Why isn't consumerization of information and knowledge the KM way as simple as the three-step process listing your book on Amazon that lasts for minutes or the simplicity offered through most online banking? Project, program, and operations information needs to be appropriately analyzed and contextualized to help knowledge workers find what they need to make decisions faster and smarter. In search of project templates for my projects, I went to PMI.org and found some great templates, but they were too broad for my project. Someone out there in my organization already had a charter template that I could customize for my project. I didn't need the frustration of looking for information. I needed to do my job as part of my project. This extra task of combing through multiple repositories for lessons learned, tools, and templates is outside the project scope and may not be part of my project's requirements. A living, easy-to-access central repository is like a café, where every knowledge agent or user converges for knowledge exchange.

When knowledge workers live in the mindset of the café, their information will also café. We create a KM environment. "In this environment, organizations have evolved to become decision factories, operated mostly by knowledge workers. Yet few enterprises organize these knowledge workers to enable quick, efficient decisions amidst rapid, ongoing change" (Martin, 2019). Knowledge workers create the space for the future of work in our ever-increasing project delivery landscape and in the project economy.

When I finally created templates for project management, I realized weeks later that other knowledge users in my organization had created similar templates. Knowledge workers work best with a free flow of information. This helped to ignite my passion for a paradigm shift in the way knowledge users use information. There was a need for a café for different repositories, content, organization, curation, and indexing in hindsight. A café relational mindset will make the information available one or two clicks away.

This experience led me to ask why there is little or no flow of knowledge and information across the organization. Accurate data are the indisputable foundation for the right information; the correct information is essential for knowledge that enables an organization's right decision. Knowledge and information need to flow freely in an organization. In an age of Big Data and information overload, retrievability of the right information has become a hard-hitting task. Many employees waste an enormous amount of time looking for and retrieving information and accessing the knowledge they need to do their jobs. Café is finding what you need to do your work. Everyone gives and receives at the café.

The Forrester Consulting study commissioned by Microsoft, "Extending the Value of AI to Knowledge Workers," revealed that "knowledge workers depend on the free flow of information. When they can't find the information they need, knowledge workers often make subpar decisions that affect the business as a whole. When graph information is properly analyzed and contextualized, it can help knowledge workers find the information needed to make decisions faster, find relevant expertise more easily, and make decisions more confidently" (Microsoft Corporation, 2019). It's fair to say that Microsoft is specifically addressing the value of AI in supporting decision-making and contextualization and how AI can help knowledge workers, not strictly about knowledge sharing.

Every stakeholder is a knowledge user. Project managers and, indeed, all knowledge workers are the users of the project information and knowledge. That's why we need to get people thinking in a café way. Dr. Ed Hoffman, a strategic advisor to the Project Management Institute and senior lecturer at the Columbia University School of Professional Studies, has a motto: "People, People, People." People are the most crucial leg of your KM program.

Knowledge users are participants in the knowledge economy and knowledge society. Knowledge Café provides the right environment for these assets to exchange and barter knowledge and ideas. They fill the dual role of applying knowledge in their work tasks and contributing their expertise and insight to the enterprise's knowledge content (Gartner, n.d.). Knowledge users are impacted by identifying, capturing, using, reusing, acquiring, organizing, communicating, sharing, exhilarating, and creating new knowledge.

According to a Global Deloitte survey, over 80 percent of Deloitte Knowledge users indicate that sharing knowledge leads to competitive advantage and adds a real client value to the organization (Alithya, 2020). Also, "Knowledge management remains one of the top three issues affecting company success and has become even more essential with the COVID-19 pandemic's scattering of staff among homes and work sites. However only nine per cent of business leaders feel ready to address it" (Weiss et al., 2021). For instance, "sustainable competitive advantage is a function of knowledge management infrastructure, knowledge quality, knowledge management systems properties, organization environment, task environment and general environment" (Halawi et al., 2005). When you share knowledge, you unleash creativity and value. Knowledge sharing is infectious! Knowledge workers are part of the precious assets of the organization. The most critical knowledge assets of an organization are human capital.

> More than 80% of a company's information exists on individual hard drives and in personal files.
>
> —Gartner (n.d.)

Some employees believe that sharing knowledge is additional work for them. Therefore, they think that it is a waste of time to make information available to other knowledge users or transfer their knowledge to others. Some think that the information or knowledge is their advantage and superiority over others or control and manipulative tool. Experience resides in people—employees, customers, suppliers, other stakeholders, and in technology. Your workforce, databases, documents, guides, policies and procedures, software, and patents are repositories of your organization's knowledge assets (Baldrige, n.d.).

Retaining and reusing the knowledge in the products or services we provide—and the ones provided by consultants—adds value. Knowledge exists in relationships among the stakeholders on projects or operations. The richness and depth of this café and the shared knowledge determine the strength of the team. Organizational memory and process assets, along with knowledge in the processes, answer the questions, "Do we know what we know?" and "Do we know what we need to know?"

Knowledge management epitomizes building a knowledge competency for a high-performing organization. Knowledge competency is the emerging desired capability to cultivate, share, and transfer the organization's know-how; this happens in the middle of laissez-faire and structure. The café is an agile KM. Imagine a Knowledge Café atmosphere.

5.2. CASE STUDY: EMPATHY, ENGAGEMENT, AND KNOWLEDGE EXCHANGE AT THE CAFÉ—MONTE LUEHLFING, DHA, PMP

This case study is written by Dr. Monte Luehlfing, DHA, PMP, a senior IT project manager at the University of Mississippi Medical Center. Here's his experience:

Knowledge transfer is critical in today's environment of multiple generations in the workplace, a move towards project-based roles, a hyper-competitive global economy, and the incredibly fast pace of technology change. Using straightforward processes and interactions is important to help less experienced team members understand the nuances of corporate culture and "why we do the things we do here." This should not be in the toxic "we've always done it that way" standpoint, but the "here's what we have learned along the way, and we want to continue leveraging these best practices to continue to improve."

Managing projects and change management, in general, must incorporate the "three-legged stool" of "people, process, and technology." The tendency to focus on technology causes us to miss the important perspectives of how our way of working will change and how we need to adapt to benefit from those changes. As most of our natural states are to fear change, change leaders must work with team members to ease those fears and create an environment in which change will be embraced. Being empathetic with those affected by the change and those who are part of the knowledge-transfer process helps our "targets" of the knowledge transfer to understand the "What's in it for me?" better and more effectively. Modeling empathy before, during, and after the café also helps develop a growth mindset and a mindset of abundance. In this mindset of abundance, knowledge sharing freely occurs without the concerns that the person sharing is not giving away some of their perceived power. Manage people-knowledge before you manage people-process.

Dr. Luehlfing summed it up: Project, KM, and change management processes start with people. So, start with a café, and engage people before you can manage knowledge. Simple processes and interactions are critical to knowledge exchange. Managing knowledge involves modeling empathy, which helps in developing a growth mindset and a mindset of abundance. Before the café space, there must be a café mindset.

CREATING THE MINDSET OF SHARING

To create this mindset of sharing, knowledge workers must understand three simple points:

1. Empathy. Bring empathy in the knowledge-exchange café and thinking process
2. Process. Simplify the process to incorporate all knowledge agents and users; have a goal and action plan before the café
3. Interaction. Make your café a productive knowledge interaction

5.3. SHARE A CUP OF COFFEE OR TEA OR DRINK IT ALONE. SHARE IT OR LOSE IT!

Café mindset is all about creating a shared space for sharing knowledge transfer. Undoubtedly, there are two critical thrusts when we share experiential knowledge from project, program, or operations:

Sharing Existing Knowledge: "Knowing What You Know"
Existing knowledge is the precondition for future knowledge. So, we share what we know at the café. Even machines learn from existing knowledge assets. Humans need machines to access, retrieve, manipulate, and add to the body of knowledge. According to Dr. Ismail Serageldin (2013), the founding director of the Bibliotheca

Alexandrina (BA), the new Library of Alexandria will no longer be able to add or interact with the cumulative knowledge without the enablement of the machines. You'll be amazed to know how much the project team knows when you converge at the café. You'll be amazed to know how much we know that we don't know that we know. We share existing knowledge.

Knowledge for Innovation: "Creating and Converting"
Existing knowledge is the foundation for conversion and creation of innovation. The convergence of what we know sparks off new knowledge. Imagine the outcome of putting together pieces of knowledge from different members of the team. You will identify gaps, missing links, and new thoughts. What we do with existing knowledge determines the germaneness of creativity and innovation.

It's not enough to know what you know. Creating and converting existing knowledge is not an end, but it preserves what we know as we share and observe and prepares us for future disruptions. Knowledge Café provides us the right environment for knowledge sharing and connects us to the future.

Knowledge Café is the connection between the past and the future of knowledge management. Today's knowledge may be out of date in five years. Therefore, it stands to reason that if we don't learn to capture and retain enduring wisdom, the end results will be like swimming as fast as you can in a pool of new technologies only to stay in the same place! Enduring wisdom can never be obsolete. The concept of a Knowledge Café, a relational knowledge sharing mindset, is a current, cross-generational, social ecosystem designed to retain and manage relevant knowledge.

5.4. KNOWLEDGE REVOLUTION: KNOWLEDGE SHARING IS THE NEW SUPERPOWER!

According to Dr. Ismail Serageldin (2013), the digital revolution is one of the most extraordinary things that has happened to humanity. However, we live in the most profound revolution in the structure of knowledge since the invention of writing, not just in terms of communication.

> The most important contribution management needs to make in the 21st Century is to increase the productivity of knowledge work and the knowledge worker.
> —Peter Drucker (Wartzman, 2014)

Knowledge work and knowledge workers are the best assets of an organization. Organizations that are leading in innovation and market share are leading because they have increased knowledge work and knowledge workers. Knowledge workers create new knowledge—the formula for innovation.

Is knowledge power? If it is locked up in people's minds and not shared, knowledge is useless, irrelevant, and anything but compelling! For the past 20 years, I have been exploring managing project knowledge and other institutional knowledge—our collective responses to their identification, capturing, sharing, retaining, leveraging, adapting, transferring, reusing, and creating new knowledge and being rejuvenated by it. I've observed the massive brain drain of skilled workers because of generational retirements and unstable and volatile job mobility. I've come to realize that knowledge that is not shared is encrypted; it goes to the grave with the owner—and means nothing to humanity—a trifle, good-for-nothing! Knowledge needs to revolve! Knowledge should orbit and not fly! This evolution and revolution of knowledge sharing are what I call the knowledge revolution.

Sir Francis Bacon, referring to the central importance of knowledge, said, "Knowledge is Power" (Bohn, 1994).

Knowledge is power, but how powerful is the knowledge in a pigeon hole, unshared, untransferred, unrejuvenated, and dead? There are people whose existence and success depend on the tacit and implicit knowledge locked inside of them. Any knowledge that cannot induce change is trivia and meaningless. Waiting for it to be perfected? It cannot be perfect until you let it out! Write it! Share it.

Share your knowledge today! "Indeed, knowledge is of limited organizational value if it is not shared" (Alavi & Leidner, 1999).

FACTS ABOUT KM

A knowledge revolution fuels the productivity and throughput of knowledge work and the knowledge worker. Experts, researchers, and industry leaders believe:

- Knowledge capture, sharing, and retention are the most significant challenges facing organizations today.
- You cannot force people to share their knowledge; you just have to create an environment for knowledge workers.
- KM is a top competitive advantage for high-performing organizations.
- The brain drain of 76 million baby boomers in the next nine years is going to be disruptive.
- Knowledge management is intentional—it should be an organizational strategy.
- In this political economy of information, knowledge sharing is the new king!
- No organization is immune from the disruption of knowledge flight—private or public sector—doers, makers, sellers, or a combination.
- There is a revolution and an urgency for knowledge innovation management strategies across the globe!
- KM is like eating an elephant, one bite at a time—it is multifaceted.

Effective knowledge management is a top competitive advantage for high-performing organizations, but KM seems to be on life support in many organizations today. So, the soon-coming brain drain of baby boomers in nine years is a considerable danger to organizational knowledge infrastructure. Knowledge management is intentional. Beyond the prima facie and truism, the adage "knowledge is power" may not have overstayed its welcome. On the contrary, this knowledge economy of information and knowledge sharing is the new king! Whether your organization is in a private or public sector; if you do things, make or sell things, you are one or all of the following: innovation, growth, change, and customer knowledge focused. There is a revolution of knowledge management strategies across the globe! There's an escalation of the importance and urgency of KM. The concept of knowledge management is massive.

There is a clarion call for knowledge project managers. Dorothy Leonard, William J. Abernathy Professor of Business Administration Emerita at Harvard Business School, opined in their research on knowledge transfer that they have seen companies significantly disadvantaged, if not crippled, by knowledge loss (Leonard et al., 2015). Indeed, some expert knowledge may be outdated or irrelevant when its possessors are eligible for retirement, but not the skills, know-how, and capabilities that underlie critical operations—both routine and innovative. This is critical! Organizations cannot afford to lose these deep smarts. Some of these SMEs have worked for more than 20 years and are the exclusive custodians of specific, critical business knowledge. Many have retired and left the organization without passing on these vital skills.

On the other hand, according to Steve Jobs, "Creativity is just connecting things. When you ask creative people how they did something, they feel a little guilty because they didn't really do it, they just saw something. It seemed obvious to them after a while. That's because they were able to connect experiences they've had and synthesize new things. And the reason they were able to do that was that they've had more experiences or they have thought more about their experiences than other people" (Doepker, 2017).

Creativity, like Knowledge Café, is just connecting things. Knowledge revolution means ease and creativity, and retrievability and accessibility of knowledge. In some corners, everyone is project-driven to the detriment of process and knowledge identification, transfer, reuse, and innovation. Knowledge Café is a knowledge revolution. Knowledge revolution is the intelligent application of knowledge. Knowledge revolution cannot be discussed in isolation—there is a connection with intelligence, creativity, and wisdom in this Knowledge Café revolution. Intelligence is classically defined as "the ability to acquire and utilize knowledge" (Christensen, 2013).

> So, intelligence matters; it demonstrates your ability to gather knowledge and effectively use it. Creativity is the ability to go beyond the intelligence frame and capitalize on seemingly random connections of concepts.
>
> —Tanner Christensen (2013)

Knowledge is power, but knowledge sharing is the new superpower. It determines the evolution of knowledge, creativity, and innovation. Organizations that put high premiums on their intellectual capital or collective knowledge—people power, process, and technology—are the most powerful. They will always win. This revolution avers and insists that knowledge assets are the most ostentatiously opulent of all organizational assets, with a grandiose façade.

5.5. EVERYONE IS A KNOWLEDGE CREATOR AND CAN BE A SHARER

To be without knowledge is not to have lived at all. I'm very compassionate, but I have a powerful personality. I can hold in my emotions. I can count to a handful of times that I've lost it in my adult life and rarely cried after watching a video. There are probably two videos that have reduced me to tears—*The Passion of the Christ* and *America's Got Talent*'s audition of Kodi Lee. Kodi is a blind and autistic 24-year-old singer. Rather than disabled, he is "knowledge-abled." He has lost his sight, but his insight is still intact. He is autistic, but he is a stable and unshakable source of knowledge and inspiration to millions. When Kodi's mother brought him to the stage, little did the world know that there remained greatness and knowledge resident within this young man. Despite his appearance, he played piano and when he opened his mouth to sing the audience shouted and cried. Physical disability is not a limitation to knowledge transfer. Those who tell me in workshops and conferences that they have nothing to share, Kodi has proved everyone wrong. We all have something to share.

> If you can't fly then run, if you can't run then walk, if you can't walk then crawl, but whatever you do you have to keep moving forward.
> —Martin Luther King, Jr.

You are unstoppable. There's a wealth of knowledge within you, and you cannot afford to go to the grave without releasing the deep smarts within yourself!

In fact, there are people whose existence and success depend on your knowledge; thousands of people depend on your knowledge. Don't keep them waiting.

6 ▪ Knowledge Culture and the Café

Chapter Objectives

- Explore how to create the right environment for KM
- Understand the relationship between data, information, knowledge, and wisdom
- Learn how organizational culture affects the knowledge-sharing environment
- Recognize different environments for knowledge fairs and café
- Knowledge retention and learning organization

6.1. CASE STUDY: AFFECTING REAL CHANGE IN CROSS-CULTURAL KNOWLEDGE-TRANSFER PARADIGMS—KOJI KODAMA, MBA, PMP

I would like to introduce a cross-cultural knowledge-exchange experience of Koji Kodama, MBA, PMP (児玉光治). He is experientially multicultural, natively bilingual, technologically analytical, and strategically successful. Koji is a past president of the PMI Austin Chapter and currently the Global Executive Management (GEM) specialist in Saitama, Japan, Kodama Operations. Here is Koji's story.

Nearly three decades ago, as a young electronics design engineer in Tokyo, Japan, I worked for a very well-known global semiconductor behemoth headquartered in the United States. I was suddenly thrust into the world of technology-knowledge transfer with a special assignment to temporarily move myself and my family to the U.S. headquarters for memory and microprocessor chips in Austin, Texas. I would find out later how monetarily expensive and mission-critical this significant project investment was to this corporation.

My mission: My mission is to formally lead my department in transferring technology information and methodologies from the U.S. "parent" company design center back to Japan, the "child" company design center.

My challenges and observations: Overcome intercompany/departmental silos and ongoing communications gaps. The knowledge-transfer challenges, very similar to those I overcame, to a large degree, to the success of my specific mission several years ago. Silos and communication gaps still exist today in diverse ways in many organizations throughout the world, and in most cases, take longer to overcome than first planned.

The good news: There are tangible solutions to affect real change for the better in both realms of challenges.

Case in point: As a technology nerd who natively spoke both Japanese and English, I first naïvely thought to myself as that mission was assigned to me, "How difficult could this assignment possibly be?" Little did I and my Japan-based management know at the time that the answer would eventually manifest itself in this assignment. What was initially planned for seven months turned into a full two years before the mission would be deemed a success and before we finally moved back to Japan.

THE COROLLARY OF LESSONS LEARNED

1. The challenges and gaps associated with knowledge transfer are overcome less because of such obvious hurdles of language or cultural differences alone, but rather due more by comprehending and enabling a real change in paradigm from an individual or team stuck in a mode of an inward mindset ("owned-knowledge") to a mode of an outward mindset ("shared-knowledge"). That is, knowledge management sets the correct path in bolstering important behaviors aligned to creating, organizing, and reusing owned-knowledge, upon which foundation individuals and teams can then work efficiently toward ultimately attaining the desired results of the transformation of such to shared-knowledge.

2. Similar to the application of an agile mindset in software development, project management has become streamlined. Improved traditional norms with greater enablement of efficiency and sense of urgency, the iterative application of methodologies to knowledge-transfer projects resulting in improved visibility, adaptability, risk mitigation, and business value will affect real paradigm change toward a more collaborative, efficient, adaptive, and as necessary, predictive knowledge management culture.

The discovery of this essential paradigm change is the fundamental essence of the very subject matter as set forth crucially and urgently in this book. It is the how of such knowledge transfer eloquently discussed elsewhere herein.

As pointed out by my friend, Koji Kodama, organizations struggle to overcome intercompany/departmental silos and ongoing communication gaps. Culture plays a critical role in all KETs. Organizational culture will determine the intensity of knowledge exchange and transfer. A lesson learned in one cultural context or organization is different from another. Koji's lessons learned experience connotes moving knowledge from the domain of owned knowledge to shared knowledge. Koji identified an agile mindset toward knowledge exchange typical of a café. This mindset will streamline traditional norms, enable greater efficiency, and improve the sense of urgency. The iterative application of methodologies to knowledge transfer projects results in improved visibility, adaptability, risk mitigation, and business value and will affect real paradigm change toward a more collaborative, efficient, and predictive knowledge management culture. Learning lessons occurs during and after the project—learning is the key.

6.2. CAFÉ CULTURE: DATA ≠ INFORMATION ≠ KNOWLEDGE

The next society will be a knowledge society. Knowledge will be its key resource, and knowledge workers will be the dominant group in its workforce.

—Peter Drucker

In 1969, Peter Drucker, founding father of "modern management," masterfully coined the phrase *knowledge economy*. Decades later, he describes a profound concept of a *knowledge society*, citing that the critical resources of this knowledge economy are knowledge and knowledge workers. Drucker's prophetic description of 2021 could not be more accurate.

Exactly how might Drucker's knowledge society play out in the world 50 years from now? At what point does the knowledge economy produce a knowledge society? Maybe, when there's knowledge in every café, and there's a café in every knowledge. Knowledge societies create a knowledge culture. Knowledge culture creates a café environment. The knowledge society is a café culture. It's a knowledge exchange and transfer (KET) environment that I'm espousing. Imagine a workplace where conversation, interactive displays, team-building days, Kanban's Trello boards, Google's office collaborative tools, huddle rooms, new media, stand-ups, video conferencing, and hot asking are the language of work. This is that mindset that affects organizational shared values, beliefs, understanding, and behaviors. The culture is the enabler of a free-flow KM, where people rendezvous or converge at the café. You cannot talk about creating an environment of KM without establishing a knowledge culture. Symbols, language, norms, values, and artifacts are the known significant elements of a culture.

In the knowledge economy, it is not the quality of data or information that matters but conversion and accessibility and converting information to knowledge and contextualizing it for decision-making. In a knowledge society, the creation, dissemination, and utilization of information and knowledge has become the most critical production factor (Encyclopedia.com).

Most innovative economies are both knowledge economies and societies. An example is South Korea—which Bloomberg ranked as the most innovative country in 2019 (Jamrisko et al., 2019). Finland is another example of a knowledge economy. Finland has the widely acclaimed transformative capacity to become a leading knowledge-based economy in the late 20th century. It transformed from an agriculture-based economy in the 1950s into one of the top innovation-driven, knowledge-based economies and high-tech producers in the 21st century. I recommend the Knowledge Economic guidebook, *Finland as a Knowledge Economy 2.0: Lessons on Policies and Governance* (Halme et al., 2014). This is also mainly due to Nokia and strong government support of the tech industry. In a knowledge economy, growth in knowledge-intensive service sectors like education, communication, and information is exploding. According to the Knowledge Management Working Group of the Federal Chief Information Officers Council (2001) in its publication "Managing Knowledge at Work: An Overview of Knowledge Management,"

Data = Unorganized Facts
Information = Data + Organization + Context
Knowledge = Information + Explanation + Judgment

Knowledge culture within the café space means that organizing data, explaining information, and applying knowledge will be intentionally communicated and become business in an organization. When data is organized, it becomes information; when explained, it becomes knowledge, but we need wisdom. Science provides us data, information, and knowledge. Wisdom is hard because it needs insights into humanity's social sciences and wisdom to reflect upon it and bring upon it a pattern of experience to get understanding.

You cannot create a café culture without a proper understanding of the data, information, and knowledge and their interfaces. In traditional project management, work performance data are the raw, not-yet-analyzed data. This "unclean" data become work performance information after they are codified, processed, or analyzed. Then and only then does data become usable. On the other hand, work performance information builds upon data by giving it meaning and making it actionable. Knowledge, including project knowledge, is explained or contextualized business-critical, relevant, actionable, and partially based on experience (Leonard, Swap, & Barton, 2015).

For a better understanding of the integration and correlations among data, information, and knowledge, let's consider the Pyramid to Wisdom, according to Ackoff's (1989) model.

Quezon City (QC) Weather in Data, Information, Knowledge, Wisdom (DIKW) Context:

- If you see the weather forecast for QC but don't live there, then it has no direct connection to your life—so it's *data*
- If you happen to live or work in QC, then this same set of numbers becomes *information*—because it informs you of what the weather is like—even if you can't do anything about it.
- If you live or work in QC and can use the information as a basis to make a decision (e.g., will you bring an umbrella or shades because it will be hot?) or take action (e.g., you won't water the plants or wash the car because it might rain), then it becomes *knowledge.*

- *Wisdom* is the experience that comes with using knowledge repeatedly (e.g., you know that if the weather report says 26–31 degrees C and partly cloudy, then it won't rain—so it's okay to wear your new shoes to go to school or work). Wisdom is the ultimate goal of knowledge. It is the application of knowledge.

In this chapter, I'll try to simplify the KM continuum of DIKW. I regret that many discussions of KM seem to be very academic and too esoteric for a wider audience. But it shouldn't be. We all learn, identify, share, and transfer knowledge daily. I utilize a Knowledge Café mostly outside work. I have two friends, Brad and Lue (not their real names), who can never talk without shouting at each other. I had an idea for them. We went to a café to sort their differences out. To my amazement, they were shouting every time we initiated an exchange in their home to resolve matters, but when we went to the café, it was a different ball game—no one raised his or her voice. This environment offered us an amazing opportunity to learn our differences, exchange knowledge, solve problems, and improve. We established ground rules for this café meeting, and the choice of venue was agreed upon by all.

Spaces and places that support knowledge circulation and increase its velocity are "breeding" grounds for innovation. Today's Knowledge Café was like the Sunday dinner table of the 1950s, when so much innovation happened among newly graduated engineers.

Information refers to data or facts that have been organized and presented with the context necessary for use or application. In contrast, knowledge is typically characterized as something within a human brain, built over time from learning and experience and used as a basis for judgment, prediction, and decision-making. A convergence of knowledge management, information architecture, and data science is necessary to convert data to knowledge (Meza, 2016). You can have a lot of process and documentation, but it takes data science to give meaning to your strategy or process—it transforms data into knowledge. If the collaboration of people is excluded, it becomes mechanical.

How Do You Create a Knowledge Café Culture?
According to a global survey in 2014 and 2017, answered by over 700 KM professionals by Knoco (Milton, 2017), barriers to creating a KM environment are (1) cultural issues, (2) lack of prioritization and support from leadership for KM, (3) lack of KM roles and accountabilities, and (4) lack of incentives. There will not be a knowledge-sharing environment in a culture of short-term thinking, excess competition, super secrecy and confidentiality, disregard for re-use of knowledge, and resistance to new ideas. Also, KM will not thrive where there is a lack of honesty in sharing, empowerment, or performance drive.

To overcome these barriers, you must have an intentional KM program that is well planned and executed and part of the organization's strategy and reward system. KM activities must be embedded in the workflow. Take baby steps.

If we want to create a culture and environment for knowledge management, we must apply knowledge to give meaning and context to data and information. There will never be a knowledge culture unless the corporate culture allows it. There must be a change in the paradigm—and how we think, perceive, communicate, or view the world of KM. Organizational cultures are hard to change. A café event can begin the discussion to evaluate, challenge, and improve our paradigms for KET. There are several ways of creating an interactive knowledge-exchange environment. Organizational culture is one of the most influencing factors that enables knowledge workers to live in the space of knowledge exchange in the workplace. Hence, fostering such a café culture in the workplace is essential in facilitating and stimulating employees to use all available platforms for information sharing and KET.

Many authors, such as Dana Youngren (2017), Laura Lynch (2020), David Gurteen (1999), and Ehsan Memari (2017), have written about how to implement a knowledge culture in an organization. They cover elements such as designing the physical environment for conducive conversation and collaboration for the knowledge workers, using various KET techniques, motivating knowledge exchange and transfer, creating the space and time for KET, incentives or rewarding knowledge sharing, and re-examining training and on-boarding methods. Other considered elements incorporate the right technology enablers for KM, keeping the communication transparent, scheduling, investing in a long-term KM strategy, building a knowledge library, engaging people via conversations, telling success stories, creating a knowledge base, implementing an open-door policy, and so on.

For example, "There are 1,500 rattlesnakes in your county" is data. "That's a rattlesnake" is information (rattlesnake, in context). "It's a rattlesnake, it's dangerous, and it can kill you" is knowledge. "It's a rattlesnake, it's dangerous, and it can kill you. Run!" This is wisdom. Both knowledge and wisdom are in the abstract realms of the KM continuum. The knowledge process starts with people, and the café culture is built on people and intellectual capital.

KM is not information management! Some people confuse knowledge management with information management or data management. I've attended workshops on KM that talked about everything but knowledge management. In fact, one was an information management workshop. Data and information create the necessary conditions for knowledge continuum. According to Warick Holder (n.d.), "KM is a JOURNEY, not a DESTINATION." It's important to understand your KM roadmap.

Another way to look at this is the number 5,121,000,000 or 5121000000. As data, the number itself doesn't tell us anything unique about it. However, 512-100-0000 is an Austin, Texas, phone number; this is information. Information is data and documents that have been given value through analysis, interpretation, or compilation in a meaningful form. You can save this information on your phone contact list—that's what we do with the information. But if you take further action to research to see if the number is accurate, call the contact to interact with the number's owner, create a connection with this number, and ask for more information and email address, this is acting upon information—it is knowledge.

Knowledge is the basis for a person's ability to take effective action or make a practical decision—if I use that number or call that number, communicate with someone over time, gain knowledge about this number and the owner of the information. You gain understanding and wisdom from this exercise after you've done this repeatedly.

Everything begins with data and facts, which have little meaning until you compile, analyze, and interpret them into meaningful information. When you use this information for decision-making, it becomes knowledge. When you apply knowledge, it becomes wisdom, and when wisdom is clearly perceived, it becomes enlightenment.

A strong and knowledgeable workforce is critical to success. Transforming information to knowledge reduces vulnerability to loss of institutional knowledge and essential sets of skills that an organization needs to conduct its business. Everyone at the café has some facts (data), information, knowledge, or applied knowledge (wisdom)—DIKW.

The café, which is a mindset, is the space where all of the DIKW elements converge. Activities and interactions at the café give birth to insight, experience, and, when applied, wisdom for direction and guidance. This is what I call the knowledge leadership continuum. I have conducted several Leadership Cafés. This is not just leadership gathering a café designed for leadership action, like taking the outcome of the café to formulate a strategy. I have dedicated the last chapter of this book to the Knowledge Leadership Café.

6.3. REWARDS, INCENTIVES, AND RECOGNITION AS KNOWLEDGE SHARING STRATEGY?

> Our approach to KM is far more than stick or carrot. We say, "Knowledge Sharing is your job. Do it! As a reward, you may keep your job."
> —Bob Buckman (quoted in Gurteen, n.d.)

Bob Buckman, a KM enthusiast and former board chairman of the Applied Knowledge Group in Reston, Virginia, takes a diametrically opposite position to incentives and rewards for knowledge sharing. He advocates that KM is your job. Your reward for KM is keeping your job (Gurteen, 2019). David Gurteen in his online blook—a hybrid of a blog, a website, and an online book, *Conversational Leadership* (2019), contends that,

> If I had a penny for every time someone suggested rewarding or incentivizing people to share their knowledge, I'd be a rich man. But like Alfie Kohn, I do not believe rewards work!
> —David Gurteen (2019)

Alfie Kohn (1993), in his book *Punished by Rewards*, sees rewards and incentives as counterproductive. He argues that they are artificial inducements to motivate people and are like a short-lived bribe. This strategy ultimately fails and does lasting harm. Kohn drew his conclusions from hundreds of studies (according to him) that demonstrates that people do shoddy work when they are enticed with money or other incentives.

Kohn Provided Five Reasons Why He Thinks That Rewards Fail

1. Rewards punish. Rewards are manipulative. "Do this, and you will get that" is not much different to "Do this else here is what will happen to you."
2. Rewards rupture relations. Excellence depends on teamwork. Rewards destroy cooperation.
3. Rewards ignore reasons. To solve problems, people need to understand the causes. Rewards ignore the complexities of the issues.
4. Rewards deter risk-taking. People are less likely to take risks, explore possibilities, or to play hunches.
5. Rewards undermine interest. Rewards are controlling! If people focus on getting a reward, they tend to feel their work is not freely chosen and directed by them.

David Gurteen (2019) added a sixth one:

6. Rewards are gamed. People will manipulate the system to win the prize at the expense of doing what is right.

So, are programs that use rewards and recognition to change people's behavior similarly ineffective over the long run? This is debatable. Like the previous authors, I agree that rewards and incentives are not a magic bullet to motivate the project team or knowledge workers. Before we throw the baby out with the bathwater, I have always resisted the concept of *or* and prefer *and*. I believe that we can employ a café strategy with rewards, incentives, and recognition and produce a great result. Yes, a combination of all these strategies will suffice. We treat ourselves at the café, and that is okay. I have conducted several scientific surveys of attendance at my café events and workshops and found out that more than 78 percent believe that incentives and rewards will motivate them to share more of their knowledge or engage in knowledge transfer activities.

Professor and researcher Prakash Baskar and K. R Rajkumar, in their research in the *International Journal of Science and Research* (2015) in a study on the impact of rewards and recognition on employee motivation, discovered that there is a direct and positive relationship between rewards and recognition and job satisfaction and motivation. Hence, if rewards and recognition offered to employees were to be altered, there would be a corresponding change in work motivation and satisfaction.

The direct translation of this could be that the better the rewards and recognition, the higher the levels of motivation and satisfaction, and possibly, therefore, the greater the levels of performance and productivity.

Research published by Bersin (2012) in *Forbes* reveals that 83 percent of the organizations studied suffer from a deficit in "recognition." And these companies are under-performing compared to their peers. Generally, recognition and incentives motivate and drive performance. I think that the same is the case in a café setting and KM ecosystem. Recognition and incentives motivate people.

Within the context of a café, it's the environment you create that will enable free sharing of knowledge and information. Rewards alone do not and will not produce the right conditions for a workplace where knowledge sharing as a culture thrives. I contend that the absence of a reward may be a setback. Like the authors mentioned previously, I share my knowledge because I derive more benefit from sharing by personal motivation than providing it because of recognition, incentives, and rewards. In my research, I have not seen a successful KM program that completely ignores incentives and recognition.

During one of my knowledge fair café events, some engineers explained that their work revolves around projects. Many employees work from project to project and make little or no time for process—and that includes knowledge sharing. I don't think it's productive to add to employees' work with additional KM activities. However, KM should be enshrined in the work process. On day one, a new employee should be made to know the value of KM and its place in the organizational strategy and the rewards for sharing knowledge. KM should become a fundamental aspect of the way an employee performs his or her work. Against the backdrop of a successful KM, implementation and practice are less about reporting and sharing knowledge.

Knowledge is the new unidentified asset of an organization. You cannot innovate faster than your knowledge assets or more than you manage knowledge. You cannot reap the rewards of KM unless you invest in it. Reward, incentivize, recognize, and make it a café experience.

According to a white paper on the Incentive Research Foundation Incentive Benchmarking Survey, in which 900 top-performing organizations were reviewed:

- 90 percent of the highest-performing companies use incentives and rewards to retain and encourage employees.
- 99 percent of employees have unique reward preferences, which makes incentives an excellent alternative to a traditional reward system.
- 80 percent of employees prefer strong incentives over a bigger paycheck.
- 78 percent of employees are willing to remain with their current employer due to the competitive perks and incentives it offers.

The bottom line: Because of the increasingly competitive nature of attracting the best talents today, organizations are modernizing their incentive programs. When I made a business case for an enterprise KM strategy for my organization, incentives were a significant element of the program.

You cannot force people to share their knowledge, but it would be best if you made the environment conducive to knowledge sharing. Remember that the goal of human relations is to create a win–win situation; this can be achieved by appreciating and respecting the employees' knowledge while at the same time achieving organizational objectives. According to Stephen Covey (2004), abundance mentality means believing there is plenty for everyone. Both the knowledge workers and the organization can win. Knowledge workers must be motivated and incentivized to share their knowledge and be recognized for sharing, too; this only happens in an environment of collaboration and trust, as I discussed earlier. An African adage says to use a token or gift to retrieve the banana from a monkey's hands. You don't just demand that he offers you his stuff.

6.4. KNOWLEDGE CULTURE: CITY IMPACT ROUNDTABLE CONFERENCE

People choose not to change their behavior because the culture and the imperatives of the organization make it too difficult to act upon the knowledge.
—Michael Schrage

Etiologically, the word "culture" derives its meaning from a French term, which originally derives its meaning from another Latin word "colere," which means to tend to the earth and grow, or cultivation and nurture (Zimmermann, 2017). A culture is a way of life of a group of people—the behaviors, beliefs, values, and symbols that they accept, generally without thinking about them, and that are passed along by communication and imitation from one generation to the next. Culture is symbolic communication. Culture is the system of knowledge shared by a relatively large group of people (Hofstede, 1997). Culture can be a way of life or the midst of life. Structural capital is all about the knowledge within a group, community, or organization. Understand your group, city, or organization's prevailing culture if you want to create a KM environment.

I began to connect with nonprofit organizations in Austin, Texas, in 2002. Some of the nonprofits and compassion organizations in my network were feeding the homeless and taking care of the needy and helpless by responding to the physical, emotional, and spiritual needs of those at the edge of society. Cities, communities, and nations, just like organizations, can have a lot going for them but lack a culture where knowledge, not just information and data, freely flows. In many cities, you have villages of silos. People cannot work together for a common cause because there's no knowledge-sharing space. What if there were a space for those who knew a lot and those seeking to know, those who have ideas, and those looking for ideas to advance our communities to converge?

Let me tell you a story about homeless boys at the café. One day I met Larry Ball. This man had about eight young men in his van. Larry told me that he picks up homeless kids from the street, gives them a home, rehabilitates and trains them, and sends them back as meaningful members of society. Some of them don't even know their parents. He takes them to his house. His organization provides these young men with a home, care, and emotional and spiritual support to get them back on their feet. They are mentored, educated, and then seek jobs. They begin to earn a living, and finally, become independent. He replaces them with other homeless kids. I asked him, "What is your success rate?" His response was an outstanding 98 percent!

I asked Larry how he gets support in doing this full time. His answer: "I receive little or no support. I've never received grants or major donations. I believe that I'm called to do this, and it's producing fantastic results." I met people from several other nonprofits from 2003 to 2008 through the nonprofit I founded, Apostolic Bridge Builders, Inc. I was also connected with several industry leaders and people in government who sincerely appreciate the roles and success of nonprofits like Larry Ball's Hungry for God organization. I thought that I needed to bring these knowledge players into a café meeting. I had several such knowledge exchange/connection meetings. Somewhere, I felt that we need to have an intentional roundtable conference to know what's going on in different communities and how nonprofits, governments, and leaders of industry can come together in a Knowledge Café–style roundtable and share knowledge and build synergy for greater community transformation. I needed to have a café and fair project for city transformation.

THREE TYPES OF CAFÉ ATTENDEES

Bringing diverse people into a café is not as easy as you may think, but it is possible. It's a way to organize knowledge workers to enable quick, efficient decisions amidst a fast-changing work environment. I have identified three categories of knowledge owners or managers:

- Those who will not come to a Knowledge Café meeting unless there's a detailed agenda (menu) with predictable outcomes. This violates David Gurteen's original concept of a Knowledge Café.
- Café enthusiasts will not café with anyone until a relationship has been developed.
- Social animals just want to meet.

On the citywide or community level, how do you bring these players together? Like in a typical Knowledge Café, some people will have their own agendas. I believe that a café provides the right atmosphere for knowledge owners and visionaries to collaborate, share knowledge, and build synergy for the community's greater good. We had several successful café meetings we called roundtables. They were less structured. Everyone's opinion counted. We celebrated the successes of the participants. We identified with their challenges—those who had more resources willingly shared. I began to see the need to facilitate or coordinate nonprofit organizations, faith communities, media, local governments, elected officials, and businesses across Texas.

Mission America has already started City Impact Roundtable (CIR) conferences. I attended the conferences in New York; Fontana, California; and Chicago, to name a few.

We didn't have to reinvent the wheel. Yearly, we had a fair and café, a City Impact Roundtable, to connect, communicate, and collaborate for strategic partnerships—leading to measurable city and community impacts and transformations. These produced dozens of strategic partnerships that changed the face of various communities in Texas. In part, Austin Disaster Relief Network (ADRN) is one of the significant results of this endeavor under my leadership. During our last CIR in Del Valle, Texas, we resolved to empty these efforts into ADRN under the leadership of Executive Director and founder, Daniel Geraci. I have been an advisory board member since its inception—providing guidance, counsel, and strategies. ADRN has coordinated and managed over 13,000 volunteers in disaster response since 2008. It deploys and trains volunteers in times of disaster in multiple areas such as incident command, trauma and emotional care, chaplaincy, case management, sponsoring surviving families, HAM Radio communications, call center operations, warehouse, clean-up, and more. ADRN has made central Texas disaster-ready, more than any other organization in Texas.

In the end, behaviors can change because of a culture shift, and the imperatives of the organization make it too easy or too difficult to act upon the knowledge. The culture must shift for knowledge to flourish. That's the right environment for KM.

6.5. MANAGE PROJECT KNOWLEDGE TO CREATE A CAFÉ CULTURE

Roger Martin, a professor in the Rotman School of Management at the University of Toronto and considered by many to be the world's number one management thinker, believes that projects are the organizing principle for work and the indefatigability of knowledge workers in the project economy (Martin, 2019). A project has remained the most effective way to organize work in most organizations. Before a KM program is activated and deployed, it should be initiated, planned, managed, and executed like a project. Behind every project is an idea—whether you want to improve process or management efficiencies, increase margins or customer satisfaction, drive innovation, or manage knowledge. As I would for any project, I developed a charter for our KM program and a charter for various techniques we implemented and deployed. We intentionally introduced processes such as CoP, knowledge interview, knowledge fair and café, lessons learned, Wiki, and more. The project management discipline grounds the process and provides the necessary elements from management buy-in, business case, stakeholder engagement, communication planning, risk management, scope management, and value realization. Our membership, connection, and learning agility in various management, research, and KM organizations such as PMI, TRB, AASHTO, APQC, KM World, NASA, the U.S. Army, and more were instrumental to our success.

Knowledge Café culture connotes the understanding of managing project knowledge. KM implementation is a project that adheres to the basic principles of project management. According to PMI's *PMBOK® Guide*, sixth edition (2017), the Manage Project Knowledge process is performed throughout the project, is concerned with explicit and tacit knowledge, and has primarily two purposes: reusing existing knowledge and creating new knowledge to improve performance on the current and future projects (Project Management Institute, 2017).

What is a project? According to PMI's *PMBOK® Guide,* sixth edition (2017), "A project is a temporary endeavor undertaken to create a unique product, service, or result. The temporary nature of projects indicates that a project has a definite beginning and end. The end is reached when the project's objectives have been achieved," or further, "Temporary does not typically apply to the product, service, or result created by the project."

ATTRIBUTES OF A PROJECT
• Projects have a definite start
• Projects have a definite end

- The start and end define the project life cycle
- Projects start with the charter
- Projects end with a closing
- Closing happens after turnover and acceptance

This definition is mainly for the project implemented using a waterfall project methodology. Operations are not projects, even though specific projects have some elements of temporary operations. To ensure the realization of benefits for undertaking the project, a test period (such as a soft launch in services) can be part of the total project time before handing it over to the permanent operations.

We bought a house in the fall of 2017. Before then, we had to sell our old house. When I met with my realtor, I told her that I had 45 days to close on the new house and therefore had to sell my old house within 30 days. The problem is that to get the most out of my 12-year-old house, I'd have to renovate it. So, how long would it take to renovate the house, list, sell, and close? We would have to finish the renovation in three weeks. This was a very aggressive timeline. I told her that I am a project manager and would manage the project.

LESSONS FROM A RENOVATION PROJECT

Here are some of the things I needed to get done to accomplish this project, ready for listing in three weeks. Without getting too complicated, I needed to initiate this project. I didn't have a formal charter, but I had a written business case with the project's objective—renovate my house to get the best value from the sale.

1. Design and planning. I secured the funding needed for the renovation. We didn't need a permit. I contacted contractors recommended by my realtor to make sure that we met the deadline. I developed a work breakdown structure upon what needed to be done to accomplish this project and developed a schedule and budget.
2. Identified and made repairs. Since these tasks wouldn't impact subsequent activities, I scheduled some of them to run side-by-side with other activities.

3. They inspected, updated, and repaired electrical and plumbing systems.
4. Completed finishing touches such as flooring, surface finishing, and trim.

I integrated all the processes, helped every contractor or player accountable, and accomplished the task in 16 days, listed the home on day 18, and had two offers on the same day. I sold the house on day 21. This is project management at work! I wish I could say that "this ain't my first rodeo" in terms of renovation and selling a property. But I learned a lot, and applied, used, reused, and widely shared what I learned with my mentees. We manage the project daily by what we do at work or at home. We learn a lot from these activities. If I ever need to renovate again, I have lessons learned from the previous experience. Knowledge is information gained based on experience and education.

Within the context of KM, the most critical organizational knowledge is confined in the minds of individuals. As stated in the definition of tacit knowledge (hard to codify), specialized knowledge in employees' hearts and minds is hard to exchange and share. You may know how to manage your projects, deliver values, and how to get things done, but it isn't very easy to communicate this kind of knowledge or know-how and know-why. Consider the five generations of knowledge workers working together in the project management space! Every generation speaks its own knowledge language. Managing this knowledge means creating a conducive café environment to make sharing possible.

Knowledge management training, awareness, café meetings, and motivations will open the minds and hearts of the knowledge managers to see KM's big picture and freely embrace the café inkling. Managing knowledge also involves rewarding knowledge workers for sharing their knowledge rather than penalizing them.

KM processes intentionally, systematically, and actively manage and leverage the knowledge assets in an organization, thereby creating new knowledge and innovation through collaboration.

Knowledge that is shared multiple times creates new knowledge, but the knowledge that is not shared dies and is useless! We live to share. When we learn and do, we share what we know. When we stop sharing, we stop learning. The new winners in the marketplace economy of ideas are those who recognize, identify, plan, and effectively manage their knowledge assets. Effective management of organizational knowledge assets is crucial for securing a competitive advantage in an emerging economy. Effective management of knowledge assets is a key requirement for securing competitive advantage (Boisot, 1999).

6.6. KNOWLEDGE CAFÉ EXCHANGE INCREASES RETENTION

Knowledge is a company asset, hidden until the knowledge worker releases it. The key to generating the best returns from your KM Program is to implement a well-planned methodology and ensure that your organization facilitates this release of information.
—Mike Bagshaw, Development Director at Trans4mation Training Ltd.

As I pointed out earlier, most organizations' knowledge assets are hidden in and by people, the knowledge workers. To retain knowledge assets, you must know what the knowledge workers know—they are the keepers of knowledge who must release that knowledge. The 2000s may have advanced the most incredible job mobility in human history. Before then, many employees spent their entire careers in one job and with the same employer. That is no more. Many people will change jobs 6 to 20 times in their lifetime. They will leave with their knowledge unless it is captured. So, it should be a top priority of top-performing organizations to implement a well-oiled process, methodology, and plan to ensure the release, leverage, and exchange of knowledge. This should be an organizational strategy for continuity, resilience, sustainability, and innovation.

Knowledge Transfer Is the New Bacon!
In January 2017, the Minnesota Department of Transportation (MnDOT) initiated the Knowledge Retention Pilot Project called M.A.S.K. Method (Method for Analyzing and Structuring Knowledge) to capture experts' knowledge in three subjects and develop knowledge retention books. Approximately 31 percent of MnDOT's workforce is or will be retirement-eligible within five years. Retaining the tacit knowledge of vital technical experts is a high priority. They are developing knowledge books to retain their agency's knowledge; preserve deep technical, organizational knowledge; share individual expertise built over the years; and make it accessible to all—a living document for successors that is easy to follow, with intuitive format e-learning platform capabilities.

There are two dimensions of knowledge retention. One is the retention of knowledge by the learner, the knowledge worker, and the retention of the organizational knowledge based on its knowledge workers' minds and heads.

It is my opinion that an individual's retention increases when they share their knowledge more frequently. German psychologist Hermann Ebbinghaus pioneered the experimental study of memory and discovered a phenomenon called overlearning during his study on the forgetting curve. His basic idea is that if you practice something more than what is usually required to memorize it, the effect of overlearning takes place. Overlearning, just like continuous knowledge exchange or sharing of what you learned, the information or knowledge is now stored much more strongly. Thus, the effects of the forgetting curve for overlearned information becomes shallower (Shrestha, 2017).

National Training Laboratories Institute's learning pyramid is unsupported by empirical research. However, it shows that we typically retain 5 percent of knowledge transferred through formal or informal classroom lecture after 24 hours. We retain 10 percent of the knowledge we acquire through reading, like reading this book, after 24 hours. When knowledge workers acquire knowledge from audiovisual, retention doubles to 20 percent. If there are demonstrations during the learning, retention increases to 30 percent. When group discussions are involved in knowledge transfer, retention increases to 50 percent. If the knowledge worker practices what they learned, like learning at the café, retention increased to 75 percent. If the knowledge worker teaches and implements (immediate use) what is learned, retention increases to an astronomical 90 percent. So, the more interactive the learning process, the more retention increases? Consider that repeated recall of information improves retention capabilities to about 80 percent. For instance, learners can have a post-course discussion or debriefing, such as conversing with their manager about how they intend to use new skills or with peers on lessons learned implementation.

Organizations like Project Management Institute (PMI; www .PMI.org), American Productivity & Quality Center (APQC; https:// www.apqc.org/knowledge-retention-and-transfer), Knowledge Management Institute (KMI; https://www.kminstitute.org/), and Knowledge Management Consortium International (KMCI) agree on developing strategies to retain and transfer organizational knowledge assets. There is also a consensus about a set of tools that can be leveraged in converting the knowledge in people's heads into processes and the hands of other employees. Some of the tools include, but is not limited to, lessons learned exercises, which is like an after-action review activity performed during and after the project. Lessons learned are utilized during and after the project and consulted by other project managers in future projects.

Also, communities of practice cafés, simple café conversation about leveraging of retirees' expertise and hire-backs, storytelling programs, knowledge interviews, exit knowledge interviews, social media and technology collaborative platforms, mentoring and apprenticeship programs, including more accessible access to subject matter experts, knowledge maps, and so on, are great approaches for knowledge transfer. Knowledge café mindset is the people side of KM. Café facilitates a casual environment for increased findability/ discoverability of knowledge and information, a conversation about expertise locators, and other tools, making it easy for employees to find people with the expertise they need, regardless of geographic and departmental boundaries. Organizations utilize these tools for knowledge retention and transfer. We draw café questions from these tools. Café conversations increase retention. I'll discuss extensively the role of each of these knowledge-transfer tools and more later. The ultimate purpose of these tools is to enable knowledge retention and transfer.

6.7. CAFÉ FOR LEARNING ORGANIZATIONS

According to Workforce 2020 (Gregory, 2014), 65 percent of employees say that development and training opportunities would increase their loyalty to the company. A highly skilled workforce is undoubtedly a strategic differentiator in the marketplace. Skilled knowledge workers flourish in a learning organization.

But training is not enough! In 2012, U.S. organizations spent a whopping $164.2 billion on employee learning and development, according to the findings of ASTD's 2013 *State of the Industry* report sponsored by Skillsoft and the CARA Group, Inc. (ATD, 2013). There was no evidence that this learning alone translated into a knowledge workforce.

Training alone isn't enough to retain knowledge, considering that baby boomers are leaving the workforce in droves, the increasing job mobility of today's workforce, accelerating market volatility, and intensified speed of responsiveness to change and technology. Learning organizations can become café organizations and must translate learning into knowledge.

A learning organization facilitates the learning and development of its employees and continuously transforms itself to remain competitive in the business environment to create a competitive advantage. Because of the pressures facing modern organizations, every learning organization continually manages its learning processes to its advantage. Knowledge management makes it possible to measure or evaluate learning, translate knowledge, uncover what we know, and create new knowledge learning.

Being a learning organization is not enough. Companies must embrace learning agility. Researchers at Teachers College, Columbia University, and the Center for Creative Leadership defined learning agility as a mindset and corresponding collection of practices that allow leaders to continually develop, grow, and utilize new strategies that will equip them for the increasingly complex problems they face in their organizations. They contend that learning-agile individuals are "continually able to jettison skills, perspectives, and ideas that are no longer relevant and learn new ones that are" (Mitchinson & Morris, 2014). Knowledge management is at the center of the metamorphosis of organizational learning. Learning-knowledge organizations learn, steward, and manage knowledge. Learning organizations are agile learners. Learning agile, versatile feedback, making meaning of our experience, and collaboration are woven into these high-performing organizations' fabric.

Data, information, and technology inform the learning, training, and mentoring culture. Learning organizations transfer information and knowledge to the knowledge worker. This knowledge is caged in the minds and brains of the employee until the learning is contextualized. Also, context and perspective are the things that make a collection of related data knowledge.

In many circumstances, the learning circle ends here. But learning organizations with a culture of knowledge exchange try to go beyond this threshold to codify what is known by the employee, sharing, transferring, and reusing the knowledge. At this point, the learned employee becomes a knowledge employee. However, when new knowledge is created through analysis, practice, and evaluation of what is known and what the organization should know, thereby creating new knowledge, this circle is completed by moving toward new data and information that needs to be expanded and relearned. At this point, the knowledge worker becomes a knowledge manager. The learning and exchange paradigm has to change as we get people in a café mindset or physical café.

Having discussed the differences among data, information, and knowledge continuum, I would like to say that their integration will ultimately result in wisdom and enlightenment from learning organizations. Learning-knowledge organizations have integrated personal mastery with team learning, mental models, shared learning, and system thinking.

6.8. CREATING A KNOWLEDGE-SHARING ENVIRONMENT

Dr. Denise Bedford (2019), author and Georgetown University professor, said that "Moving to a knowledge culture is going to be a huge disrupter. A traditional culture rewards competition and knowledge theft over-sharing and reduces the visibility of knowledge to what is necessary."

Knowledge culture will disrupt the ways we have learned, shared, and exchanged knowledge. The reward patterns and structures are changing forever. To create an environment of knowledge sharing, you may want to know what I mean by the environment, how to create it, and what is shared.

Organizations have spent millions of dollars on the Internet and for capturing information. Dan Remenyi, a visiting professor at Trinity College Dublin, Ireland, contends that "The belief behind this approach was that if we could capture knowledge and put it in a computer, then it could be shared. This sharing would ensure the highest possible utilization of knowledge across the entire organization" (Ramenyi, 2004). How realistic has this become to organizations today? It's like putting a suit on a monkey. Is the problem of KM technological issues or human interaction issues? If it's merely a technology issue, it will be a breeze. You must show people where the knowledge is and make them interested in using the knowledge. The environment determines whether folks will use these. Environments are not created by default. We create an environment for Knowledge Café exchange. Maybe you work in a dog-eat-dog industry, where everyone seems to be snapping at your heels, and you are running out of napkins! Knowledge Café offers the impetus for redirection, reciprocity, and rationality, thus turning competition to coopetition. Knowledge, which is information explained by itself, is entirely inadequate to bring transformation! Knowledge exchange creates energy. Honest conversation, reflection, interchange of ideas, sharing, trust, and reciprocity are the building blocks of a knowledge-sharing environment.

In an environment of shared knowledge, sharing that knowledge is natural. Knowledge managers find joy in sharing what they know because they feel a sense of fulfillment in doing that; they trust the culture; they feel rewarded for sharing. There's a reciprocity in sharing knowledge. In a KM environment, will you trust knowledge workers to do the right thing? Of course. How you create this environment varies from one organization to another. There's no one answer or magic bullet. Based on my research and experience, the approach isn't top-down or bottom-up; the approach can be either, both, or neither. During the 2019 Transportation Research Board Information and Knowledge Management Committee's Summer Webinar, Dr. Moses Adoko contended that KM should be federated, with each part of the organization having its own autonomy under an organizational KM program. There is no one-size-fits-all approach to creating an environment of KM (Adoko, 2019a).

What Is Knowledge Shared?

Simply put, you share what you know, and you don't share what you don't know. However, you don't wait until you fully understand what you know before your café. There are things you have a partial understanding of that you can only come to grips with if you embark on "caféing" the idea—bringing it to shared conversational space. New knowledge and innovation are made possible when knowledge is shared. We come to a café to know what we know, challenge what we know, understand what we don't know, and unlearn what we've learned, and relearn Agile.

You can use the café knowledge sharing environment to solve, resolve, or discuss any issue. I once caféd with the DevOps team to define and improve the role of security in DevOps. DevOps, development, and IT operations are an enterprise software development phrase used to describe the type of agile relationship between two business units. The goal of our café was to change and improve DevOps relationships by encouraging better and café-like communication and collaboration among knowledge workers across units. I am a subject matter expert (SME) in project management, not necessarily in all aspects of the project, for example, software development. When you challenge the team to a café, facts come to light, and the team forms a common understanding. Café provides the meeting point of ideas in any setting.

We can know what we know, but we cannot know what we know until we capture and share it. When a knowledge mindset is embedded into an organization's DNA and becomes its organizational strategy, workers become knowledge workers, the workplace becomes a knowledge workplace, performance improves, and competitive advantage accelerates. KM is not another program to be adopted but a philosophy that changes culture and a way of life. Café and demand for knowledge create knowledge sharing habits. Participants in a KM café are colleagues willing to learn from others to create a learning process and knowledge culture.

There has to be an environment of innovation and collaboration with a strategy for knowledge sharing for there to be a knowledge culture. For there to be a knowledge environment, you have to create it. It's a Herculean task to share knowledge in an environment where there's no culture of knowledge sharing. The culture of knowledge sharing creates a knowledge workforce. Just like change, human beings and organizations don't just embrace knowledge management. It has to pass the common sense test.

> You can't force people to share their know-how or what they know. You do create an environment that enables knowledge culture, where knowledge sharing is not punished but rewarded.

Knowledge is the most critical asset of an organization. Being able to preserve organizational knowledge determines profitability, sustainability, competitiveness, and the ability to grow. No organization can afford to lose its knowledge base. According to the World Economy Forum, 95 percent of CEOs claim that knowledge management is a critical factor in an organization's success, and 80 percent of companies mentioned in *Fortune* magazine have staff explicitly assigned to KM (Kampioni & Ciolfitto, 2015).

LITTLE STEPS OF CONTINUOUS IMPROVEMENT

As I said earlier, KM is like eating an elephant—one bite at a time. It's one brick on top of another. We are peeling an onion. As in continuous improvement, we take baby steps. Valparaiso University's senior research professor, Dean Schroeder (2019), was right when he answered the question about small ideas and baby steps in continuous improvement.

- "Small ideas are less costly and less risky—learn as you go.
- Big improvements need lots of small ones to be successful.
- Going after smaller ideas builds an improvement culture from the bottom up.
- Small ideas have a huge impact."

He concluded by saying that small improvements repeated over time accumulate to huge savings naturally.

My prescription for creating a KM environment is to incorporate a Knowledge Café into a way of life. There are several tools and techniques for implementing a KM program. I contend that techniques like knowledge fairs and cafés, and communities of practice are some of the most effective ways of implementing a KM culture. I have introduced these concepts in several organizations, including TxDOT, and have seen KM passion erupt.

Create an environment of openness and willingness to help and share. Identify some knowledge enthusiasts, project managers, or employees who are willing to share what they know. They must be excited by what they know and be glad to help and share with others.

PRACTICAL THINGS YOU CAN DO AS YOU CREATE
AN ENVIRONMENT OF KNOWLEDGE SHARING

- Embody team values and incorporate shared values in your fairs and cafés.
- Normalize vocabulary and develop KM-specific training.
- Allow for organic growth as practitioners show interest in KM and some form of CoPs.
- Start small. Small teams lend themselves to agile knowledge sharing.
- Leadership needs to lead in overcoming fear of sharing and show how unshared knowledge becomes obsolete.

- Use knowledge exchange as a legacy builder; for instance, those who have developed a successor should be rewarded instead of being punished.
- Recognize your opportunities to share knowledge.
- Identify KM elements and all opportunities for knowledge exchange in your organization.
- Schedule regular and recurring cafés.
- Try planned SME presentations (call for presenters and facilitators, CoP lead, new ideas, etc.) to initiate or supplement the conversation.
- Incorporate café into conferences and workshops; emphasize two-way learning and knowledge exchange as opposed to one-way presentation style.
- Share tools and technology enablers used by different units to organize, share, and invigorate knowledge.

KM ENABLERS BEYOND PEOPLE, PROCESS, TECHNOLOGY, AND CONTENT

Knowledge management enablers—people, process, technology, and content—allow the organization to develop its knowledge, stimulate the creation of knowledge within the organization, and share and protect it. According to Yeh et al. (2006), these are the most critical enablers required to create a KM environment.

- Management buy-in and continued support
- Designated KM lead, personnel, and budget
- User-friendly technology enablers
- Clear roles and accountabilities
- A business case to show evidence of KM value
- Significant process and clearly defined KM approach
- A personal belief of the champion, brokers, and KM leads
- Enterprise KM strategy
- Championship and support from teams and champions
- Incentive system

In the organizations where I have managed knowledge, we have succeeded because we first secured an executive champion. Getting an executive sponsor was a good beginning that gave us leverage. Once our charter was signed, we had the authority to activate the program, take baby steps already defined in existing KM elements, and implement enablers. We had some pilots for KM techniques, such as CoPs.

HOW DO YOU DEVELOP AND EXPAND
THE KNOWLEDGE ENABLERS?

- Have a governance structure
- Employ change management principles
- Incorporate KM in training and development
- Employ the right measurements (multidimensional)
- Utilize technology tools
- Utilize rewards and recognition

WHAT IS RIGHT FOR MY COMMUNITY?

Consider your community's preference for communication and knowledge transfer—pick what's right for your café and community!

- Expand knowledge enablers. Share those technology enablers that have proved to be effective and make them accessible to knowledge users.
- Provide governance to knowledge-sharing communities like CoPs or café sessions.
- Incorporate change management principles into your journeys for a KM culture.
- Measure your progress through multidimensional measuring or gauge the result of knowledge sharing through surveys and other means.
- Use the right technology tools to enable KM. Create the right balance of people, process, content, and technology.
- Create a system of rewards and recognition. Rewards, not punishment, accelerate the knowledge culture's intensity.
- Work with each domain owner and champions to mature your knowledge practice areas and CoPs.
- Work with information management to identify collaborations and knowledge-sharing platforms and necessary governance levels.

- Include integral skill sets for an organizational knowledge-sharing culture (e.g., IT, HR, Communications, Library and Information Science, change management).
- Identify the most critical ways the knowledge culture can add value to your organization. Examples are connecting people through communities (CoPs) and networks, business transformation through big data, artificial intelligence (human-machine collaborations), innovation (new knowledge), improved enterprise document management, content management, findability and searchability, knowledge retention, the convergence of best practice, knowledge-based engineering, improving market share, safety records, customer relationship and satisfaction, cost efficiency, lessons learned management, social interaction and idea generation, a collaboration of content, capturing and disseminating information, content, and knowledge, searching for people, and so on.

Café and KM culture should be incorporated into enterprise training and development; one-way learning is the antithesis of a café culture, which is a two-way exchange. Knowledge culture creates a KM environment: you must be intentional, plan, and execute well, and make the process an organizational strategy.

7 ▪ Knowledge Café Environment: Trends, Future, and Disruptive Technologies

---

Chapter Objectives

- Discuss the interface of the changing world of work, project knowledge transfer trends, automation, AI, and disruptions
- Explore the present and the future of KM
- Analyze innovation, knowledge co-creation, and the café
- List KM software in the market today

7.1. CHANGING WORLD OF WORK: TRENDS, ARTIFICIAL INTELLIGENCE (AI), AUTOMATION, AND DISRUPTIVE TECHNOLOGIES

Consider these statistics about our changing world of work from McKinsey Global Institute's manpower group survey (Manyika et al., 2017).

- 60 percent of occupations have 30 percent of automatable activities
- 45 percent of today's tasks could be automated by adopting proven technologies
- 84 percent of businesses use AI as 'essential to competitiveness'
- 70 percent believe AI's greatest impact will be in functions such as Marketing, Customer Service, Finance, and HR.

Will Automation Enhance a Knowledge Culture?

According to builtin.com, artificial intelligence is a wide-ranging branch of computer science concerned with building smart machines capable of performing tasks that typically require human intelligence. AI is an interdisciplinary science with multiple approaches, but advancements in machine learning and deep learning create a paradigm shift in virtually every sector of the tech industry ("Artificial Intelligence. What Is Artificial Intelligence? How Does AI Work?," n.d.).

In today's ultra-competitive global and knowledge economy, businesses across every vertical segment are riding the automation wave to cut costs, boost revenues, increase employee satisfaction, provide a superior customer experience, and save time on other matters such as business and information strategy and knowledge culture. I believe that replacing repetitive tasks with automation will be critical for businesses and will speed up processes, cut costs, improve efficiencies, and free knowledge workers to concentrate on the big issues.

LEVERAGING AUTOMATION

While automation will enhance KM, several conversations need to be caféd if we want to create an environment of knowledge transfer and exchange. Andrew Filev, CEO and Founder of Wrike, outlined this step-by-step guide for leveraging automation (Filev, 2017).

- Bring all data in one single source of truth.
- Recognize repeatable patterns emerging in your work so you can oversee at a program level.
- Create templates and workflows.

- Automate the repeatable bottlenecks, such as requirements gathering/work intake, reviews and approvals, and monitoring consistency of data and process.

A KM café may be a one-off or a continuous event. A KM environment has a culture of excellence built on continuous improvement, team commitment, and flawless execution. It is also one of conversation and collaboration that ensures that individuals can work efficiently as a team.

Single Source of the Truth?

Every organization is sitting on piles of information, disparate knowledge in systems and people. But these treasure troves don't create value unless employees can find, use, and reuse them. Painless accessibility of information is key to success. When information is stored across different repositories, in all other formats, in the minds of varying knowledge workers, it has a ripple effect across the organization—like delayed projects, longer time to resolve the issue, duplications of efforts and tasks, frustration, expensive errors, and reworks.

Truth: We need a complete enterprise search solution—a single source of truth that is easy to access like a café. *Café is a convergence and conglomeration of knowledge and ideas.* In the case of information, there's a need for space to give employees a single, personalized place to access all relevant information and insights wherever they live. This will save employees' time and impacts strategic priorities, including cost savings, revenue increases, and risk mitigation.

How do we manage our data? What is our effort to create one single source of truth or at least have a simple way to integrate all the data sources in the organization so they can talk to each other? In a KM environment, we have a single source of truth for our main work. We can connect with other vital systems and sources of records, as knowledge workers connect with ideas. Data and information strategy must align with the business culture.

We cannot overlook the process and delivery of agility and personalization. KM environment means we can adapt quickly as we deliver personalized and customized experiences. It means we can deliver consistent, predictable high-quality results. It means we build automation into every aspect of our work and manage knowledge.

In 2020, we have seen an incredible advancement in AI, knowledge overload, and disruptions such as capsule network, clinical enrollment, back-office automation, check-out free trials to high industry adoption, and market strength of threatening AIs like autonomous navigation, connected and automated vehicles, global pandemics like COVID-19, Bitcoin, 5G, and network optimization.

Will AI and Automation Replace Project Knowledge?

There is a rise in industry adoption of AIs, such as face recognition, edge computing, an open-source framework, predictive maintenance, conversational agents, cyber threat hunting, and so on. Where is knowledge in the midst of all these? KM filters and delineates certain work or tasks for automation so that critical knowledge that cannot be automated is reserved for innovation. Automation freedom is catalytic to value-added tasks and increased capabilities for managing risk and problems, opportunities for greater efficiencies in relevant areas like communications, increased scalability, and shaving off routine and mundane repetitive tasks. Automation of program and project knowledge will help improve knowledge exchange and co-creation of new knowledge. A McKinsey Global Institute report in 2017 stated that 60 percent of occupations have 30 percent automatable activities, and 45 percent of today's tasks could be automated by adopting proven technologies. This will leave the remaining skill sets and knowledge required for 55 percent of the innovation tasks (Manyika et al., 2017). Automation doesn't mean that projects will become easy. The project and program manager will be acquiring more skills to match the complexities of the new project knowledge environment. Automation and AI will not replace the project manager. It will complement him or her.

Knowledge is the acquisition of skills, experiences, and information. The application of this knowledge requires intelligence. Everyone can apply intelligence to provide solutions in a project, program, or operational activities. The Knowledge Café mindset enables the harnessing of collective intelligence and the co-creation of new knowledge. Automation enables knowledge workers to move into those skills that have an increasing value, such as creativity, strategy, empathy, executive communication, and analytical thinking. The advancement of technology and artificial intelligence has increased KM in the project management space, research, academia, and across industries. The knowledge assets of yesterday are becoming quickly irrelevant today.

Strong Business Acumen = IQ + EQ + XQ
Successful leadership requires intelligence (IQ: new knowledge and understanding), emotion (EQ), and execution (XQ). Project managers and all knowledge workers must pursue those skills and knowledge that have increasing value: leadership skills, business acumen (IQ + EQ + XQ), executive communication, emotional intelligence, and technology skills. Those who don't have or develop these skills will become irrelevant in the face of disruptive technologies in the years ahead! Organizations that leverage their knowledge workers and assets share, and new knowledge creates innovation value to their organization and provides better solutions to their customers.

What are some of the results of automation?

My point is that the technology aspect of knowledge is transient because techniques, technologies, and KM strategies are transitional, as seen in table 5. Still, intelligence—the application of knowledge—is not. I often tell my knowledge leaders that the experiential knowledge that brought us here cannot keep us here. The strategy that brought us here is insufficient for the future. If we run with footmen and we are worn out, what will happen when we run with the horsemen of AI? We have to manage knowledge sharing and transfer with future trends in mind.

Organizations and individuals have never before been exposed to the amount of data that is available today. The data sources are made available by today's technologies, including the Internet, email, video, cell phones, social media, IoT (Internet of Things) sensors,

Table 5. Results of Automation

From . . .	To . . .
One size fits all	Increased segmentation, scalability, tailored to the customer
Unmodified enterprise legacy systems and process	Enterprise digital strategy
Legacy applications	Modernized systems and digital transformation
Poor user experience	Increased Net Performances Score (NPS)
Manual and repetitive processes	Automation, advise, and judgment
Fax and printers	Electronic signatures
Limited insights	Strategic focus, customer centricity, organizational agility
High cost	Low cost
Human error	Reduced error and high accuracy
Legacy process	Real-time, omni, 24 X 7 monitoring, centralized and more efficient process, greater capabilities, and high compliance
Paper	Digital assets

and call centers. Data literally come at an organization from every direction. Most of this data are converted to information, and few organizations can convert both data and information to knowledge. It will advance human-machine collaborations in any knowledge-centric organization.

What is extraordinary in organizations that embrace Knowledge Café, embark on intelligent conversations on how to curate data and information, and convert them to knowledge, applying them for a pearl of enduring wisdom, is the Café environment they create—an environment where knowledge is cherished and flourishes.

Artificial intelligence will free knowledge workers for creativity and innovation. Imagine a world where the designers of the Internet of Things, 3D printing, mixed reality, robotics, 5G, blockchain technology, quantum, cognitive AI, and robotic process automation get together in a café and become co-creators of knowledge.

Microsoft recently commissioned studies with Forbes Insights and Forrester Consulting to take a closer look at the mission-critical benefits of AI for knowledge workers and help organizations harness Everyday AI's full potential in Microsoft 365. The discussion is compelling. AI has come to stay, and there's a critical interface between knowledge workers and AI. In fact, knowledge workers will make AI possible, and AI will free project managers and knowledge workers for creativity and critical thinking activities while streamlining processes. The café opens the possibilities and discussion for mastering the art of human–machine collaboration. Artificial intelligence is irrefutably transforming the way we manage projects and work.

Global GDP will increase 14 percent by 2030 as businesses adopt AI, contributing an additional $15.7T to the global economy (Rao & Verweij, 2019). According to Gartner, in 2021, AI augmentation will generate $2.9 trillion in business value and recover 6.2 billion hours of worker productivity (Gartner, n.d.). According to a report by the McKinsey Global Institute (Manyika et al., 2017), nearly two-thirds of all jobs could have a significant chunk—at least 30 percent—of their activities automated by 2030. This will affect about 800,000 jobs and means that we'll soon be sharing cubicles and offices with robots! We've got to get used to AI because that will be the business language in the days ahead. Machine intelligence will present another interesting knowledge-sharing atmosphere and challenges. Most of our job learning is not formal training but observation and knowledge sharing, two indispensable processes. Today, we are sacrificing learning and knowledge sharing for productivity.

This is how NASA responds to machine learning advanced algorithms to be used to further its mission-critical goals:

Uses of Machine Learning for Auto Generation of Pre-Task Safety Information

- When an employee is assigned to a new project, operation, or task, a machine learning algorithm could review safety and mishap databases and compile relevant safety information about that task (latest Agency and Industry information).

• The system would send a summary email highlighting lessons, learned documents, and videos based on the system and project life cycle.
• The system would identify potential experts or others working on similar projects across the Agency.

Uses of Machine Learning for auto-generation of knowledge sharing opportunities

• When a meeting is scheduled through the Outlook shared calendar, a machine learning algorithm system would read the topic, agenda, and attendees.
• Compile and summarize the latest Agency and Industry information about that topic.
• Learn of people at other Centers working on similar projects and then identify other potential attendees/ experts (Northey, Meza, Bell, & Barnes, 2016).

Machine learning will radically change how we work, as research shows that we have the inclination to outsource expertise to machines and automation. When this happens, young learners are likely going to be cut off from the learning process. As Ford's Model-T motorcar symbolized the death-knell for the horse-drawn economy, AI may pose a severe challenge to knowledge sharing, which is still strange to many people in the different professions, including the project management space and the workplace.

In the new knowledge economy, we live in a stretch of three inescapable whiplashes or blows of technology-based changes: computers, the Internet, and machine learning. For example, algorithms dictate the automated trading of trillions of dollars' worth of assets in the financial markets.

According to American technologist and commentator David Weinberger (2018), "There is, of course, a lot of human intervention in this process, from deciding which data to feed in, to optimizing the algorithms to get useful results, to checking the outcomes to see if the system is perpetuating or even amplifying the biases inevitably expressed by the data."

In call centers around the world, artificially intelligent chatbots are replacing the role of humans. The Global Tech Council contends that chatbots "are yet not equipped to understand human emotions like sarcasm, stress-full situations among others" (Sharma, 2019). However, "The University of Texas, Austin team is incorporating artificial intelligence into its machines so that they can deal with real-world situations" (Ghosh, 2018).

Machines like Flippy, built by Miso Robotics, are flipping burgers and using image-recognition capabilities to flick away unripe tomatoes on a high-speed sorting machine (Mogg, 2018). International Data Corporation Manufacturing Insights reveals that robotics is ranked the highest priority for technology investment in its 2017 report; this is based on the survey of companies from manufacturing, retail, health, and utility sectors ("Key Insights from IDC Worldwide Robotics Survey," 2017, cited in "IDC Latest Survey Ranks Robotics as Top Priority for Technology Investment in 2017," 2017). In the construction industry, machines lay bricks and open doors. 3D printers can now build concrete houses. Welcome to the fourth industrial revolution! These astounding realities are transforming everything—our lives, business, and knowledge management forever! Machines will undoubtedly learn from experts and experienced professionals who are custodians of organizational intellectual capital. Are we going to be learning from machines, or will there not be a need for knowledge sharing? The most mind-boggling development is the machine's ability to program itself.

Machines can do all these things in a fraction of the time humans can. Does this eliminate the need for expertise and knowledge sharing? In the days of connected and automated vehicles (CAV), smart roads, and unmanned planes and drones, our learning and knowledge sharing are taking on a new dimension. Given this perspective, you probably think there will be no need for knowledge sharing because machines will replace human knowledge—but not so fast.

Machines don't learn by themselves. Humans teach them. Think of knowledge sharing and learning for professional drivers and pilots. When machines take over our jobs, the knowledge we refused to share will vaporize!

Human knowledge is required for machine learning, and when we lose the aspect of knowledge that cannot be obsolete, there will be disruption. The Knowledge Café concept addresses the current absence of a theoretical, collaborative system by which all generations of workers can impart mission-critical business knowledge. The Knowledge Café suggests that most revolution happens outside the home and office, and indeed, at the café. The conversational and collaborative space to build connections between learners has never been this essential. I struggle to believe that the classroom is the best vehicle for future knowledge when today, 98 percent of all information in the world is in our palm (electronic device).

Shelley Goldman's work is an excellent illustration of the richness of the interpersonal interaction that is usually either overlooked or deliberately disrupted in the classroom setting. For Goldman, there is an overlapping world in which students, in conversation with one another, construct their understanding and identities. If these are curtailed, then so is much of the learning potential. As knowledge workers, students are eminently capable of "accomplishing work with each other, on their own terms" and learning on their terms outside the dictatorship of conventional presentation style at conferences, workshops, and classrooms. She contends that as learners, our social work is not counterproductive to accomplishing our science work and may even be a necessary prerequisite (Goldman, 1992).

"When the group engaged in conceptual learning conversations, they became very close, focused, and unified" (Goldman, 1992).

The classroom, fortunately, tends to be too well secured against knowledge theft. Knowledge workers can steal their knowledge from the social periphery made up of other, more experienced knowledge workers and ongoing, socially shared practice from the community of practice.

—Brown & Duguid (1996)

For decades, robots have been doing all kinds of repetitive work in our factories. The bottom line is that automation, AI, and other disruptive technologies will create new sets of roles, along with corresponding problems. Solving these problems will require the expertise of current project managers, knowledge workers, and employees to understand them, create solutions, and share the knowledge of the know-how, know-when, and know-whys of the new solutions. Every solution creates new problems for new knowledge challenges. Share your knowledge today, or it will become extraneous soon.

7.2. INNOVATION, KNOWLEDGE CO-CREATION, AND THE CAFÉ

Chiyoda-ku Kioicho of the German Institute for Japanese Studies, Tokyo, contends that "especially when introducing new products or when entering new markets, knowledge creation and transfer and intra- as well as inter-firm collaboration prove critical to project success" (Kohlbacher, 2008). One of the best ways to foster innovation is through collaboration and knowledge sharing. Knowledge management, co-creation, and innovation involve managing knowledge within the organization and its consultants, customers, suppliers, and competitors. In today's project and knowledge economy, companies cannot afford to isolate any outside entities. "Collaboration and joint creation of knowledge and value with external stakeholders and other entities in the business ecosystem are becoming increasingly important" (Kohlbacher, 2008).

Several elements will facilitate this collaboration that enhances the co-creation of knowledge and innovation. Co-creation is a collaborative initiative that operates like crowdsourcing by seeking information and ideas from a group of people. Knowledge co-creation means that the knowledge created is a joint effort.

Leadership and organizational culture set the tone for knowledge co-creation that gives birth to innovation. It also provides governance. Leadership promotes collaboration at all levels of the organization, leveraging new social technologies for collaboration. According to Wikipedia, social collaboration "refers to processes that help multiple people or groups interact and share information to achieve common goals" (Social collaboration, 2020). Wikipedia means that social collaboration is natural or organic and is group-centric.

Rewarding knowledge sharing and recognizing it at the leadership level stirs innovation. In its simplistic terms, the culture or environment in such a workplace gives project managers and, indeed, all knowledge workers the space to communicate openly and honestly. Employees can freely form meaningful bonds with one another. Collaboration and knowledge sharing are intentionally infused in the organization's culture and reflected in its daily operations.

Learning and applying lessons for programs and projects is another critical element. There is a mad rush for new learning, new ideas, innovations, and new knowledge. How many people reflect, search, and learn from their mistakes? How many people have taken inventory of what they know? Build on these lessons, sharpen them, and watch and see new knowledge and innovation explode! Some noticeable cultural change happens due to leadership and culture incorporating innovation, invention, new ideas, aesthetics, increased rights and freedom, process improvement, lessons learned implementation culture, cost-efficiency culture, and increased knowledge sharing that has been accomplished.

At the Texas Department of Transportation, there is a set of positions designated as operational excellence. This team is charged with the responsibility of business transformation, operational excellence, and innovation. I happen to hold one of these positions. While multiple divisions and districts have a designated function for this role, we have a branch under Strategic Planning under the Strategy and Innovation Organization of the agency. Based on my research, it's crucial to establish a function within your organization that is specifically charged with fostering innovation and knowledge sharing. For there to be co-creation of knowledge and innovation, these designated positions must have specific objectives tailored toward innovation and co-creation of new knowledge, with specific collaborative activities and success factors. Some organizations have designated functions such as innovation project manager, futurist, enabler, innovation scout, innovation manager or strategist, innovator, process improvement manager, idea finder, or manager. This ties into the intentionality of KM I discussed earlier. The designation of function also means delineating objectives and activities associated with those functions.

Knowledge Café means creating a knowledge-sharing community. This means multiple formal or informal ways of getting the organization together for learning, development, and information sharing; documenting new knowledge created; measuring results; and sharing institutional history or experience stories.

7.3. KNOWLEDGE MANAGEMENT SOFTWARE

One size does not fit all when it comes to KM software. Know what works for your organization. Here are some criteria to consider:

- Friendly user interface (UI); easy to learn and use
- Self-service customer support
- KM mobile application for tablets and smartphones
- Mature indexing and search functionality
- Integration with other systems and software

KM SOFTWARE

The following are the recommendations for the 20 best knowledge management software for 2020, according to FinancesOnline (n.d.).

1. Zendesk
2. Atlassian Confluence
3. Document360
4. LiveAgent
5. Igloo
6. Zoho Desk
7. Bloomfire
8. Bitrix24
9. ProProfs KnowledgeBase
10. ServiceNow Knowledge Management
11. Inkling Knowledge
12. Remedy Knowledge Management
13. Guru
14. Inbenta Knowledge Management

15. Tettra
16. KnowledgeOwl
17. Helpjuice
18. RightAnswers
19. ComAround Knowledge
20. MyHub

7.4. CASE STUDY: THE FUTURE OF KNOWLEDGE TRANSFER IS NOW OPEN TO SURPRISES—GABE GOLDSTEIN, MPM

This case study is by Gabe Goldstein, MPM. Gabe served with me as the director of vendor relations on the PMI Austin board. As Gabe pointed out, everyone is involved in the art of knowledge transfer.

From my work experience, with the recognition of organized and systemized material, Knowledge Transfer is often performed as tasks within activities of departments, for the performance of contractual (or organizational) benefit. Perhaps a mental graphic would paint a shared knowledge between horizontal and vertical levels of organizations. I see Knowledge Transfer as contextualized information (know-how) virtually directed, to the right users, within organizations when it is needed. One could attribute this to merely performing daily duties. The future of KM is KET as part of our daily job.

Many organizations have decided to make KM a unique and dedicated ritual, under the forms of professional training, succession planning, knowledge interviews, continuous learning, new media collaborations, and sharing. These steps are executed via seminars or work meetings, where the transfer of knowledge is conducted under the eye of senior management or facilitated by knowledge leaders. Agendas are drafted, and work knowledge is made available within certain circles, depending on the organizational chain-of-command or authority level. Depending on the hierarchical organizational position, knowledge transfer is often done at the basic organizational level by simply giving instructions, guidance, and close supervision. At the middle management level, knowledge transfer is more complicated. It includes, at a minimum, information gathering, assessment, and analytical computations. The purpose of this knowledge transfer is to sort and select relevant information for decision making. The senior management level is using more leadership traits than management skills in transferring knowledge. This skill set falls mostly under decision-making, turned into items action lists to be carried out by the levels below.

In my career and KT experience, perhaps, the most widely used method of transferring knowledge is the work meeting, stand-ups, café-style collaboration for knowledge sharing. Whether in-person or virtual, those meetings heavily rely on knowledge exchange between parties for the purpose of providing the needed information used at various work levels. Machines of all sorts are using data to analyze and spring into the desired action. Here, knowledge is less transferred; it is used to create output. For now, humans transfer knowledge by using machines to execute programs. The future of knowledge transfer is now open to surprises, be it from humans or machines.

Gabe's most effective KM tool is collaborative café-style meetings and stand-ups, and he believes that KM should be part of our daily routine. He is right! KM should be part of our daily duties. It needs to be enshrined in our processes. The rise of automation and machines will force humans to unbridle human capabilities in the KM space. When robots replace the repetitive roles in the project, the accumulated wisdom, experiences, or deep smarts will become predominant. Human core capabilities such as curiosity, imagination, emotional intelligence, teaming, empathy, resilience, creativity, social intelligence, sense-making, adaptive thinking, and critical thinking will become hard to transfer except through human interactions. Café is a human interaction component of KM. Conversation in a café and other social interactions become prime. A machine will never aid us in transferring curiosity or empathy. I submit that we start managing knowledge today before AI makes it unmanageable.

8 ■ Knowledge Café Environment for Dealing with Tough Conversations

---

Chapter Objectives

- Propose how to address complicated situations like security in development and operation environment with a café
- Illustrate knowledge for responding to pain associated with change

---

8.1. "I DON'T SEE COLOR" IS NONSENSE: RACIAL RECONCILIATION THROUGH KNOWLEDGE CAFÉ DIALOGUE

I have called for a Knowledge Café to focus on the topic of understanding racial justice. Do you think you know the other race? Unapplied knowledge is useless. Applied knowledge is wisdom. With wisdom, you build a house that accommodates a family with different personalities. But the house will fall apart without understanding. You establish, rejuvenate, and freshen up the house—now home with knowledge.

One of the wisest men who ever lived, King Solomon said,

> By wisdom, a house is built, and by understanding, it is established; by knowledge, the rooms are filled with all precious and pleasant riches.
>
> —Proverbs 24:3–4 (NKJV, 1982)

The emphasis is on wisdom, knowledge, and specifically *understanding* as the sole tool to establish what we build. There is also righteousness and justice. They go together.

Everyone agrees that race is probably the most challenging conversation. That is because there is a right way and a wrong way to handle it. Some people respond to it from a righteousness perspective, especially whites, but black and brown people discuss it from the justice angle. Some people on both sides of the debate respond from a self-righteousness point of view. However, my call is to be a bridge-builder—a reconciler. From this vantage point, I have witnessed some people, quickly and simultaneously, go into their enclaves whenever there's a discussion about race. Some keep silent, which is understandable because they don't want to say the wrong thing and be bashed as racists.

Many honest white friends sincerely talk about race but don't understand how the other side perceives their honesty. They think that they understand black and brown people so well that they often unintentionally make terrible and offensive comments. Some even believe that the more honest you are, the more politically correct you become, which is not true.

Some honest black and brown people make others feel guilty about their ancestors' racial injustices, causing them to walk on eggshells for the rest of their lives. I'm afraid that's not right either. Hence, the efficacy of understanding. I've brought people of all races together for the past 18 years to a café dialogue. Because of my café mindset, I believe that I understand and empathize with each side very well. There's no such thing as "I don't see color." We all have biases and prejudices, but it doesn't make all of us racists. We lack understanding. We lack action.

There are several ways that a community can begin this difficult dialogue, rather than just talking about it or taking sides. We need knowledge and wisdom, but the most important tool is understanding to tackle racism and its demons. Honesty. I know some guilty people who mask their real selves with bumper stickers and slogans and cannot come to the table. Knowledge leaders need to take the lead. Come to the table.

How many times have you kept quiet for fear of saying the wrong thing or becoming defensive, saying, "I'm not the problem"? In this instance, you better know what you are talking about or shut up! Others become a chameleon—fearful of revealing their true nature. The solution to bridging the breach between races can be as simple as stating, "I want to understand how people in your community feel, think, talk, and why." Aha! You got it now. Now summon your courage. Challenge your fears. Accept the realities. We all see color, whether intentionally, unintentionally, or instinctively. Let's have a café. Listen. Listen. Listen to each other. Ask questions, understand, dialogue—this café.

8.2. KNOWLEDGE CAFÉ, SECURITY IN THE RISE OF DEVSECOPS, AND AGILE/WATERFALL PROJECT MANAGEMENT

The cafés provide nonjudgmental spaces where we can voice crazy ideas, have others think about them, and test them out. Without space where we can take risks, innovation will not happen. You can also argue that a Knowledge Café is an "idea safe space" rather than just a place.

As stated earlier, the café is a simple mindset. This mindset can help to design a KM environment. With a café approach, any conversation in response to a complicated and challenging situation is possible. You can use this mindset and space to respond to security in the rise of software development and IT operations (DevSecOps).

In 2019, ransomware attacks on the City of Baltimore, ASCO Industries, and The Weather Channel were just a few issues dominating the headlines. According to *Cybercrime Magazine* (Morgan, 2017), ransomware is projected to attack one business every 14 seconds by the end of 2019, up from every 40 seconds in 2018; global ransomware damage costs is predicted to hit $11.5 billion by 2019. In 2020, the COVID-19 global pandemic scrambled our health care systems, revealed our vulnerabilities, and shone a spotlight on health care research's critical role in national security. Researchers across all industries are forced to adopt holistic security controls that hold device manufacturers accountable to security requirements, incentivize security by design, and train all personnel to be cyber hygienic by default and security conscious.

We shop, bank, and even find love online, and hackers are having a field day. Should security be left only for certain stakeholders like IT operations teams? Where is the interface of security in software development and IT operation (DevOps)? DevSecOps? Kanban (Just in Time) and Scrum Agile methods are DevOps friends that organizations can use to speed and improve development and product releases. So, how do we stay a step ahead of hackers?

How do you create champions between competing and diametrically opposite but complementary team approaches—DevOps or Waterfall/Agile? The waterfall is a traditional or structured project management methodology. Its outcomes are predictive and often very rigid. On the other hand, Agile is seen as a mindset based on an incremental, iterative approach, mostly for projects with unclear requirements like software development. Agile is a project methodology and approach that is derived using Lean thinking. Agile software development methodologies are open to changing requirements over time and encourage constant feedback from the end users.

My friends, you can create security champions on your company's development team, Agile champions on a waterfall team, and project champions on an Operations team. For instance, IT security teams and software development teams share a common goal of putting quality code into production. However, how often do we see clan control, unrealistic expectations, and wars between them?

Figure 4: DevOps life cycle.

DevOps is a set of practices, mindsets, or cultures that combine software development (Dev) and IT operations (Ops) to shorten the software development life cycle. Like other business ideologies, the goal of DevOps is to deliver features, fixes, and updates frequently with programming agility and customer-centricity. This brings post-implementation operations to the development life cycle early to ensure the new products and systems' supportability. In the IT software development orbit, teams are challenged to work together more effectively and innovate more freely and collaboratively. As seen in figure 4, the DevOps life cycle is based on:

According to MarketsandMarkets (2018) research, "The DevOps market size is expected to grow from USD 2.90 Billion in 2017 to USD 10.31 Billion by 2023."

BENEFITS OF DEVOPS

DevOps offers many benefits over a more traditional separation of development and operations. Hence, it provides many services, including

- greater automation through early identification of automation opportunities;
- greater visibility into system outcomes in the right culture;
- greater scalability and availability in the right culture;
- greater innovation;
- better resource utilization;
- faster, better product delivery;

- faster issue resolution and reduced complexity; and
- more stable operating environments.

Agile and DevOps is the organic pairing that creates the framework, the right mindset, unified responsibility, culture, and an environment that facilitates innovation and digital transformation. Also, they provide greater visibility and more readily realized cost savings (or avoidance).

In today's world, increasingly prevalent cyber threats and erudite hackers, whose tools and practices have grown increasingly sophisticated, are outplaying everyone and eating our lunches! Hackers have been very good at agile programming for a long time—much longer than mainstream software developers. Organizations and individuals now face unprecedented security vulnerabilities, even as applications are becoming more complex and organizations grow ever more entangled in the networks. In the knowledge economy, every area of our lives is going digital.

Why Not Hold a Café for Security within DevOps (DevSecOps)?

Without security woven throughout the process of DevOps, it's a joke! Much of the IT operation works can be planned, such as moving between data centers, significant system release change, or performing system upgrades where you have the luxury of planning ahead of time. However, much of the work in operations is unplanned—we don't have the luxury of time to prepare—when security has been compromised, there's a system outage, or even performance spikes. These issues that demand immediate response can't wait for the next sprint planning session or iteration. So, it's time to embrace Patrick DuBois' DevOps thinking that looks beyond Scrum to Kanban. DevOps helps the team track both kinds of work and helps them understand the interplay between them. According to Atlassian Agile coach Ian Buchanan (n.d.), the team may adopt a hybrid approach, often called Scrumban or Kaplan (kanban with a backlog).

The most common problems stem from the fact that there are uncertainties about dev and ops responsibilities. DevOps teams are under pressure to build and deploy software as quickly as possible. The proverbial goat jointly owned by multiple teams dies of hunger because each team expected the other team to feed it! Frankly, it's easy for one faction of DevOps to think the other has completed the necessary security tasks. How much more effective would your software development be if your IT developers are also security champions advocating security mindfulness in their peers and promoting security knowledge across the enterprise?

A Knowledge Café brings teams into a fellowship or camaraderie for a deeper understanding and appreciation of each other's demons— pressures, priorities, and competing interests—to say, "We are on the same team." The job is easier for everyone when we understand each other's roles. In the inexorable march to DevSecOps, we can use a Knowledge Café approach to push security into the development organization further and instill security earlier in the development cycle (Whitley, 2019). A Knowledge Café mindset to manage and leverage our collective knowledge will be a home run!

According to *TechRepublic*, 50 percent of companies are still in the process of implementing DevOps (Brown, 2017). According to Gartner (n.d.), 90 percent of organizations will have implemented DevOps by 2023, and 90 percent of DevOps initiatives will fail to meet expectations—not because of technical reasons entirely but due to leadership approaches' limitations. Remember these knowledge management enablers: people, process, content, and technology/information. Any process, including DevOps, fails if people and culture are not upfront. Engage people in a Knowledge Café. Sort out people's issues first to ensure a safe and secure foundation for success.

Security is the responsibility of all stakeholders. In project management, everyone is responsible for quality; in the organization, everyone is responsible for safety. We have moved from silos to cross-functional space, collaborative innovation, shared security responsibility, continuous integration, and continuous development (CI/CD). Compliance is being operationalized, and security is dashboarded. We are changing behavior on how we respond to time to market and risk reduction.

A Knowledge Café as the Space Where Security Meets DevOps
I'll show you how a Knowledge Café mindset may be an answer. Developers must adapt to new incentives like enterprise-wide collaboration, branding, and metrics. A Knowledge Café mindset is a silo buster. Get all DevSecOps teams to the café today! A Knowledge Café brings different teams to a space where they will begin this discussion and leverage collective knowledge.

There is a difficult conversation. A Knowledge Café brings a Dev and Ops team to the café with the objective of putting security at the center. Here, there is an open, creative conversation on the topic of security, process improvement, speed to market, innovation, and so on. Security is a topic of mutual interest to everyone; their café is to uncover both groups' collective knowledge, share ideas, and gain a deeper understanding of the issues involved. Everyone knows something, but knowledge resides in the network (café).

The café can connect employees, DevOps, Agile and Waterfall teams, and SMEs; improve interpersonal relationships; break down organizational silos, improve trust, idea generation, innovation, and engagement. This kind of Knowledge Café is driven by a robust question, like how do we move security to the left of development? Where is the interface of security in DevOps? Where is the interplay between DevOps? What does DevOps think that looks beyond Scrum to Kanban? Where is the place of the waterfall and Kanban, and so on?

How do you preserves the flow of natural conversation? The café is a dialogue—not a debate—that provides an ecosystem that eliminates fear and preconceived outcomes. The critical environmental factor is that everyone in this space has an equal voice and it's a safe learning space: it should be as simple as walking into a café for a coffee or tea.

8.3. PRACTICE CAFÉ: RECOMMENDATIONS AND LESSONS LEARNED IN ACTION
In this practice café session, I would like you to be part of the exploration of the simplicity and agility of a café. Share the lessons you have learned as you compare them with mine.

1. Grab your cup of coffee or tea.
    a. I'm not advocating for a stand-up meeting (there are too many meetings already) or for lessons learned (we haven't learned anything yet) or after-action reviews (we need to start and end with security, safety, and quality in mind—as a culture) for DevOps teams. No, I'm not prescribing another process or methodology.
    b. I'm presenting a café mindset that can address the culture and relationship between all stakeholders vis-à-vis security. It's a space to address culture, not process or technology, a place to appreciate the role each stakeholder plays toward a secured digital transformation, a place to see the big picture.
    c. In my experience, healthier knowledge management ecosystems foster an interactive space of various interests and diverse patrons. The café brings eclectic and random—and sometimes strangers—into one location. I invite practitioners to the Knowledge Café to brainstorm, investigate, aggregate, and optimize the multiple available knowledge levels. The ultimate goal is to formalize and institutionalize KM processes.
    d. I've learned more in a café setting than in any traditional classroom or boring meetings. The best and the most significant people I've met have been where I was volunteer-ing—in a café setting. The best ideas that I have turned into reality came from the café. My greatest fears are let go at the café. I've met the best of friends at the café.
    e. The café is the gateway-drug to knowledge management. It's that mindset for the superiority of tools and space that accelerate and scale casual conversations over those focusing on documents, artifacts, and cumbersome formality.
    f. During the café, ask questions such as, "Which team is more important, the development or the operations team?" The rhetorical response, of course, is, "Kidding! Both teams are equally important."

g. Possible questions to ask for a DevSecOps café:
- Who is responsible for security?
- How does your role impact mine, and how can we share security responsibilities?
- How do we jointly reduce risk and vulnerabilities in the system?
- Where does security meet DevOps, and how do we channel our efforts to win in the digital transformation process?
- What is the role of Agile and DevOps in efficient innovation?
- How do technology innovators enhance digital transformation in your organization? Examples of innovators, identified by International Data Corporation (IDC), are the Internet of Things (IoT), cognitive/AI systems, next-gen security, 3D printing, augmented and virtual reality, robotics, and drones, blockchain, connected consumers, and connected and automated vehicles (CAV).

2. Use a DevOps and Agile mindset to fail fast and double-down on collaborative innovation.

3. All stakeholders are responsible for security, safety, and quality—enshrine this in the teams' culture.

4. Adopt a café mindset—a conversational approach to problem-solving rather than finger-pointing.

5. Innovate efficiently, too.

6. Hold a WAgile Knowledge XChange—a knowledge exchange café to understand how and when to integrate different project management methodologies to meet ever-changing customer demands and achieve results in your project life cycle. Use a Knowledge Café to consider how/when to integrate life cycle approaches according to *PMBOK® Guide,* sixth edition (2017).

a. Predictive Life Cycle: A form of a project life cycle in which the project scope, time, and cost are determined in the early phases of the life cycle.

b. Iterative Life Cycle: A project life cycle where the project scope is generally determined early in the project life cycle, but time and cost estimates are routinely modified as the project team's understanding of the product increases. Iterations develop the product through a series of repeated cycles, while increments successively add to the product's functionality.

c. Incremental Life Cycle: An adaptive project life cycle in which the deliverable is produced through a series of iterations that successively add functionality within a predetermined time frame. The deliverable contains the necessary and sufficient capability to be considered complete only after the final iteration.

d. Adaptive Life Cycle: A project life cycle that is iterative and incremental.

8.4. KNOWLEDGE CAFÉ TO DEAL WITH THE PAIN ASSOCIATED WITH LOSS FROM CHANGE

You may ask where in the KM ecosystem is the place of "dealing with the pain associated with a change." Deploying a café or any other KM element brings about change in an organization. Many changes have temporary or permanent discomfort as a side effect, and it is essential to understand how to deal with these pains. Different people handle changes differently. I remember working for an organization several years ago. There was a massive organizational change that had to do with a change in management. The number of retirements spiked by 42 percent. Several people left the organization for other jobs. Lessons learned from changes are an essential aspect of KM that must be explored. Here is how I used the café concept to deal with changes in a family and organizational setting.

We lived in this one-story house for 12 years. Two of my kids were born while we lived there. During that time, they had been admiring a two-story building all the while. In the fall of 2016, my kids objected, even resisted our selling the house for a bigger and better home in a better neighborhood. Since the kids don't run the house (at least in mine), we made the strategic decision to move. The new neighborhood schools are the best in the county, both in academics and sports. A year later, my seventh grader's girls' volleyball and basketball teams were the teams to beat—they were almost undefeated and won all the regional championships. My eighth grader's boys' football team were also undefeated champions. The academic standard, compared with others in the region, was very impressive.

I know that my kids lost some of their friends when we moved, but now they confess to having lots of friends and enjoy the neighborhood. Our neighborhood now is more peaceful, with more amenities, and the list goes on. However, every time I drive past our old house with the kids, they are just melting down. In their minds, they still prefer our old house. They are still in pain from losing their childhood home. This is very emotional.

FAMILY CAFÉ

I can either tell my kids to suck it up—we live in a better place—which is appalling to do, or bring the kids to a Knowledge Café and do the following:

- Identify with their pain
- Accept their pain
- Walk them through the process of managing and getting over the pain
- Move them into the now and the future

They say that if you can't beat them, join them. However, joining them doesn't mean that you have changed. Sometimes, change is just a locational move, yet our emotions and spiritual state are still stuck in the past. The fact that you have changed doesn't mean that the pain associated with the change is gone. It may always be there, and you may live with it for a long time until you are healed from it. Obviously, we need the knowledge to deal with all the problematic situations in life.

A café mindset is an excellent prescription for demystifying complex and sticky issues like change and the painful residue it leaves behind. The attitude and atmosphere of a relational café provide the simplicity, passion, and the ecosystem to begin a discussion—investigate, share, and café. This applies to both our work and personal lives.

In this section, I want to concentrate on pain associated with the loss that people incur due to change. Make no mistake, change naturally leaves people bleeding, not just because of the change but because of what they have lost. The losses may be insignificant to you or me, but people may be dealing with the pain from those losses for a long time. So, even as we implement a knowledge-sharing culture, some people are simply wired to function within silos. The change will cause them to lose their silos, privacy, and emotional and spiritual attachments to things. If change and the possible painful outcome are discussed in the café KM program, it may become a white elephant project.

I happen to be a change champion for a $375 million campus consolidation project, where I shared some of these principles to other change champions—I thought that it was very effective. This consolidation would be a significant change to about 2,200 employees as the new campus will be a cutting-edge 21st-century work environment. While most of the employees are excited, there are still a few people who seem to be silently feeling some pain due to the impending changes.

LEARNING LESSONS AT THE CAFÉ

Engage stakeholders in a café style to discuss lessons we are learning for the change and hopefully avoid some of the change's pains. Dr. Moses Adoko (2019a) calls it "lessons learning," as opposed to lessons learned.

1. Change is planned and executed like a project.
2. Everyone absorbs pain differently. Some are chicken when it comes to handling changes, while others have the skills and knowledge to manage change. Café brings them together for relational knowledge sharing rather than a transactional one.
3. Change is like surgery; you need to administer anesthesia. Plan ahead of the change. If you cut people and they

begin to bleed, don't act surprised. Give them time to process the change.

4. Don't be presumptuous about change, no matter how little or insignificant you think it is.

5. Bring those who will be affected by the change into the planning and executing processes.

6. Give those who will be affected by the change ownership of the change project. People don't resist or oppose something they have ownership of or contributed to its success.

7. Consider combining waterfall and agile methodologies when managing change. I worked in an organization that implemented large enterprise software. This project lasted for two years, and the implementation lasted for six months. Before deployments, several employees left the organization because the change was so fast and overwhelming. Project teams planned and executed the project. The end users were barely involved. If they utilized an agile method, maybe the software could have been implemented incrementally rather than all at once. Iterations resulting in short-term successes will guarantee end users' engagement and participation throughout the project and improve buy-in.

How Do People Handle the Pain from Change?

People of all tribes, races, gender, ethnicities, and economic classes go through change and pain, and everyone handles it differently. When people are in pain, it tends to manifest through their actions. Pain can lead to bitterness sometimes. People in pain can say some terrible things as a display of their internal frustrations. In popular culture, when some segments of our society (white suburban, neglected majority, middle class, minorities, or the disadvantaged) show signs of pain, the pundits quickly call them ugly names and school them to get in the game. Some people are gracious in their response to pain, while some are anything but graceful. Consider how people grieve when they lose a loved one, a pet, a job they have held for several years, a cubicle or an office space they loved so much, or even changing to a flexible work schedule when they telecommute. Some people become sick and depressed when they lose something or someone dear to them, especially if they have an emotional or spiritual attachment to what they lost.

LOSSES THAT CAN BRING PAIN BECAUSE OF CHANGE
- Freedom
- Flexibility
- Friends
- Proximity to work
- Decorations
- Articles and memorabilia
- Spiritual and emotional attachments
- Familiarity
- Silos
- Privacy
- Ownership
- Peace
- Comfort zone

HOW DO YOU KNOW THAT YOU ARE IN PAIN BECAUSE OF THE CHANGE?
- Headaches, backaches, or stomachaches, especially when you remember the change
- Loss of appetite or changing your eating habits
- You want to retire early or look for another job because something is unsettling about the change
- Feeling irritable and edgy with colleagues and people you love
- Sleeping more than usual
- Drinking more alcohol
- Daydreaming
- The feeling of anger and frustration

No matter what the loss, we must be understanding with people if they are in pain. There are different types of pain. You would be amazed at what brings emotional and spiritual pain to people when change occurs. Don't tell people to suck it up if they grieve for losing their pictures on the walls, old coffee pot, or individualized trash can and copier, even though the change may include a better and centralized copier, 21st-century office space, and more. For instance, Mag has worked an 8 a.m. to 5 p.m. work schedule for 27 years, within a small personal space. Within that personal space were a coffee/tea kettle, individual trash can, family pictures, and memorabilia on the walls and tables. Now, we want her to consolidate, telecommute twice a week, share cubicles in a living workspace with not-so-fun and sometimes weird strangers, use a centralized copier and a centralized trash can, and—the most painful—accept the decoration in the new modern and sophisticated cubicles. Whoa! What a transformation! For some generations like the millennials, this is not a big deal, but it may be a significant concern and painful for older generations.

Mag feels that she has lost her identity, history, and freedom. She is now suffering internally because of the emotional attachments to her previous surroundings, team, and work schedule at the current workspace. We have to admit that this pain is real. My choice is to face the pain with her because I recognize it as genuine pain.

There is no better place to talk about pain and healing than in a community of others who are facing similar pains—a community of practice. There are several café events devoted to this kind of knowledge exchange and interaction.

8.5. PRACTICE CAFÉ: RECOMMENDATIONS AND LESSONS LEARNED FROM DEALING WITH PAIN FROM CHANGE

Here are some recommendations for coping with the pain of moving to a new location, a career change, losing a friend or a loved one, or pain associated with whatever you lost because of change.

1. Bring those affected by the change to the café. During my family's move in Austin, Texas, I brought the kids to a café-style negotiation and mindset. At this café, I let the kids choose the café style of their choice (they had no idea that it was a café event). We established ground rules that included

"everyone's opinion is valuable." Believe it or not, we had decided that we would move, but I needed to bring the kids along. However, when we met at the café, we didn't have a preconceived plan of action. I wanted them to be part of the healing process since they were not in the original plans to move. The remarkable thing about the café is the liberty to answer questions, connect, hear different perspectives, exchange technical know-how, and test ideas without the limitations of formality and conventionalism. You'll be amazed at how much you can learn about a matter in a café.

MORE QUESTIONS AT THE CAFÉ

Here are some questions we discussed:

    a. What are the examples of changes we have made in the past 10 years, and why do we have to make those changes?

    b. Why do we have to move?

    c. Why can't we stay here?

    d. Why do people move, and why do we have to change?

    e. How do we bring those involved in change into the change process?

2. Some choice conversations at the café:

    a. We shall identify with you.

    b. Your pain is real.

    c. You didn't make it up.

    d. We completely understand why you feel that way.

    e. If we were in your shoes, we wouldn't feel any better.

    f. Your pain shows that you are human, grown-up, and realistic.

    g. You are not a faker.

    h. You are real.

    i. We would like to listen to you more so we can appreciate why you are in pain.

3. We would like to discuss what is reversible and what is permanent in this situation.

    a. What can we do to ameliorate the pain?

    b. Any suggestions?

       c. What are other alternatives?

       d. Can we remind you that you've gone through similar changes in the past?

       e. Take a minute to think about it. We believe that you are equal to the task. You can walk through this pain.

4. Talk about change and its antecedent pains. You may agree with me that the only constant thing is change ("Change is the only constant," said Heraclitus.) We are always changing. It's more beneficial to change at the right time rather than later. When my kids went through similar pains, I showed them the pros and cons of moving to a better neighborhood, the financial ramifications of the move, and emotional and other implications. They were convinced that we were not going to live in the old house forever.

5. Develop a change management plan—how are we going to make the change? For instance, in the campus consolidation project, I was a change champion. We are taking the time to understand the components of this move. We have mapped out the stages of the move. Everyone deserves to be prepared for change. Plan change and carefully manage it. Change is like a project that needs to be managed. It has initiation, planning, execution, monitoring and controlling, and closing phases. Don't just execute change. Manage it!

6. Believe. We would like you to believe that there's light at the end of the tunnel, the belief that something good is going to come out of this. When I realized that I don't have an option, my comfort has always been to believe for the best. You don't need reasons to believe. However, part of our growing process is to have a positive attitude toward things that naturally look awful, like change. Believe that it's going to be alright. Let's make lemonade out of this lemon.

7. Confess and do something about the pain! It's helpful to make a daily confession about some pains we are strug-

gling with daily. A CoP can facilitate these confessions in a café.

a. Accept the reality that this change has come to stay.

b. Discuss your pain with someone who can listen and empathize with you.

c. Remember how you coped and worked through significant changes in your past.

d. Exercise by going to the gym, run, or take a brisk walk.

e. Re-energize yourself with family, friends, pets, or nature.

f. Sing, dance, or even cry to release emotional energy.

g. Use a good sense of humor to put your reality into perspective.

h. Name three things you are grateful for this morning.

i. Name three things you are thankful for this evening.

j. Pray if you are inclined to prayers.

The community of practice is one of the most effective ways of delivering a KM system because CoP is organic and not mandated. When they are learning and sharing culture, knowledge workers become passionate about sharing within the community. Hence, practitioners have fun sharing and will not feel overburdened.

8.6. CASE STUDY: KM IS ABOUT CONNECTING KNOWLEDGE BROKERS, SEARCHABILITY, AND FINDABILITY—AHMED ZOUHAI

This case study is from Ahmed Zouhai, PMP, a consultant with comprehensive global experience in project, program, and product management.

As a consultant, I have worked with many organizations. Most of these organizations do not have a formal knowledge Transfer Program. Some of the departments seemed to be very territorial. They don't like the term "share, collaborate and or transfer" of information, especially when dealing with global organizations operating in the United States and vice versa. I must say, there are valid and legitimate reasons for not sharing some of the information because of the IP and so forth.

To my knowledge, I hardly heard the term KM used. But instead, we use SharePoint and/or network drive by the department. There was no one source of truth for knowledge and information. In terms of knowledge transfer, my challenges are based on our competitors' use of the info if employees leave their current position. In retrospect, is there anything wrong with some Knowledge Transfer technology tools that don't talk to each other? KM tools we used were internal, and most of them were not easy to use, and most of the employees didn't like to have access to them, nor were they updated frequently with shared information. Companies seemed not wanting to spend money on these KM tools as well as training.

It could take minutes or hours to get the information you need to do your job, depending on the searched information, especially in a new technological context. Sharing my knowledge means time-saving, efficiency, and staying competitive.

KM is both a challenge and fun, depending on which department you work in. Sometimes, leadership makes it difficult to share information and sometimes more natural and more fun, especially for new employees.

Before Google and other search engines, it was virtually impossible to find and share knowledge management. Nowadays, most organizations realize the importance of ease in searchability and findability, connecting knowledge brokers, creators, and sharers. Many companies are raising their capabilities by making knowledge transfer less painful and more fun because they know that it increases efficiency and competitive advantage. It is important to remember that knowledge comes in different forms and shapes. People's experiences, know-how is the most crucial aspect of knowledge. IT departments and project management teams are utilizing search function and face-to-face collaborations to advance projects and value. KM enables the contextualization of information. Employees spend much time searching the World Wide Web for information that may or may not be valid and accurate.

As Ahmed stated, context is the key to KM. Remember that knowledge is the information that has been contextualized. In today's gig economy and project economy, many organizations are coming to grips with an efficient KM system's efficacy. It's a race to the finish as companies raise their capabilities by making knowledge transfer less painful and more fun. As Ahmed pointed out in his personal experience, a simpler KM system that connects people and systems increases efficiency and competitive advantage. Experiences and knowledge in knowledge creators and sharers' heads is the most critical aspect of knowledge management.

In terms of one source of truth, some argue that there are precise models available, perhaps found in academic sources, that delineate the knowledge management landscape more broadly. For instance, the "information sciences" as an academic (graduate professional) degree is expanding, and the questions of knowledge management, archiving, retrieval, and making sense of information are well studied nowadays. Companies are actively studying knowledge management, and as pedagogy, the librarians of the past have now become knowledge managers. So, information architecture (IA) is the art and science of organizing or designing information to make it accessible, usable, and relevant to all end users. IA includes, but is not limited to, shared settings and methods of naming and arranging online communities, software, intranets, and websites to make them easier for users to access, retrieve, use, and reuse. Taxonomy is an aspect of IA that seeks to define relationships between components.

However, knowledge management is not information management because, while information is organized data, knowledge is information that has been given meaning or explained. Information sciences and information architecture can help to bring distinctions between codifiable and non-codifiable knowledge. Information science considers the relationships between people, places, and technology and data from those interactions. It is primarily concerned with analyzing, collecting, classifying, manipulating, storing, organizing, retrieving, moving, disseminating, and protecting this information.

Simple processes and interactions are critical to KET. Managing knowledge involves modeling empathy, which helps develop a growth mindset and a mindset of abundance—a café mindset of sharing.

Again, you can't manage the process until you have managed people-knowledge. You need to learn from the people and the organization before you can manage and lead. Let's assume that you just joined the organization. The next day, you are providing guidance and making intelligent suggestions on running things better? I'm sorry, but you don't know what you are talking about. You need to understand the people, the culture, the Organizational Process Assets (OPA), Enterprise Environmental Factors (EEF), and then apply what you learned to the environment—and lead well. Every organization is different. What works for one may not work for another. I once worked for an organization where my office was involved in processing hundreds of millions of data bits. We used Mainframe. In my second week, my supervisor wanted me to provide feedback for their process since I had fresh eyes. I told her that I needed a few more weeks to learn the process and organizational culture. To be frank, I identified many gaps during my first week.

It's appropriate to know before you lead. Here are some reasons why you shouldn't be quick to jump into leadership before you acquire knowledge. If some people were born to lead, why didn't you elect them to become your city mayor when they were in kindergarten—when they haven't even learned to spell their names or write a letter? No. Instead, you wait for them to learn, acquire knowledge, make mistakes, and learn life lessons. Would you want to follow someone who hasn't followed anyone? Every leader is, first, a follower. If you can't follow, you cannot lead.

LESSONS LEARNED AT THE CAFÉ

- You'll be seen as arrogant and presumptuous if you start pointing out what is wrong in the new organization you joined.
- You are not in a hurry. Relax. You'll have all the time in the world to provide guidance and lead.

- You don't want to be eaten alive by politics. You have to understand they are persisting in politics, or you'll be caught in the crossfire. If your new workplace is one where everyone is in a camp, dog-eat-dog workplace, and rival groups, your suggestion may lead to siding with a specific political camp.
- A leader should spend 80 percent of his or her time learning, knowing, and listening, and 20 percent leading. This will be more effective.
- Willingness to learn from other knowledge workers is a mark of leadership.
- Humility is a mark of leadership. "Humility is not denying your strengths. Humility is being honest about your weaknesses."—Rick Warren (Close & Close, 2018)
- The business value of having knowledge practices are simplification and more engagement.
- It's better to ask questions before you answer one.

When you create a Knowledge Café environment, possibilities for free exchange and transfer of knowledge are endless.

9 ■ KM Roadmap, Value, and Knowledge Stewardship

Chapter Objectives

- Describe the value of a KM environment and necessary knowledge stewardship
- Evaluate the right organizational strategy for KM (Café) environment
- Explain critical steps and roadmap for a KM system and environment
- Explore practice café: How do you start a KM Program: Knowledge Café or audit?
- Outline what it means to implement a KM program after the café

9.1. KNOWLEDGE MANAGEMENT VALUE
AND KNOWLEDGE STEWARDSHIP

VALUE OF KNOWLEDGE

- GE has realized $35 million (USD) in documented savings and 180 communities of practice with 130,000 engaged members. There are three key success factors—enterprise KM strategy, governance, and measurement. (American Productivity & Quality Center [APQC], 2019)
- Hoffmann-Roche, the Swiss pharmaceutical saves over $1 million per day due to its KM activities (Yelden & Albers, 2004)
- Hewlett-Packard's knowledge efforts aimed at customer service have reduced average call times by two-thirds, and the cost per call has fallen by 50 percent (Yelden & Albers, 2004)
- Chevron Corporation saved an initial $150 million plus at least $20 million annually by instituting KM; Dow Chemical's efforts saved it over $40 million (Yelden & Albers, 2004)
- Over a six-year period since its investment of $72 million, Schlumberger Corp. has realized an ROI of 668 percent on its KM programs (Swanborg & Myers, 1997).
- Teltech, a firm that specializes in aiding companies to implement knowledge management programs, reports that its clients enjoy an average ROI of 12:1 for their effort (Abramson, 1998).
- Fortune 500 companies lose roughly "$31.5 billion a year by failing to share knowledge" (Babcock, 2004)

Note: the result of the ROI analysis indicated a 1,014 percent return on annual investment in the KMX, based on time savings attributable to use of the application (about $11 in savings resulting from each dollar invested in the KMX, a Global Consulting, Inc. company's primary global KM repository (Association for Talent Development, 2019). Truth be said, companies struggle to put a value on customer satisfaction, job satisfaction, quality service, or even captured intellectual capital. But with the right benchmark, we can always show added value and calculate ROI in most cases of KM.

How do physicians keep up with 10,000 diseases and syndromes, 3,000 medications, and 400,000 articles added to biomedical literature each year? Knowledge stewardship and exchange. The value of KM can be seen throughout the pages of this book. Davenport and Glaser (2002) contend that by leveraging and focusing all of your organization's knowledge—information, experience, and insight— you will be able to improve your individual, team, and organization performance and deliver value to your stakeholders and your entire organization. This knowledge creation paradigm will ultimately improve an organization's ability to develop the best solutions and make the best decisions. There is value in a KM environment.

Knowledge management is the new competitive advantage for high-performing organizations.

Some people spend their time reinventing the wheel. I don't think it's productive. I would rather spend my time making wheels that can fly. When knowledge is not shared, and when there are silos in the organization, other knowledge users will end up reinventing the wheel. Organizational process assets (OPA) "are the plans, processes, policies, procedures, and knowledge bases specific to and used by the performing organization" (*PMBOK® Guide*, sixth edition, 2017). OPAs include historical information and lessons learned, repositories, organizational standards, policies, procedures, portfolios, programs, project governance framework, monitoring and reporting methods, and templates. Knowledge workers work smarter, not harder, by using the organizational tools and processes rather than reinventing them. Then you'll use your time wisely, cut costs and waste, improve efficiency, and gain a competitive advantage.

"If you think education is expensive, try ignorance." This saying was first featured on August 28, 1902, in an advertisement in *Ottumwa Semi-Weekly Courier* for a Conservatory of Music in Ottumwa, Iowa (1902). In 1978, Ann Landers attributed it to Derek Bok, the president of Harvard University ("If You Think Education Is Expensive, Try Ignorance," n.d.). Bok later disowned it. In 1874,

The Statistics and Gazetteer of New Hampshire provided a prolix passage: "Knowledge is less expensive than ignorance. Ignorance is a dangerous and costly factor in any form of government." There are countless justifications for a KM program. Knowledge doesn't manage itself—we must manage knowledge and be knowledge stewards.

KM provides both tangible and intangible benefits to an organization. Benefits from enterprise-wide KM program implementations have been known to save organizations millions of dollars.

How Do We Calculate the Tangible Value of KM?

Let me make some assumptions about the value and savings of a KM program. This is the assumption I made when I was making a business case for enterprise knowledge management some years ago. Several of my peers have reviewed it and validated my methodology. If your organization has 12,000 employees, and if 40 percent of employees (3,600) participate in KM's knowledge exchange like a community of practice, knowledge fair, and café, or Wiki knowledge exchange, there's an assumption that 30 percent of these participants (1,080) could gain as little as 30 minutes of efficiencies per week in the first year, and this increases by 10 percent per year. But let's assume that there's a rough order of magnitude (ROM) increased efficiencies of .5 hour per week. Each employee worked for 48 weeks in a year at a labor cost per hour, assuming a base rate of $50/hour and applying a multiplier of 1.6193. If we invest $2 million into the knowledge management program in the first five years, there will be a total saving as a result of .5 hour (30 minutes) of increased efficiencies, resulting from some increased knowledge sharing activities through KM. This will be resulting in a net savings of $16 million, net present value (NPV) of $20 million, and return on investment of 310 percent.

Organizational knowledge, as intellectual capital, is confined in the minds of employees; if an employee leaves, they will go with this knowledge unless it is captured and shared. KM enables the accessibility of information and knowledge across the organization. It provides knowledge, platforms, and tools for sharing knowledge with others. Much organizational knowledge is scattered across the organization and in various repositories such as file shares, SharePoint, the intranet, and Outlook email. Employees often store data on personal hard drives, where they may be inaccessible to others. The most difficult aspect of introducing a KM program is making a business case for it. Dr. Ed Hoffman stated that all the top global organizations (including PMI) that he advises have one problem: sustaining knowledge. He added that measurement is essential, but leading organizations are not waiting until they measure the intangibles (benefits) before advancing in KM programs (AASHTO, 2019). Knowledge management and stewardship are valuable for all organizations.

HOW DO YOU MEASURE THE VALUE ADDED
BY A KM PROGRAM?

1 hour saved per person per week = 50 hours/year
X number of employees
(e.g., 1,000 employees × 50 hours = 50,000 hours)
That could mean:
50,000 hours × average cost per hour, assuming that an
  employee works for 2,000 hours per year
50,000 hours / 2,000 hours = 25 people. This is the number of
  new employees that could be hired with the savings, or we
  saved one whole year's work of 25 employees.

TANGIBLE AND INTANGIBLE BENEFITS
OF A KNOWLEDGE TRANSFER

Here are some tangible and intangible benefits of knowledge management and stewardship.

- Transforms your organization into a knowledge workplace with knowledge workers
- Builds bench strength to improve organization effectiveness and resilience
- Fosters the reuse of intellectual capital, creating conditions for innovation
- Enables better decision-making
- Leads to competitive advantage and adds real client value

- Innovation: creation and conversion of new and valuable knowledge into innovative products, services, processes, methods, and strategies created and converted into products, services, and processes
- Monetary savings through efficiencies

9.2. KNOWLEDGE CAFÉ ENVIRONMENT ROADMAP

My roadmap recommendation for starting a KM program is to create a conversation. The café may be the right place to connect and begin this conversation. Start a conversation with knowledge creators and users. Someone will have to lead this endeavor or project. Analyze your environment. Secure buy-in. Be curious. Many people agree that KM is essential, but few do something about it. Have you heard someone tell a family member that smoking is bad for your health? The usual response is acknowledging the fact, but acknowledgment has never been a deterrent for anything.

The Café is a simple way to bring a small knowledge-curious group of people together to have a slightly structured conversation on a topic of mutual interest. It can be adapted for various purposes. Although you'll get the best out of a face-to-face café gathering, it also works exceptionally well in virtual settings and platforms such as Zoom and Microsoft teams with break-out room capabilities as we adapt to the new normal. A Knowledge Café is a highly adaptable face-to-face conversational process that can be used in many different business nonbusiness situations to bring a group of people who know something together to have an open conversation, cross-fertilization of ideas for a specific purpose.

> I'd like to reinforce that you do not need to be a professional presenter, facilitator, or moderator to design and host a café. If you can have a conversation in a café, you could host a Knowledge Café for the exclusive purpose of knowledge exchange and rejuvenation.

Follow a few critical steps to implement an intentional KM program. The sequence is not essential, and all of these activities show intentionality.

- Who is the project manager or knowledge strategist that will facilitate and manage this program? Chief knowledge officer, knowledge strategist, knowledge project manager, or lead?
- Secure an executive sponsor(s), champions, and stakeholder buy-in.
- You may conduct a knowledge audit.
- You may conduct a strategic workforce analysis.
- Identify, prioritize, and engage potential retirees and stakeholders.
- Identify already existing KM elements or methods, tools/techniques, and best practices in your organization.
- Develop KM goals and strategies.
- Design and select KM methods, tools, and techniques from the recommendations provided by the knowledge leadership. Leadership Café formalizes Knowledge Café outcomes. I will discuss Leadership Café in detail in chapter 11.
- Develop a compelling business case for KM.
- Make small incremental steps.

Dr. Schroeder (2019) said that "small improvements, repeated many times, accumulate to huge savings—invisibly." This means that

- most opportunities to improve are buried deep in the processes and procedures used to perform daily tasks, and
- front-line workers see lots of problems and opportunities that managers don't.

In our value delivery landscape, how do we scale without the proper knowledge brokers and a roadmap? I asked Sunil Preshara, PMI CEO, about how KM fits in with project management paradigm. He thinks that organizations like Project Management Institute could be a one-stop shop for anyone who wants to get things

Figure 5: Café Environment Roadmap.

done and that making KM relevant for people of all ages is the next strategy. A roadmap defines how we shall get there. As seen in figure 5, Café Environment Roadmap, knowledge is power: There will be no power without knowledge, no knowledge without the right environment, no knowledge environment without leadership, no leadership without curiosity and passion.

So first, curious and passionate leaders initiate knowledge-exchange with a Knowledge Café conversation to establish an environment where knowledge is stirred up, applied, and flourishes. Then, there will be power. "The power of knowledge is a very important resource for preserving valuable heritage, learning new things, solving problems, creating core competences, and initiating new situations for both individual and organizations now and in the future" (Liao, 2003).

We must start with knowledge leadership, including securing management or executive buy-in. Knowledge leadership is made up of knowledge architects and governance of a KM program. Like the knowledge architect, passionate knowledge leadership defines knowledge processes; formulates policies; identifies the appropriate technology requirements and knowledge gaps and needs; enables the environment for creating, capturing, organizing, accessing, and using knowledge assets; and enlivening knowledge. Leadership Café in my model, oversees the implementation of a KM program and its maturity; I will discuss this later in chapter 11.

9.3. KNOWLEDGE MANAGEMENT ORGANIZATIONAL STRATEGY
Designing a KM strategy means defining what the organization hopes to accomplish through KM techniques, methods, and activities, and how that will be realized. It also involves engaging and aligning key players in the organization and providing an opportunity for the leadership to establish accountability for moving forward.

The knowledge management program should be in consonance with the organizational strategy. What is a KM strategy? It's a plan of action that outlines how an organization manages its information, data, and knowledge; creates a knowledge culture; improves productivity; and realizes organizational resilience and efficiency. The organizational strategy is typically aligned with the critical path of the organization's mission. So, emphasis should be placed on how to manage this critical knowledge of the organization. Café is connecting the dots between people and knowledge.

KM OBJECTIVES

When I was managing a KM project, I completed a survey that required me to rank sets of KM objectives in order of importance to my organization. Here are the possible objectives:

- Preventing knowledge loss
- Data and/or information management
- Knowledge transfer/sharing
- Collaboration/socialization of knowledge
- Succession management/building bench strength
- Productivity and performance improvement
- Breaking down silos, supporting knowledge flow across the enterprise
- New knowledge creation and innovation

My ranking of the enterprise KM objectives was slightly different from my sponsor's ranking. It is essential to discuss and come to a consensus on the KM strategy and priorities.

The knowledge management strategies of an organization cannot be divorced from its business strategy or organizational cultures. In their research, Mojibi, Hosseinzadeh, and Khojasteh (2015) found significant relationships between four dimensions of knowledge management strategies (creation and transfer of knowledge) and organizational culture in the organization they studied. There is no one-size-fits-all approach in KM strategy. The knowledge management environment we create must consider existing business strategy and business culture. The culture of the organization must be put into considerations, or the whole system will collapse. According to Jasimuddin and Zhang (2014), optimal knowledge management strategies can cultivate or support the organizational cultural fit and maximize organizational profit. Bottom line: KM strategy must align with the business strategy and culture. As I stated earlier, culture eats strategy for breakfast every day of the week.

I think that business strategy dictates where and how KM strategy should be formulated or developed. Culture determines what is valuable and what is not. A few years ago, PMI conducted national research on program and project management professionalism and efficiencies, published by PMI's *Pulse of the Profession*. The report uncovered that only 64 percent of government strategic initiatives ever meet their goals and business intent—and that government entities waste $101 million for every $1 billion spent on projects and programs. The existing business culture is the elephant in the room. We can't ignore it anymore if we want a vibrant knowledge exchange and transfer environment.

QUESTIONS FOR ORGANIZATIONAL READINESS

Demarest (1997) identified six key questions an organization has to answer to participate in KM effectively. In summary, they relate to

- the culture, actions, and beliefs of managers about the value, purpose, and role of knowledge;
- the creation, dissemination, and use of knowledge within the firm;
- the kind of strategic and commercial benefits a firm can expect by the use of effective KM;
- the maturity of knowledge systems in the firm;
- how a firm should organize for KM; and
- the role of information technology in the KM program.

POSSIBLE ROADMAP

Part of the roadmap is identifying KM activities, methods, or techniques that fit into your business strategy and culture.

- Seek executive endorsement and resource commitment
- Create goals and objectives for your KM program

- Identify strategies to meet goals
- Develop a CoP maturity model
- Rank identified CoPs based on the maturity model
- Outline characteristics of each level
- Identify metrics and evaluation methods
- Develop a detailed plan for the first pilot
- Develop a communication plan
- Identify resources needs and develop a budget
- Establish a schedule of milestones
- Set up tracking and evaluation process
- Establish realistic success criteria
- Form a working group with broad organizational representation
- Identify resources for the first 6 to 18 months

9.4. KNOWLEDGE MANAGEMENT RECIPE AND PLAN

RECIPES FOR STARTING A KM PROGRAM

In his beautiful piece, *Knowledge Management and Maturity Models: Building Common Understanding,* at the Second European Conference on Knowledge Management, Gabor Klimko (2001) posits that there are various recipes on how and where to start building a knowledge management program in an organization. Here is a list to illustrate:

- Wiig discusses several broad, top-down methods, technical, and general methods that range from knowledge charting to knowledge-based systems development (Wiig, 1993c).
- Allee draws attention to quality-based approaches (Allee, 1997).
- Davenport and Prusak distinguished among knowledge management projects based on their objectives, i.e., whether it is an attempt to create knowledge repositories, to improve access to knowledge resources, or to build knowledge culture (Davenport & Prusak, 1998).

- Brooking, emphasizing corporate memory, stresses the need for starting with soft approaches and warns us to avoid a technology-focused start (Brooking, 1999).
- Drew promotes knowledge management into the building of business strategy (Drew, 1999).
- Hansen, Nohria, and Tierney observed two different strategies identified as codification and personalization in the practice of consulting firms (Hansen, Nohria, & Tierney, 1999).
- Bukowitz and Williams suggest going for diagnosis first, then creating an agenda action (Bukowitz & Williams, 1999).
- David Gurteen espouses conversation leadership through a Knowledge Café (Gurteen, n.d.).
- I will add: bring knowledge workers to the café.

Create a Knowledge Leadership Café. This is a formalization, "strategization," and "policicization" of the Knowledge Café mindset, conversational leadership, and World Café outcomes through Leadership Café—converting ideas to reality and plans to policy in a café style.

According to Klimko (2001), there are a variety of approaches and best practices for KM. Such a proliferation of tested KM approaches from respected and influential writers makes the case that there's no single normative model for building up a KM program. A clear-cut research roadmap is critical for exploring, implementing the KM function, creating new knowledge, and rejuvenating the knowledge process.

So, what's your knowledge management plan? We have a project management plan for planning and executing projects. Depending on your organization's size, there may be a need for a plan for managing your KM system. Do you need a plan to convene a Knowledge Café or call your first CoP meeting? Still, you can start a CoP at lunch today or call a café meeting for next week. Because of my organization's nature, I needed to develop a charter with a business case before we launched a KM effort.

POSSIBLE KNOWLEDGE MANAGEMENT PLAN

A knowledge management plan is a document that defines how knowledge leaders will plan, execute, monitor, control, and mature the KM system. This plan comes into the picture when you want to institutionalize your KM program. The plan may include the following:

- Communication management plan
- Risk management plan
- Schedule management plan
- Change management plan
- Stakeholder engagement plan
- Integration management plan
- Tools and technology management plan
- Scope management plan
- Procurement management plan
- Value realization plan
- New knowledge implementation registers and plan

You can see that these plans are tailored toward the project management waterfall methodology, but I utilize a combination of the Agile and waterfall methods for the most part. So, could you show me your knowledge management plan? No time? There's so much "terrible" learning out there which in actuality is not really learning at all because most learning is one-dimensional. Sharing has been replaced with technology—KM texting and emojis!

How much does your organization know? What is its intellectual capital? What's your budget for KM? Could you show me the money? Has your organization captured its knowledge assets? Does it create an environment for sharing and rejuvenating in knowledge? Do you reward knowledge users for sharing their expertise, or do you think it's part of their jobs—necessity is laid on them to share what they know? What is your knowledge culture?

Practice Café: How Do You Start a KM Program:
Knowledge Café or Audit?
What is the first step toward knowledge management? A café or knowledge audit? It's a matter of preference and the needs of your

organization. My recommendation is to begin with a Knowledge Café. Knowledge audit is a systematic and scientific examination and evaluation of explicit and implicit knowledge resources in a company, including what knowledge exists, where it is, how it is being created, and who owns it (Hylton, 2002a, 2002b, as cited in Yip et al., 2015). A knowledge audit is knowing what you know, what you don't know, what you should know, and what you should unlearn—and then prioritizing it all. The audit is for formalization. I have used a knowledge audit to understand my organization's needs and understand the knowledge gaps. Knowledge audit or evaluation of the organization's knowledge management can begin in a café.

Start with a Knowledge Café mindset. Incorporate iterative, adaptive, and predictive approaches. Simplicity. Try to convene a Knowledge Café for knowledge interchange and shared learning. Convene a casual café with knowledge enthusiasts—knowledge managers, knowledge users, and knowledge creators.

Disciplined Agile for KM Implementation

I'm a WAgile (waterfall and Agile hybrid) project manager. Incorporating an Agile mindset has helped in implementing various KM tools into our KM program. I manage KM implementation like designing and deploying software with some Agile methodologies and grounded in a waterfall, making simplified process decisions around incremental and iterative solution delivery. Candidly, ignoring Agile and neglecting waterfall is ignoring sound balance. You don't want to miss out on some of the basic project management concepts that every PM should know.

A better evangelist of project management is someone who dwells in both worlds of waterfall and Agile. To be a super project manager but ignorant of the basic PM concepts and terminologies lowers the bar too low. It's like being a history expert who has a mastery of all current events, but not so much on the events that have happened in the past. I believe that a professional project manager should be able to use PM competencies and methodologies to manage all kinds of projects, ranging from technology/software projects

to construction/building projects to process improvement or program developments, design projects, and KM projects. The same
principles and methodologies apply. If you can only function within
the circumference of stable teams that routinely deliver releases, just
like operations, it may limit your capability scope. Having said that,
if you are still stuck in the waterfall world and ignoring Agile, you'll
find yourself irrelevant soon!

> Usually people begin a KM project by focusing on the technology
> needs. But the key is people and process.
>
> —Shir Nir

*Practice Café: What Technology Tools Have Proved Successful for
Knowledge Capturing and Sharing in your Organization?*
How do you make your organization a knowledge-centric one? What
are your knowledge-sharing challenges during disruptions?

9.5. WHAT DOES IT MEAN TO IMPLEMENT KNOWLEDGE MANAGEMENT?

To implement a KM program and system, you need to know leadership and governance, organizational strategy, and measurement
that is sure of value and progress. In a 2019 national TRB KM Task
Force Summer Webinar, where I co-presented with Dr. Moses Adoko (2019b), 75 percent of attendees did not have a formal KM program. Attendees were drawn from public sectors, including 52 U.S.
state departments of transportation, research and educational institutions, and the private sector.

In her research for the book *Critical Knowledge Transfer: Tools for
Managing Your Company's Deep Smarts*, Dorothy Leonard, professor of business administration at Harvard, conducted a survey and
found that 42 percent of companies try to address this problem of
knowledge retention by hiring retirees back as consultants to do the
same jobs they have always done but with double pay (Leonard,
2014).

Some organizations have a fully implemented KM program and deployed the KM system. A knowledge management system is designed to store and retrieve all the organization's knowledge. LIU Post Professor of Knowledge Management Michael E. D. Koenig (2017) wrote, "KM, historically at least, is primarily about managing the knowledge of employees and in organizations." There are several techniques and tools or KM activities. It would be difficult and unnecessary to simultaneously deploy all these tools and techniques in an organization. After you have conducted a forensic analysis of your organization, identify appropriate tools for your organization that align with your organizational strategy and culture, then test the water to the secure buy-in of critical stakeholders. Assuming you are starting with a Knowledge Café, call the first meeting. Take one step at a time. Focus on café conversation on business issues and tangible values.

The first KM technique I implemented in our organization was communities of practice. My executive sponsor approved a KM plan that included taking a snapshot of our organization. I visited some divisions, districts, departments, regions, and offices to identify existing KM activities. I visited seven divisions and presented their leadership with the efficacy of KM, inquiring if they have any KM activity like CoP going on in their divisions. It was amazing to find out that some divisions had up to three functioning CoPs. While I was making a presentation to these leaders, I was hearing comments like, "it looks like what we've been doing for the past several years," "we've begun running CoP without knowing it," and "we didn't know it was called CoP, but the intention was exclusively to share and transfer knowledge." At the end of my initial KM exploration visits to seven divisions, I identified 17 CoPs at different maturity levels. Today, we have more than 50 CoPs.

I took the results of my investigations into a Leadership Café. The enterprise KM lead analyzed the results, developed a maturity model for the CoPs, developed a CoP charter, and created organizational templates. We provided resources to assist the CoPs in organizing more formally and grow. We guided them on how to convene, lead the CoP, and measure results.

WHAT DOES IT MEAN TO IMPLEMENT KM?

- Conduct knowledge audit and gap analysis
- Align knowledge and business strategies
- Identify opportunities
- Evaluate value and business benefits
- Identify and select KM tools appropriate for your environment
- Implement enterprise governance—develop a KM workgroup
- Pilot a technique like communities of practice (CoP)
- Develop maturity model
- Measure outcome

An investment in knowledge pays the best interest.

—Benjamin Franklin

9.6. CASE STUDY: KM IS FOR PROFESSIONAL AND PERSONAL GROWTH, ORGANIZATIONAL EXCELLENCE, AND NEW OPPORTUNITIES—RAM DOKKA, PGMP PMP PMI-ACP CBIP SSBB

Ram Dokka gave this case study, PgMP, an Enterprise Agile Transformation Coach, Sr. IT Portfolio/Program/Project, past president of the PMI Austin Chapter, and a board chair of the PMI Educational Foundation. Ram has certifications as a project management professional, program management professional, and PMI Agile, among several others.

I'm not sure if we have a formal program in all the organizations I've worked for, and I'm not aware of budget allocation for KM. Some of the challenges I encounter in transferring or sharing knowledge include readiness and willingness to share and receive, lack of purpose and drive, and not seeing the big-picture benefits. In terms of knowledge Transfer technology tools, it is not the tools that are the problem most of the time; it is the silos created and the effort involved in managing multiple repositories.

I share my knowledge of professional and personal growth, organizational excellence, and new opportunities. Knowledge Transfer is both a challenge and fun at the same time. Challenge to identify the proper resources and fun to give and receive. In my experience, some of the painful results of poor or no Knowledge Transfer program or strategy include lack of innovation and growth, resistance to change, rework, and to reinvent the wheel, and total business failure in extreme situations.

Ram Dokka identified that KM enhances professional and personal growth, organizational excellence, and new opportunities. He contends that the silos created and the effort involved in managing multiple repositories are the problems of KET rather than technology. A knowledge transfer program or strategy makes possible innovation and growth and eliminates resistance to change, rework, and the tendency to reinvent the wheel.

10 ■ Café Interfaces with Other KM Methods and Techniques

Chapter Objectives

- Describe the interfaces of the Knowledge Café with other KM methods like CoPs, lessons learning, oral history, after-action review, etc.
- Explain the practical application of some KM techniques

10.1. THE CAFÉ FOR COMMUNITIES OF PRACTICE (COP)

TWO METHODS OF KM

Generally, there are two methods of knowledge management:

- Knowledge capture (codification). This involves capturing a technical expert's enduring wisdom, a summary of important lessons, and techniques they have learned to do their work. This will, in turn, be made available to others in the knowledge community.

- Knowledge transfer (person to person). Here, knowledge transfer can be through social interaction like CoP or the use of KM technology enablers.

Most of the knowledge in an individual's mind cannot be captured or transferred except through social interactions like mentoring, job shadowing, coaching, observations, brainstorming, or collaborative opportunities offered in a fair or café. There are several techniques I've encountered that include communities of practice, knowledge fair and café, storytelling, wikithon, appreciative inquiry, knowledge retention interviews and exit interviews, positive deviance, yellow pages, project lesson capture meeting (large scale), enterprise content management, new media, after-action (small scale), knowledge-sharing roundtable, peer assist, coaching and mentoring, action learning, innovation deep dive, crowdsourcing, open space, and so on.

The CoP construct tries to bring people together with mutual interests and who want to collaborate and share knowledge. The space—the venue for the convergence of CoPs, the mindset, and the environment—is the café. Where do we meet? At the café. What do we do there? Talk, listen, think, learn, make sense of what we know, and maybe, build knowledge-driven relationships.

Differences between the Café and CoP

- Different CoPs converge in a place for a Knowledge Café, but CoPs can connect without meeting in one place.
- A café or a series of cafés does not necessarily constitute a CoP.
- A CoP will adopt many ways of interacting rather than just the café format (e.g., less structured conversations, open space technology sessions, and online discussion forums).
- A Knowledge Café is a powerful conversational tool that can be employed by a CoP, but it is not the same as a CoP.

- A café is unstructured, informal, fun, relaxing, creative, social, collaborative, nonthreatening, and time-bounded; a CoP can be structured and is not necessarily time-bound.
- Cafés cover one purpose, like best practices among CoPs; the CoP covers a community or communities of practice.

Communities of practice can be a KM tool, technique, element, or activity or practice. The concept of communities of practice most likely originated with Lave and Wenger (1991), based on their study of situated learning in the context of five apprenticeships: Yucatec midwives, Vai and Gola tailors, naval quartermasters, meat cutters, and non-drinking alcoholics. Others contend that the idea of communities of practice has a long history in community-based and mental health and other learning-based communities. They defined CoP as "a system of relationships between people, activities, and the world; developing with time, and in relation to other tangential and overlapping communities of practice" (Lave & Wenger, 1991, p. 98). The community of practice is a consortium of knowledge and shared culture, scalable learning, shared repertoire, common problem-solving, and free flow of information.

How Do You Know When You Need a Community of Practice?
I worked for a project-driven organization. I was about to manage a complex project that could not afford to fail. The Project Management Office (PMO) was a young one. *PMBOK® Guide,* sixth edition (2017) calls this a supportive PMO, a repository, with low control—a PMO that provides a consultative role to projects and provides support in the form of on-demand expertise, templates, best practices, access to information, and expertise from other projects. I called our PMO for project management templates, including risk, communication, stakeholder, management plans, RACI, risk register, status report templates, and so on. The PMO didn't have these templates. I visited PMI.org, adapted some templates, and customized my templates.

Before long, I realized that other project managers were developing their own templates. If there were a connected community of project managers, there would have been one true source for all project management templates. CoP brings professionals who are encountering similar challenges in a community to learn from and support each other. There would not be a reason to duplicate our efforts if we had a CoP. We could have shared the same organizational process assets, saved time, and leveraged each other's strengths. There was no community to inform us of what others were doing or the challenges they were facing.

When teams within the organization are defined by location, job function, process area, or other factors, there will be natural silos, and these are functional silos. However, these natural barriers create independent cultures by the group. CoP enriches the organizational learning process and knowledge exchange. I called for a project management CoP.

Communities of Practice Can Create a Single Source of the Truth with a CoP Café

CoP invites knowledge brokers who encounter similar challenges to come to a conversation and learn from each other. The CoP is a rendezvous of colleagues doing similar projects from different functional silos; these birds of a feather usually flock together due to what they do. In a CoP café, practitioners build leverage, share common problems, and reinvigorate knowledge. New ideas and solutions emerge at the CoP café. The more excellent knowledge belongs to the community, and no one is left behind. It's like a "you scratch my back, I scratch your back" mentality. We all give and take. There's no need to reinvent the wheel.

In terms of digital transformation, CoP connects the digital workplace and other knowledge-sharing tools and approaches. It provides a single source of truth for all digital collaboration, from one central Wiki to new media interactions—a one-stop shop for all digital content and connection for all knowledge creators and users.

Here's a CoP example from General Electric (GE). Its 180 communities of practice with more than 130,000 engaged members have generated 31,000 discussion posts, 39,000 Wiki articles, 16,000 taxonomic topics, and $35 million in savings. GE communities are linked to and enabled by all of GE's other KM approaches (APQC, 2019).

> At Shell, community coordinators often conduct interviews to collect these stories and then publish them in newsletters and reports. AMS organizes a yearly competition to identify the best stories. An analysis of a sample of stories revealed that the communities had saved the company $2 million to $5 million and increased revenue by more than $13 million in one year.
>
> —Wenger & Snyder (2000)

The KM framework involves communities of practice, best practices, practice owners, and practice improvement. A CoP can be an internal, local, or global forum for exchanging best practices, technology, and business solutions, time-tested or golden standards, customer challenges, and feedback.

In a CoP, we move from "owned knowledge" to "shared knowledge," which is community knowledge. So, knowledge workers and learning organizations are driven to enhance learning across organizational units and empower people in their work. A CoP is a convincing way of doing so. "CoP meetings should be considered legitimate business functions, as opposed to extracurricular activities" (NCHRP, 2014).

If you need evolution in your organization, you may need a café to introduce CoP across your enterprise. Evolution means from individual knowledge → group knowledge → business-critical institutional knowledge → institutional resilience. Connect the right people to align with initiatives. Remember that a CoP shouldn't be an additional burden to your workload but is fun! It's colleagues connecting to build synergy, sharing what they know to solve common projects, programs, or operational problems—thereby creating new knowledge.

CoPs are easy to start. Use Knowledge Café space to begin a conversation with your professional community members or people who manage similar projects in your organization or other knowledge workers. I have templates for CoP charter and formation steps on my website, BenjaminAnyacho.com, and there are templates on the Internet.

SOME LESSONS LEARNED FROM MY EXPERIENCE WITH COPS

- Have a clear purpose enshrined in a charter.
- The purpose should match the culture and strategy of the organization. Their mission alights with the organizational mission and KM strategy.
- Deliver real benefits to the community members.
- Have identifiable leaders.
- Practitioners should agree on ways of working amongst the community.
- Even if they operate mostly virtually, use face-to-face meetings at some point.
- CoPs are designed for learning, knowledge-sharing, fun, and engagement and are not a "burnout" tool.

CHARACTERISTICS OF A COP

According to Wenger (1998, pp. 125–126), these are the critical characteristics of a CoP:

- Sustained mutual relationships—harmonious or conflictual
- Shared ways of engaging in doing things together
- The rapid flow of information and the propagation of innovation
- Absence of introductory preambles, as if conversations and interactions were merely the continuation of an ongoing process
- Rapid setup of a problem to be discussed
- The substantial overlap in participants' descriptions of who belongs
- Knowing what others know, what they can do, and how they can contribute to an enterprise
- Mutually defining identities
- The ability to assess the appropriateness of actions and products

- Specific tools, representations, and other artifacts
- Local lore, shared stories, inside jokes, knowing laughter
- Jargon and shortcuts to communication as well as the ease of producing new ones
- Certain styles recognized as displaying membership
- A shared discourse reflecting a particular perspective on the world

10.2. THE CAFÉ FOR LESSONS LEARNING

A survey by Ernst & Young (2007) of PMI members and guests at a PMI meeting revealed that although 91 percent of PMs believe lessons learned reviews on projects were necessary, only 13 percent said their organizations performed them on all projects. Only 8 percent believed the primary benefits of lessons learned reviews (Ernst & Young, 2007).

Organizations like the Control System Integrators Association (CSIA) and the Project Management Institute (PMI) cite lessons learned as best practices. The *PMBOK® Guide,* sixth edition (2017) defines lessons learned as "the learning gained from performing the project. Lessons learned may be identified at any point." The question is whether we are learning for the project or just checking off the box. How to assess long-term learning is typically considered a problem across all corporate learning and development. Several years ago, I realized that lessons learned are one of the closing activities during a project.

LEGACY LESSONS TO LEARN MODEL

- Sessions held during project close-out
- Documented as a project-specific deliverable

SUSTAINABLE KET LESSON LEARNED MODEL

- An ongoing activity conducted throughout the life cycle of the project
- Does not point fingers at anyone
- Analyzed and validated by subject matter experts (SMEs)
- Focuses on both the successes and the opportunities

- Aligns with project management processes and knowledge areas, institutionalized
- Must perennially become an organizational process asset and part of the processes and procedures for future projects

The fundamental question is not if there was a lesson, but if the lesson was actually learned. There should be lessons in learning, according to Dr. Moses Adoko. The most important aspect of the lessons learning is institutionalizing the lessons and capturing new knowledge that arises from the execution of the project.

> The "learning" part only comes when the lesson has been institutionalized (e.g., changing a policy, writing a procedure, revising a standard, issuing a new specification, improving a work process, etc.)
> —Mark Marlin, PMP, Sr. Vice President of
> Westney Consulting Group

One of the communities of practice in my organization, Financial Management CoP, gets this right. During their normal execution of a project or normal operations, if new lessons emerge or they identify a new knowledge or best practice, they apply the new lesson, update their standard operating procedures, communicate to all stakeholders about the new lessons, and demand that every member of the community follows or implements the new learning.

Agile is a mindset; Knowledge Café is a mindset. Lessons learned should be a mindset, too. Well-defined, planned, executed, and institutionalized lessons learning could be a great tool to implement knowledge transfer in an organization. The truth is that new knowledge is created every day as we manage our projects and programs. This includes Agile retrospectives, lessons learned during project product backlog, Agile project sprint backlog, daily stand-ups, and stakeholder reviews. We can turn the lessons learned mindset into a powerful KET tool.

CHALLENGES OF IMPLEMENTING "LESSONS LEARNING"

Here are some of the challenges of implementing lessons learned as a knowledge exchange and transfer technique and the reasons why lessons learned are ignored in projects and programs.

- No time for extra chores! Just like any other KET activities, many PMs work from project to project, activity to activity, task to task, and job to job, and build no time into the process for KET. KET is an intentional process. Lessons learned must be deliberate and planned into the KM strategy.
- We were playing the blame game. Lessons learned are not about everything that went well. It is not about who did something wrong. It's all about what we learned to do better or what we did better than we can institutionalize.
- KM is not part of the culture. Lessons learned fail because it's not part of the organizational culture or a lip-service.
- Lack of the lessons learned value-add. Just like the entire KM program, many overlook the tangible and intangible benefits of KET.
- Not a priority and, hence, no management reinforcement.
- No leadership. As I'll explore later, things happen or don't because of the right leadership. I've led my teams to develop the lessons learned template that makes it easy to arrange and organize lessons learned content and make it searchable and findable.
- Documentation is too complicated. Lessons learned is one of the knowledge capturing tools that require documentation. The template should enhance curation, indexing, and organization of documented lessons learned and make it possible to be found and used by other knowledge creators.
- Unorganized knowledge documentation process. There is no knowledge management strategy or governance.

DEVELOPING A "LESSONS LEARNING" TEMPLATE

The template I developed follows the elements of lessons learned according to the *CDC Unified Process Practices Guide: Lessons Learned* (2006). The template includes:

- Project information and contact information for additional detail
- A clear statement of the lesson
- A background summary of how the lesson was learned
- Benefits of using the lesson and suggestion of how the lesson may be used in the future

Knowledge Leadership, as I'll discuss in chapter 11, brings organization to lessons learned.

Level 1 is appropriate documentation, writing knowledge down, including using various knowledge-capturing techniques.

Level 2 is the organization of lessons we are learning, including analyzing them.

Level 3 is consolidation in a way to avoid repletion, including curating the captured lessons learned.

Level 4 is the dissemination of the knowledge-making process; the lessons learned available, findable, and usable.

Level 5 occurs when the knowledge from the lessons learned is applied for the benefit of the organization.

10.3. THE CAFÉ FOR AFTER-ACTION REVIEW

An after-action review is a café-style activity to discuss a project or activity that enables the project team and stakeholders involved in the project, program, or operational activity to learn for themselves what happened, why it happened, what went well, what needs improvement, and what lessons can we learn from experience. Through this activity, the team identifies new knowledge and innovations.

David Garvin (2000), in his book, *Learning in Action: A Guide to Putting the Learning Organization to Work*, contends that, "To move ahead, one must often first look behind" (p. 106).

Looking back brings innovation into the right context. Just like a café, it brings us to a reflective mode, identifying those golden moments, things that were incorrectly done or that should've been done better. After-action reviews or learning lessons are not about pointing fingers or blaming those who may have dropped the ball. It's about learning, growing, and innovating.

The U.S. Army's After-Action Reviews (AARs) are probably the industry model for an example of a knowledge management system and a culture of learning and knowledge that is unmatched. The after-action reviews are routine and have created a culture where everyone continuously assesses themselves, their units, and their organization, looking for ways to improve and innovate. After every important activity or event, Army teams review assignments, identify successes and failures, and seek ways to perform better the next time (Garvin, 2000, p. 106). We can't be too busy to ignore this critical KM activity. A café can be designated for AARs.

10.4. THE CAFÉ FOR STORYTELLING: ORAL HISTORY

Why I developed a knowledge preference register is because I have a preference for reviving and sharing knowledge. Everyone loves stories. In a corporate setting, people often prefer to obtain specific knowledge and information through stories. Oral history tools engage some knowledge brokers who tell their stories about process; events; methodologies; and lessons learned from a project, program, activity, or event. These stories are recorded, stored, and made available for the knowledge communities for use and reuse. The stores can be made available in multiple formats for consumption, for instance, video, audio, paper, and so on. Many users' learning preference is listening. Oral history captures the most difficult to capture and the most critical aspect of knowledge—tacit knowledge. Oral history is an essential tool because of the decline in readership among knowledge users and creators.

Today, almost any digital text has an audio option where you can listen to rather than read the content. More knowledge workers are listening. In 2015, "18% of Americans say they listened to at least one audiobook in the past year (up from 14% in 2016) and, for the first time, over 50% of Americans report having ever listened to a podcast" (Schwanenflugel & Knapp, 2019, p. x). It's fair to say that audiobooks aren't strictly oral history, though it's an interesting philosophical concept to consider all audio-based information to be part of the collective oral history.

In terms of learning and knowledge acquisition, oral history should be a significant player.

> For example, in the wake of the 1989 Loma Prieta Earthquake, the Bay Bridge Oral History Project documented the personal and professional experiences of 258 Caltrans employees who worked to restore the State's damaged transportation system. The interviews capture their perspectives on the Bay Bridge's engineering achievements, the maintenance challenges, and the complex symbolism of this massive structure.
>
> (AASHTO CKC, NCHRP Problem Statement, 2019)

10.5. CASE STUDY: KNOWLEDGE TRANSFER CAN BE BOTH A CHALLENGE AND FUN—LINDA AGYAPONG, PHD, PMP

This case study is by Linda Agyapong, PhD, PMP, a project manager in Newark, Delaware. She is also an author and freelance PMP consultant and trainer for corporate institutions and higher education. She is the 2015 James R. Snyder International Student Paper of the Year Award winner, presented at the 2015 North America congress. Here is her experience:

Yes, my organization has a Knowledge Transfer (KT) program, and it is formalized. The HR team leads this as it is included in our orientation and ongoing training curriculum. Some organizations I've worked for allocate a specific amount for KM within our annual budget and the amount is based on forecasted revenue for the year.

Some of the transferring or sharing knowledge, pain points, and challenges include obtaining the required logistics or resources, and where applicable, the appropriate systems are necessary for simulations. Additionally, we see KT as being a double-edged sword, because in one sense, it helps you to sharpen the skills of your employees. Alternatively, once the employees identify that their marketability skills have increased, they sometimes tend to leave for greener pastures, leading to a "pseudo-brain drain" syndrome.

I don't necessarily see it completely wrong when some knowledge-transfer technology tools don't talk to each other. One single source of truth is great, but I think there is "a place" for those tools that don't naturally talk to each other. There must be a reason why they are one-dimensional, and hence, if the user or the organization requires two-dimensional tools, those would preferably be sought for as well.

How long does it take for you to get the information and knowledge you need from people and technology to do your work? Does it depend on the amount and type of knowledge that is being requested? In terms of speed, agility, and accessibility, receiving information is applicable if it has to do with clicking a link and expecting the results to be displayed on the screen. However, suppose the results need to be sourced from a vast database or from third-party systems, which require specific authentications, or meetings and conferences are necessary. In that case, a longer time frame may be needed based on the turnaround (or ETA) policies for those parties.

I share my knowledge to ensure continuity of information, that is, to ensure that the knowledge does not stop with me. Knowledge transfer can be both a challenge and fun. The fun part is to see that someone else "gets" the same thing that you know and is running with it in a different direction or capacity than you are, which results in some form of diversity.

I would not necessarily call a lack of knowledge transfer painful. Still, just to reiterate the point I made earlier, the challenge is to invest so much in an individual only for the person to leave before you reap any benefit from them. Bottom line: As project managers, we need to brace ourselves with the challenge and knowledge-transfer efficacy. Tacit knowledge is the most critical type of knowledge.

Dr. Agyapong pointed out that knowledge transfer can be both a challenge and fun, which is true. In terms of conversion, tacit knowledge is the most challenging type of knowledge to transfer.

In knowledge management, training—just like any other single KM tool—is a little potato. However, some organizations see too much training or free flow and access to knowledge and information to be counterproductive. I remember when I developed a Professional Project Management (PMP) certification for my organization a few years ago. At the initiation stages of the project, I remember talking with a stakeholder who argued vehemently that providing a significant certification like PMP for employees at no cost is an incentive to look for greener pastures. Is this a valid argument? Since the program was deployed about seven years ago, more than 100 project managers have become certified PMPs, and hundreds have been mentored. Yet, only a handful of credentialed PMPs have left the organization for greener pasture. While the fear of "too much learning" or too much access to knowledge and information is valid, I can honestly say that the benefit of an open free flow of knowledge and information outweighs it.

Dr. Agyapong was right when she alluded that there's no one size fits all. Every knowledge environment is unique. Every tool is also different. Every tool may not fit into one single source of truth. Converting the knowledge to wisdom or applying knowledge remains a challenge at all levels, hence the importance of managing and stewarding knowledge and its availability to users when and where they need it.

11 ■ Knowledge Leadership Café

Chapter Objectives

- Describe the interfaces of the Knowledge Café with other KM methods, like CoPs, lessons learning, oral history, after-action review, and so on
- Explain the practical application of some KM techniques

11.1. KNOWLEDGE LEADERSHIP CAFÉ ROADMAP

As seen in figure 6, the origin of most knowledge is from the physical dimensions of data—things we can count, measure, observe, and touch. From this domain, we derive information. We need more than data or facts. In the age of big data, the importance of organization, analysis, and data cannot be overemphasized. When data are given

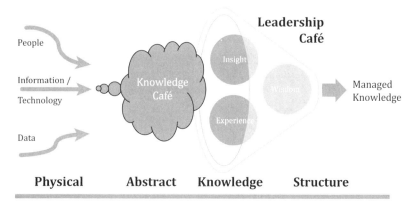

Figure 6: Knowledge leadership continuum.

meaning—and made actionable—it becomes information; it still needs to be explained to become knowledge. The café can provide the vehicle and space for this metamorphosis of data to information knowledge and wisdom. When this information is married with experience and insight and is contextualized, it scales to the domain of abstract, as seen in figure 6. This is where these data and pieces of information can be used to make decisions. When we analyze and consume information regularly, this is a sphere of knowledge. When knowledge is applied, it becomes wisdom. A Leadership Café answers the question "what next" after the café.

Dr. Richard McDermott, a Visiting Academic Fellow at Henley Business School and an Associate of the Knowledge and Innovation Network sponsored by Warwick University, describes six characteristics of knowledge that distinguish it from information (McDermott, 1999, as cited in UKEssays, 2018):

1. Knowledge is a human act.
2. Knowledge is the residue of thinking.
3. Knowledge is created in the present moment.
4. Knowledge belongs to communities.
5. Knowledge circulates through communities in many ways.
6. New knowledge is created at the boundaries of old.

Knowledge is a human act, a product of our thinking, and belongs to the community. It's almost useless in a silo but can give birth to greatness when it is caféd.

A Leadership Café–like dinner took place in early 1969 among three men at the Three Threes Restaurant, a small, intimate gathering place just a few blocks from City Hall in Philadelphia, Pennsylvania. This dinner was a continuation of several months of discussions and cross-fertilization of knowledge between two men, Jim Snyder and Gordon Davis. By the end of their knowledge exchange, it was decided that a new organization should be formed to provide a means for project managers to associate, share information and knowledge, and discuss common problems. Project Management Institute was born. Today, millions of project managers and professionals have been impacted around the world because of that Leadership Café.

Experts know how to get things done. Leadership is influence. High-impact leaders increase their influence by sharing what they know.

I intend to take a Knowledge Café to a new level—Knowledge Leadership Café—a framework, not a methodology or technique. Leadership Café becomes Knowledge Café 2.0 for validating the café experience, investing, formalizing or institutionalizing café practices, identifying appropriate KM strategy, and aligning it with the organization's mission and goals. Café 2.0 is a sequel to Knowledge Café.

At work, I plan about one Leadership Café every other month to respond to our KM community's needs and make recommendations to top management on KM. Leadership is a framework versus being a methodology. Café 2.0 is not prescriptive and is more strategic than other types of Knowledge Cafés. Café 2.0 convenes leaders to develop the strategy for a KM program.

You and I may be different in the way we see this concept, but I have developed a powerful framework for this. Café 2.0 is the café for the implementation of new knowledge. It is the formalization, "strategization," and "politization" of the Knowledge Café mindset, conversational leadership, and World Café outcomes. Leadership Café converts ideas into reality, plans into policy, and advances newly created knowledge to top management in a café style. There is a feeling of disequilibrium regarding the formalization of knowledge within an organization. How formal can we get without creating more work for knowledge users and creators? Café 2.0 establishes the framework for formalizing KM in an organization without being too prescriptive and pedantic.

A framework provides structure and direction on a preferred way to do something without being too detailed or rigid. A framework provides guidance while being flexible enough to adapt to changing conditions or to be customized for your organization.

I report to senior leadership and an executive sponsor who wants to see numbers and results. After gathering 85 leaders across the enterprise for a four-hour Knowledge Café and fair event, there should be some tangible deliverables. I know that the outcome of the café is what attendees learned in their heads. I'm customizing these principles to enable me to gain higher management and stakeholder support. I'm hoping that we shall have a virgin café that will not have a knowledge fair attached to it in the future. By the way, I have had some executives attend my café events. Believe it or not, their presence didn't stop café attendees from expressing their views or having positive and heated conversations because there was a ground rule that all attendees agreed to.

Another ground rule is that there are no preconceived outcomes. I usually have a live survey during my café events and have received tremendous feedback. We had 93 percent overall customer satisfaction. We take this feedback to the Leadership Café. In many organizational settings, you can't get 80 middle-to-senior managers together for an unstructured conversation like a café.

The Knowledge Leadership Café comprises enterprise champions and KM strategists. You can call it a project or program planning enterprise team or committee. But this team is strategic. What differentiates this team from a committee is the café mindset and the ability to see the big picture and make recommendations to top management.

Just like in all projects, a KM program has more likelihood of success if it has an executive sponsor and management buy-in is secured. People at the top have "big picture" knowledge. . . . People at the bottom have the knowledge of how things work and how to get things done," said Friedrich Hayek (1899–1992).

11.2. THE INTERSECTION OF KNOWLEDGE CAFÉ AND LEADERSHIP CAFÉ

I conduct knowledge fairs and café, incorporating about 60 percent of Gurteen's Knowledge Café elements or principles. I believe in the simplicity and principles of a Knowledge Café mindset. Remember that the café is a KM technique used to surface a group's collective knowledge, learn from each other, and share ideas and insights to gain a deeper understanding of topics, issues, and KM best practices. It's a conceptual "home base" for KM, an unstructured and interactive ecosystem for exploring, sharing, and rejuvenating knowledge. The critical environmental factor is that everyone in this space has an equal voice and a safe learning space. It should be as simple as walking into a café for a coffee or tea.

The outcome of a Knowledge Café is what attendees learned from the café, but after the café, what next? What are the plans for institutionalization? Café should be the baseline for conversational leadership—Leadership Café. I have held multiple Austin citywide Leadership Cafés during the past years. They were electric and exciting! Attendees—leaders, project and portfolio managers, "Agilest," and KM think tanks—brainstormed KM ideas using Knowledge Leadership Café as a framework. Attendees were mostly portfolio and project directors/managers in our region. Leadership café presentations were just about 15 percent of the time; the rest of the time was for questions, feedback, brainstorming, and conversations.

Why Is Knowledge Leadership Important? Because It Leads to Wisdom and Institutionalized Knowledge
Do you want knowledge or wisdom to be your identity? Do you want to be called a wise man or a wise lady? Whom do you identify with? We become identified with the things or people we identify with, and what we identify with becomes our identity. There is no wisdom

252 ■ The Knowledge Café

without first having knowledge. Enlightenment, or perception of clarity, is the product of wisdom.

Knowledge is the new gold. Knowledge is the new beacon. Knowledge has become the most significant asset of an organization. Knowledge is today's most essential resource of organizations and a prime factor of production. We are not just in an information economy; we are in a knowledge economy.

KNOWLEDGE INVOLVES

- "knowing that" (know a concept),
- "knowing how" (understand an operation), and
- "acquaintance-knowledge" (know by relation).

Knowledge is the beginning of wisdom. You cannot be more potent than your knowledge. Your conquests, victories, and accomplishments are directly proportional to the depth of your knowledge. People perish not because they are unlucky or weak but because of deficiency in knowledge or ignorance. In any society, when steadfast love, faithfulness, and knowledge exit, what will be left is anything but mercy. It's impossible to have the former without the latter. Faith, belief, reason, and knowledge work together. In all spiritualities, both organizational and religious spiritualities, you grow in grace and knowledge or become irrelevant.

Like a project, knowledge doesn't manage itself—knowledge needs to be managed. Beyond managing knowledge, knowledge leadership is required. Some persons or groups will have to provide leadership and guidance for knowledge to be identified, transferred, and reinvigorated in the organization. I want to emphasize my hunger and desire for KM's simplicity for an average knowledge user and creator, and the emphasis on people, before process and technology.

According to International Data Corp. (IDC), a Framingham, Massachusetts-based market intelligence and advisory firm in the IT and telecommunications industries, Fortune 500 companies lose at least $31.5 billion a year by failing to share knowledge (Babcock, 2004, p. 46). Knowledge Café is limited to providing this kind of measurement. Café 2.0 offers a maturity model to measure the KM activities in the organization.

As we have discussed throughout this book, Knowledge Café is my preferred technique or methodology to start the KM process—to bring people who know something and those who desire to know more to collaborate and broker intelligent ideas and share knowledge. My preferred tool is to engage knowledge creators to create new knowledge, replace obsolete knowledge, and innovate. When David Gurteen coined the term Knowledge Café, he had in mind that the café is a casual gathering to ask and answer questions. His expectations or prescription are 6 to 24 people in a café that last for about 1-½ hours. I told David that I had as many as 100 leaders in my café and that my café events last up to five hours. There's not supposed to be any note-taking in the café, but I took notes because I saw the café as a kind of crowdsourcing for knowledge within an organization.

As a project manager, I always distribute a meeting agenda, including a column for action items. In the knowledge fair and café, there is so much feedback, learning, sharing, and reinvigoration that takes place. Café 2.0 is the next logical thing to do with the outcome of the café.

A Knowledge Café evolves to Leadership Café or Café 2.0. Contrary to the spirit of the Gurteen café, we take notes from the tables, summarize and distribute them to the café attendees, and subsequently try to curate and make these learning, ideas, and new knowledge accessible and findable by knowledge users. We have developed a knowledge Wiki to capture café lessons, knowledge, and wisdom. My favorite part is reporting the outcomes to my executive sponsor or top management. But the next part is the analysis that goes with the contents of the café that occurs after the café. The café enterprise team meets at another café-like meeting—a sequel to the café to intelligently analyze and synthesize the surveys and contributions for café attendees. I utilize live polls or surveys during the café to capture the knowledge creators' and enthusiasts' sentiments.

What Do I Do with the Notes Collected from the Café?

We take notes from the tables, analyze them, and distribute them among the attendees and other interested stakeholders. We analyze the deliberations, synthesize them, and use them to understand how to develop other KM methods in the organization.

I frequently use surveys in café meetings for decision-making. The Leadership Café is the framework to deploy strategies to respond to the outcome of the surveys. In terms of the discussions and summaries at the tables at the café, we listen to knowledge creators from different CoPs and disperse what we learned to all interested knowledge creators and users.

For example, during one of my café meetings, CoP participants shared collaboration technologies in their various CoPs. During the Leadership Café, we analyzed the comments from the participants. Some of the collaboration tools used by some CoPs were not safe—technology enablers with security risks associated with them—and have not been formally deployed for enterprise use. This made us develop plans to identify and promote technology tools ready and available across the enterprise. The Leadership Café responds to and provides guidance in this kind of situation. We developed a communication strategy for the CoP participants on the collaboration tools allowable across the enterprise. Plans were also created for how to move forward with other expected collaboration tools.

11.3. CAFÉ CHALLENGES

If you have ever used knowledge, you can create knowledge. I hope that the KM process is simplified and gives the reader concepts, principles, and frameworks to approach KM in all organizations. The role of the knowledge leader is to answer the big KM questions. How do you activate intentionality? How do you manage knowledge in the minds of people? How do you make KM an organizational strategy? Knowledge leadership provides the appropriate governance needed in the café space.

We understand things through our frame of reference. Many people are incapable of coming up with something that hasn't existed. The new idea in your head may be an old idea in another knowledge leadership. Our knowledge capacities are boundless. Café surfaces what we know. Knowledge leaders or brokers are the gate-keepers of knowledge and provide appropriate leadership for KET.

Café 2.0 provides a maturity model to measure the KM activities in the organization. It applies lessons learned, makes self-adjustments, develops understanding, creates leverage, adds maturity to the process and product, and more.

11.4. MIDDLE MANAGERS FACILITATE KM PROGRAMS

In their book *The Knowledge-Creating Company*, Nonaka and Takeuchi (1995) contended that the "middle-up-down" model of organizational knowledge creation is a realistic and workable model KM. "Simply put, knowledge is created by middle managers, who are often leaders of a team or task force, through a spiral conversion process involving both the top and the front-line employees (i.e., bottom). The process puts middle managers at the intersection of the company's vertical and horizontal flows of information." They elaborated this concept with GE's, 3M's, and Canon's case studies, drawing a contrast between top-down management and bottom-up management, proposing middle-up-down management as the best-case scenario.

"In the middle-up-down model, top management creates a vision or a dream, while middle management develops more concrete concepts that frontline employees can understand and implement. Middle managers try to solve the contradiction between what top management hopes to create and what exists in the real world" (Nonaka & Takeuchi, 1995). Top management sees the big picture. The analysis and synthesis of the KM process are too cumbersome for senior management. The topic of KM is too complicated for the frontline workers and project support team members to deal with.

Even if they are organizationally relevant, the authors argued that frontline employees who are mostly immersed in the day-to-day operations or work, from project support to project support, do not have the "big picture" advantage or are equipped to drive communication of the importance of their insights about KM. If the top-down approach is a bad idea and bottom-up is not workable, we are left with the middle-up-down approach. So, middle managers become the purveyors of the Knowledge Leadership Café—the facilitators of the unstructured plethora of insights toward an intentional knowledge creation organization.

There needs to be a KM facilitator who will bring like-minded knowledge workers to the café to begin the KM discussion. They are the firecrackers of the KM. Middle managers will be the evangelists of the sensible and realistic KM model and conceptual framework for the organization. If you have found something else that works, let me know. I successfully championed KM in my organization because, by the nature of my role as an operational excellence coordinator and senior project manager, I advise executives—helping them translate organizational strategies into reality. All my projects are involved in acquiring, developing, and managing enterprise project teams. I had the luxury of leading familiarity with top-middle-down.

Knowledge leaders validate the Knowledge Café outcomes. Knowledge Leadership Café is by invitation only. I'm blessed to have a knowledge leader in my organization who has a Ph.D. in knowledge management. When we developed the guidelines and templates for an enterprise knowledge Interview program, he was one of the knowledge leaders who validated the program before advancing to the top management.

Leadership Café sits in the middle, not the top, or down the chain of command. You can only make changes within a well-defined context. I have had several Knowledge Café and Knowledge Leadership Café events within and outside my organization. In each case, I sent out several surveys to know the leadership structure of a KM program. I have conducted independent research on this. There seems to be a consensus that a KM program would be a terrible idea if it had only a top-down KM approach. On the reverse, a bottom-up approach won't work either—it dies before it gets to the middle.

Throughout this book, I have mentioned knowledge creators, knowledge workers, and knowledge users. Nonaka and Takeuchi emphasize that everyone is a knowledge creator in a knowledge-creating company, whatever their position in the organization. I liked their categorization of knowledge users and creators:

Knowledge practitioners are responsible for accumulating and generating both tacit and explicit knowledge. Those who interface primarily with tacit knowledge are "knowledge operators," while those who interface mostly with explicit knowledge are "knowledge specialists."

Knowledge engineers are responsible for converting tacit knowledge into explicit knowledge and vice versa, thereby facilitating what they describe in their book as four modes of knowledge creation, specifically socialization, externalization, internalization, and combination (also discussed in their organization science paper); I referenced this earlier.

Knowledge officers are responsible for managing the overall organizational knowledge-creation process at the corporate level.

I don't think that one person can play these roles. I also do not believe that someone in the top management will be able to fulfill these roles of knowledge leaders. Hence, the enterprise management of KM is vested in the hands of a Knowledge Leadership Café.

Knowledge management is a vast ecosystem with several activities and techniques. There is no body of knowledge like *PMBOK®* *Guide* that serves as a compendium of KM time-tested practices and methodologies. A unified theory of knowledge does not exist. Like projects, tools, techniques, methods, and KM activities are context-specific and located in open systems. Hence, the temptation for researchers is to toe the line of personal opinions. The need for a research roadmap for KM is a sine qua non for progress.

11.5. CASE STUDY: *NIGHT AT THE MUSEUM* MOVIE— KNOWLEDGE UNMANAGED

Watch this movie or the preambles on YouTube. If you are a knowledge project manager, conduct a knowledge gap analysis to identify an organization's knowledge assets (see table 6), maturity level, and needs.

Background: Cecil Fredricks (Dick Van Dyke), an elderly night security guard about to retire from the American Museum of Natural History, hires Larry despite his unpromising résumé.

The museum, facing financial challenges, is rapidly losing money and plans to replace Cecil and two colleagues, Gus (Mickey Rooney) and Reginald (Bill Cobbs), with one guard. Cecil hands Larry an instruction manual on what to do in the museum on his first night, warning him that it can get a little spooky out here at night. Cecil gives Larry an instruction booklet on how to handle museum security, and advises Larry to leave some of the lights on, and warns him, "One thing you'll have to remember is not to let anything in . . . or out." Soon, Larry discovers that the gallery comes alive when the lights go out—an epic battleground fueled with nonstop action and adventure!

LEADERSHIP CAFÉ PROCESS

Call a few other managers who are knowledge creators and users to a Leadership Café.

- Identify the museum's missing knowledge gaps.
- What is wrong with this transition and succession?
- From this movie, what do you consider as the knowledge assets of the museum?
- If you are to present a business case to the management, what will that be for knowledge management?

KNOWLEDGE ASSETS

As seen in table 6, we can identify knowledge assets as:

- Museum as its workforce, databases, documents, guides, policies and procedures, software, and patents, repositories of the organization's knowledge assets
- Number of years of experience in managing a complicated and spooky museum
- Times and methods of operations

The ultimate goal is Café 2.0, a Knowledge Leadership Café.

Knowledge Café is not the end, but a means to an end. The ultimate goal is the formalization of the process of KM; this could be done within the context of what I call Knowledge Leadership Café. Knowledge Leadership Café is a framework in the KM implemen-

Table 6. Organizational Knowledge Assets

WHAT ARE ORGANIZATIONAL KNOWLEDGE ASSETS?	
Organizational Knowledge Base	Workforce Knowledge Base
• Databases	• All Intellectual Capital
• Documents	• Information
• Guide	• Ideas
• Policies	• Learning
• Procedures	• Understanding
• Software	• Memory
• Patents	• Insight
• Consultants	• Skills: Cognitive & Technical
• Customers' Knowledge Base	• Capabilities

tation continuum. It's not a methodology. The knowledge exploration process may begin with a Knowledge Café method or technique. Still, at the Leadership Café, you bring structure, formal planning, and implementations of what was discussed at the café. Many KM programs are informal. Leadership Café brings the simplicity of the café into reality, where leaders analyze and explore methods within the framework of the organization's preferences, culture, capacity, goals, and strategy, and then execution. You cannot drive a cultural change without a Leadership Café. While I had up to 100 knowledge managers at my Knowledge Cafés, the Leadership Café is just for a few strategic leaders who can design an enterprise KM architecture for the organization.

11.6. PRACTICE CAFÉ

Will I be able to understand maturity in my KM program? What will make me implement KM? Choose one or two tools and develop a workable model.

Knowledge is the decision driver. This chapter is not intended to provide you examples but instead shows a leadership framework for implementing KM in all organizations of all sizes. Knowledge guides how much we make, spend, and pay. During one of our Knowledge Leadership Cafés in Austin, the hotel attendant told us a story of the boxing legend who was having a one-man-show in New York. He asked us how much we think he was charged per month for the towels he used during his boxing activities? We all guessed and missed the answer. He said, "this boxer paid six figures per month for the towels he used," which is insane. Knowledge is the driver for all decisions we make. Use knowledge; you'll become wise!

12 ■ Knowledge Advantage and Why You Should Share Your Knowledge

---

Chapter Objectives

- Illustrate how I stumbled onto the café and how it impacted KM systems
- Case study on the café environment through mentoring
- Explore why you should share your knowledge
- Formulate an epilogue

12.1. KNOWLEDGE CAFÉ FOR COMMUNITIES OF PRACTICE

National Football League coach Pete Carroll has said, "Each person holds so much power within themselves that needs to be let out. Sometimes they just need a little nudge, a little direction, a little support, a little coaching, and the greatest things can happen" (Doyle, 2018).

Everyone needs a mentor. We all need a coach.

Let me tell you the story of how I stumbled onto a Knowledge Café and how it impacted our organization's KM system.

I started developing CoPs. As the CoPs matured, they began to evangelize across the enterprise. Within a year, we identified 50+ CoPs, and KM activities began to grow across the organization. However, something was still missing. I needed to see some KM momentum. My curiosity increased. There were still silos, and CoPs were even duplicating activities. I thought that there had to be a way to bring all the active CoP practitioners together to know what everybody is doing. Sure enough, Knowledge Café was the appropriate vehicle for this kind of informal gathering for knowledge management enthusiasts in the organization. At the first café at TxDOT, we had about 80 percent of the divisions and districts participating. Attendees possessed different levels of maturity and sophistication. Several identified CoPs were present to discuss what was happening at different CoPs, the technology tools being used to share and collaborate, what was working and what was not working, challenges of knowledge capturing, mentoring, and knowledge sharing among CoPs.

The café was simple, with no preconceived outcome. Everyone was involved in the learning process. At the café, we learned that some of the CoPs were already advanced using some technology collaboration tools and maturing in mentoring members. One of the CoPs had previously conducted a knowledge audit for their CoP. They identified all the skills and expertise within their CoP, developing a knowledge map that traced all 150 members with specific skills and capabilities. They developed an expertise directory complete with frequently asked questions. It made my job easy. Other CoPs copied from them rather than reinventing the wheel.

One of the CoPs I support, Surveyors and Geomatics Scientists CoP, was way ahead of the curve. I provided them with guidance for a simple knowledge audit for their CoP, but they went over and above in conducting their CoP knowledge audit and mapping. A knowledge audit takes an inventory of an organization's knowledge capabilities to understand where an organization stands in terms of knowledge management and its knowledge assets. An audit identifies precisely what knowledge the organization has, what knowledge they would require in the future to meet their objectives and goals, and maps the knowledge.

Needs Analysis is to identify precisely what knowledge the organization has and what knowledge they would require in the future in order to meet objectives, goals, and mapping (Kumar, 2013).

This CoP, through their knowledge audit, can identify all knowledge produced within the CoP, who produces the knowledge and uses it, the frequency of its usage, and where the knowledge resides or is stored. KM is all about knowledge stewardship—knowing what we should know and creating new knowledge.

Innovation happens at the intersection of knowledge-sharing and intelligent-exchange of ideas.

12.2. MENTORING CASE STUDY: SINCERE MENTORING IS ONE OF THE MOST EFFECTIVE WAYS OF KNOWLEDGE TRANSFER— SANDRA JACKSON

This case study is from Sandra Jackson, PMP. Sandra was a mentee. She has CTCM, SAFe 4, and Agilist certifications and was my successor as president of PMI Austin Chapter, with a membership of 3,500 project, program, and portfolio managers in Austin, Texas. Here is Sandra's case study:

No organization I've worked for has a formal knowledge transfer program. Sadly, in terms of investment into KM, not nil to none. Regarding the challenges I encounter transferring or sharing knowledge, we are not being given enough time for knowledge sharing and transfer. For the most part, if done at all, knowledge transfer is done at the last minute when a person is leaving the organization. The time spent with the person leaving is limited and rushed due to their other commitments that they are trying to fill before they leave. Often, the knowledge has not been adequately documented, or there is no documentation at all. It's all in the leaver's head.

On knowledge transfer technology tools, it's appropriately filing the information in a way that it can be accessed. For example, on SharePoint, I have to use keywords/phrases to locate/search for information. That can be a challenge when the information you are looking for is not correctly filed or indexed.

One of my most significant challenges in the project space is getting information from other people. You have to schedule meetings and set a date/time when they hopefully will be able to talk to you for the duration of time requested. At times, it's easier to go online and get the information I'm looking for. But it doesn't take the place of asking someone who knows the intricacies and idiosyncrasies of the information and knowledge you are seeking.

Share my knowledge? It brings less stress on you—especially if you are the only one who has the knowledge. It's empowering to others. Also, when you share knowledge, it opens you up to receive knowledge. Knowledge transfer can be both a challenge or fun. Knowledge transfer can be a challenge if the other parties involved are not willing or limit what they share because they are intimidated, or it can be fun when both parties recognize the benefit of sharing and how it will add more skills to their toolbox.

On painful results from lack of knowledge transfer, I've encountered? I would say it left me feeling very disappointed with the person I was seeking knowledge from. I desperately needed their help before they left the company, and they chose to make themselves unavailable. I ended up gathering as much information as I could from the Internet—but not enough to feel confident in taking on the position's responsibilities.

It was my joining the PMI Austin Chapter board of directors that I experienced knowledge transfer through hands-on mentoring. This was intentional. From day one, I experienced knowledge transfer on steroids, feeling the importance and joy of knowledge transfer. Café style knowledge transfer simplifies the whole knowledge system. Taking a leader by hand to observe one's knowledge and leadership through sincere mentoring is one of the most practical knowledge-transfer methods.

When I handed over to Sandra as the PMI Austin Chapter board president, there was no need to provide her a formal handover note except that the boarding process required it. I literally took her by the hand to observe everything, we exchanged knowledge, and I made knowledge transfer part of our governing process. When I spoke to other speakers like Dr. John Maxwell, or contacted the police chief, mayor, or the governor, and participated in the PMI regional president calls, she was intentionally keyed into all of them as part of the KT process. I can boast that if I had stepped down halfway into my tenure, Sandra could've taken up the mantle and ran with it—thanks to the mentoring and knowledge-transfer culture we established.

One of my life's missions is to mentor one million authentic servant-leaders. You don't have to change the world; what you do is to mentor one person who changes another. One of my mentees, Chris DiBella, MBA, CSM, a passionate project manager, and Scrum Master, quipped that far too many companies have teams set up that act as individual entities within the company, which they should to a degree. Still, the issue is that some teams are stronger than others, perhaps due to a project manager handpicking whom they consider being the most qualified. There is no cross-transfer of skills or knowledge base to make the other teams better, and it almost seems like some people are unwilling to go to whom they consider a "weaker or lesser" team. This attitude only inhibits growth at the individual and team level and the cultural level of the organization.

I believe that everyone needs mentors and needs to mentor others, too. This is a dynamic knowledge-transfer tool. A mentoring environment is a KM culture.

12.3. WHY DO I SHARE MY KNOWLEDGE?

Every KM environment is a knowledge exchange and sharing environment. Most knowledge users are not aware of their knowledge

Knowledge

Explicit Knowledge
- Data
- Information
- Documents
- Records
- Files

Tacit Knowledge
- Experience/ Relationship
- Thinking/Politics
- Competence
- Commitment
- Deed/Passion

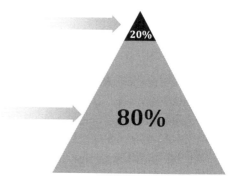

Figure 7: Knowledge assets of an organization.

or how valuable this knowledge is to other knowledge workers. Because tacit knowledge provides context for people, places, ideas, and experiences, it is considered more valuable.

The knowledge assets triangle was adapted from Allee's (2001) *12 Principles of Knowledge Management* (see figure 7). Knowledge assets of an organization are made up of tacit and explicit knowledge, and some have added the category of implicit knowledge. Explicit knowledge is easy to articulate, write down, and share. Tacit knowledge is gained from personal experience that is more difficult to express. Implicit knowledge is the application of explicit knowledge.

Eric Verzuh, in his internationally bestselling book, *The Fast Forward MBA in Project Management*, contends that it's so important to get all assumptions and agreements written down and formally accepted. He argues that the "written statement of work is a much better tool for managing stakeholders than is memory" (Verzuh, 2011, p. 51). Carefully writing down the project rules, like agreement on the project's goals among all parties involved, control over the project scope, and management and stakeholders' support, is a project knowledge process that should never be overlooked (Verzuh, 2011; see pp. 117 & 127). Capturing and reusing knowledge or lessons learned during and at each phase gate or re-view point throughout the project's life cycle is a knowledge management process.

An example of explicit knowledge would be that you write down the process or instruction for developing a software code. Contrast that with some tacit knowledge. You missed a deadline, and a customer is upset. No one could calm the customer down, so Brad was called in. He has the skill to talk to difficult customers. After talking to this customer for 15 minutes, the conversation turned into laughter as you could hear the customer on the side laughing. Brad, how did you do it? Can you write it down? Brad said, "No, I can't. I just talked to him." This tacit knowledge is hard to write down. Interaction and observation are the best way to share and transfer this kind of knowledge.

REQUIREMENTS FOR A SIGNIFICANT TRANSFER
OF TACIT KNOWLEDGE

- Extensive personal contact
- Interaction and circulation
- Tight environment
- Trust
- Question and answers

Knowing what you don't know is very important. Knowing what you don't know that you are ignorant of is more important. I propose that conversation, personal contact, trust, observation, questions, and answers effectively extract tacit knowledge and close knowledge gaps, as seen in figure 8. Knowledge is contextual. Tacit knowledge is also situational. You may never know that you possess innovative or solution knowledge unless a problem arises or you are asked about it. Everyone has a story to tell. In that story is your tacit knowledge. Learning doesn't always happen in the classroom. When you say it at the café so everyone can learn, your knowledge becomes richer. Stories at the café stir up tacit knowledge that you identify and document in your knowledge register. Various cultures and people

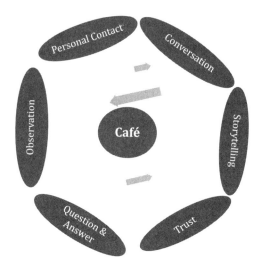

Figure 8: Café and tacit knowledge transfer.

have different ways of acquiring and communicating knowledge. Where is the knowledge we need to do our work? Knowledge resides in people, systems, culture, or the environment. How do we get this knowledge and apply it?

How do you create a collaborative team with a high level of trust without creating the space for it? You could be formal about it, but the café is a simple and informal and partially structured way of achieving the same objective—to get knowledge out of silos. It's just one effective tool to create an environment of KM.

Create a space in the café to think alone and together, in person or virtually. In our high-paced work environment, we need a safe space to come together, to think, maybe to cry it out! Environmental psychology tells us that our mental space stands in direct proportion to our perception of physical space. Great ideas are not hidden in cubicles.

Albert Einstein was right when he said, "We cannot solve our problems by using the same kind of thinking we used when we created them." We need a knowledge learning culture to succeed in today's world.

Why Do We Share and Exchange Our Knowledge?

We are not cisterns made for hoarding; we are channels made for sharing.
—Billy Graham

We share because the hand that gives is always on top! Every knowledge worker is a channel of knowledge, exchange, and sharing. The café mindset makes this possible as it stirs the culture. American activist Robin Morgan was right when he said that "Knowledge is power. Information is power. The secreting or hoarding of knowledge or information may be an act of tyranny camouflaged as humility."

Why do some knowledge users hoard their knowledge while others share theirs (see figure 9)? At a global conference on KM in Los Angeles a few years ago, someone asked me, "Why should I share my knowledge with someone who is competing with me for a promotion?" To answer these questions, I'll pose another question: Why do I share my knowledge?

I propose seven possible reasons why employees are reluctant to share their knowledge, and some rightly so.

Current economic conditions have placed a premium on an organization's ability to be flexible, quick-to-market, scalable, and responsive to unique customer demands.
—Hiatt & Creasey (2003)

1. No knowledge cultures

Hiatt and Creasey (2003) emphasize flexibility, quickness to market, scalability, and responsiveness to unique customer demands. This kind of agility can be achieved in a café environment more effectively than in other settings. For there to be knowledge culture, there must be an environment of innovation and collaboration, with a strategy for knowledge sharing—as a Knowledge Café. Knowledge

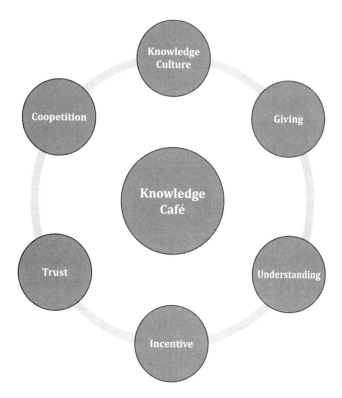

Figure 9: Why some share and others don't.

sharing is a Herculean task in an environment where there's little to zero knowledge-sharing culture. As I said earlier, KM doesn't just happen. The culture of knowledge sharing creates a knowledge workforce. Human beings do not readily embrace change. In the same vein, human beings and organizations don't just embrace knowledge management. Like an organizational mission, KM is deliberately and meticulously managed and enshrined into the culture of an organization.

Demand for knowledge creates a knowledge-sharing habit. Participants of a café and KM are willing colleagues who are curious to learn from others to create a learning process and knowledge culture.

Some employees see KM activities, such as a café, lessons learned, or communities of practice, as additional tasks that compound their daily workload. Many organizations are siloed in such a manner that makes it unnecessarily burdensome for knowledge workers to share their knowledge without feeling guilty about abandoning their regular project duties. A café mindset is making knowledge sharing part of our daily routine and our culture. Knowledge sharing should be painless if it's part of the organizational culture. In my house, we clean as we go. So, after dinner, no one drops their dirty dishes into the kitchen sink. It's natural for everyone to clean up after each meal. Knowledge sharing shouldn't be an additional burden but part of the culture and routine.

Incorporation of the café practices in the organization's business is part of organizational agility. Change has become the norm for all organizations. It has become a culture, so organizations develop a change competency and change agility, which is enshrined in their way of doing business. It becomes a way of life—a voluntary régime. Knowledge sharing creates a culture of knowledge. We explored knowledge culture in chapter 6.

2. People compete rather than complement: encourage "coopetition" and succession

We have been in prison from wrong teaching. By perceiving that cooperation is the answer, not a competition, Alfie Kohn (an American author) opens a new world of the living. I am deeply indebted to him.

—W. Edwards Deming

Employees get 50–75 percent of their relevant information directly from other people. Individuals hold the key to the knowledge economy, and most of it is lost when they leave the enterprise.

Most of us rely on information and knowledge from colleagues and teammates to do our work. There is a balance between cooperation to work together and compete in the workplace to do your best; this is coopetition. Amazon and Apple became "frenemies" when each realized, "If you can't beat them, join them." Both competitors joined forces to create the Kindle iPad app. This type of coopetition is beneficial for all major enterprise applications. Coopetition is exemplified in Project Connected Home over IP.

Apple, Google, and Amazon, who are competitors cooperating to make our home gadgets talk to each other, which is called Project Connected Home over IP. This project will work to create a new standard that will make it easier for the fragmented ecosystem of smart home products to work together—and cafés. That is the meaning the joint distribution of the coronavirus vaccine between competitors Merck and Johnson and Johnson represents. I think that this is smart.

Coopetition is cooperating with your competitors, building synergy so that everyone wins. David McMillan, of the HR Division for the Texas Department of Transportation, defending succession planning as a KM tool, said, "People don't like to succeed; they compete." This saying is true—but sad! David is right because the test of success is succession. Succession planning is a technique of knowledge management for preparing. You don't raise a successor if you are competing with them. In a public company governance survey by the National Association of Corporate Directors (2017), 58 percent of directors indicate that improving CEO-succession planning is a critical improvement priority for 2018, up from last year when 47 percent of respondents reported this as a crucial priority.

The good news is that in 2019, public company boards are more focused on long-term succession planning now than in years past. The same year, 80 percent of public company respondents to the survey reported discussing long-term (three to five years) CEO succession plans in the previous 12 months (Edgerton, 2019). This is succession rather than competition. When there's a culture of succession rather than competition, knowledge sharing thrives.

SUCCESSION PLANNING DONE RIGHT

Here are some examples of succession planning done right.

• By establishing a great professional development pathway, IBM creates a thriving and positive company culture that allows candidates to compete at the same level. Consider when IBM's senior vice president Virginia Rometty took over as its first female CEO from Samuel J. Palmisano. The company created the environment.

- Before he stepped down as CEO of Apple, Steve Jobs prepared his succession plan at Apple University. Their digital curriculum is an excellent example of how technology can be used to prepare an organization's leadership succession.
- In February 2017, the luxury retailer named the company's COO, Daniella Vitale the new CEO. Her predecessor and mentor, Mark Lee announced, "It's time to turn the day-to-day management over to Daniella, who has long been my planned successor and is uniquely qualified to take the leadership reins." (Ang, 2018)

In 2018, I was elected president of the Project Management Institute (PMI) Austin Chapter. PMI Austin is one of the largest PMI chapters in the world, with membership of more than 3,500 professional project, program, and portfolio managers. I realized that coopetition is the way—a necessary element of resilience and succession. Coopetition means knowledge exchange. It creates a win–win situation. We increased the chapter's membership by over 400 in 2018. We increased and strengthened membership, doubled the value offering to members, increased retention, generated lots of excitement among practitioners, and received 97 percent overall customer satisfaction. But in my opinion, these achievements alone do not describe our greatest success. The 2018's board leadership success is ultimately dependent on the success of the 2019 board. We are not competing with our successors!

Authentic leaders celebrate the success of their successors. A business strategy and culture that ignores coopetition and throws succession planning away will have knowledge-transfer challenges.

These leaders are happy when their successors are greater achievers or excel where they didn't—because your successor's success guarantees the sustainability of your success. Hoarding doesn't complement succession.

Competition in itself is not a bad thing. It all depends on the intention. I compete with the goals I set for myself. Unconsciously, we compete for everything. Steinhage, Cable, and Wardley (2017) identified that "some research studies suggest such competition can motivate employees, make them put in more effort, and achieve results. Indeed, competition increases physiological and psychological activation, which prepares the body and mind for increased effort and enables higher performance."

Keeping your knowledge from others may sound like a smart strategy, but it depicts a need for knowledge growth, awareness, incentive, and competitive knowledge sharing in an organization. In many organizations, especially in the public sector, in some departments or offices, one person houses mission-critical knowledge that the organization needs to conduct its businesses. I have seen situations where only one person is the subject matter expert in a particular business process like risk management, business strategy, tool deployment, specific business analysis methodology, specific metric analysis, report generation, and project or program management. This individual or project team member may be the project manager and the go-to person with unique competencies for the project or program. There will not be a knowledge culture in this kind of environment.

Why is it that if an expert or a knowledge manager goes on vacation, progress is put on hold? For instance, there are some offices where only one person develops a specific critical report on the organization's projects' critical path. This expert may have been doing this particular report for as long as many team members recall. This means the entire team has to wait for that person to return before moving forward. These experts use their specific experience and skill as leverage or a bargaining chip for individual competitive advantage. Knowledge employees will continue to hold the entire office or division to ransom because of their knowledge, expertise, and special skills until everyone convenes at the café. This mentality proves that there is a cry for a knowledge culture.

An environment where information and knowledge are siloed is dysfunctional for knowledge workers. I call the environment where employees hoard their knowledge rather than sharing it a tight-fisted knowledge environment. Everyone guards their knowledge and their jobs. Everyone knows that an unshared knowledge mindset is an unspoken culture enshrined in the organization's eternal psyche and culture. It makes employees compete rather than complement each other. Author Stan Kroenke (n.d.) was right when he said that "Economics is about creating win-win situations. But in sports, someone loses." Knowledge management is within the context of economics and not sport. We can compete and complement at the same time. I don't intend to diminish the psychological phenomenon of rivalry in the workplace. I do not believe that I'll lose something when I share my knowledge. I've always won!

Within the purview of KM, the right competition should be deemed the one where the most knowledge is shared and where knowledge transfer matches the speed of disruptive technologies and job mobility. The café creates an environment where employees are inspired to share their knowledge. They will compete on who shares the most and not who hoards the most knowledge. Know that whenever there is a competition that impedes knowledge sharing, someone loses. We should compete so that everyone wins! Covey (2004) summed it up when he said, "When one side benefits more than the other, that's a win–lose situation. To the winner, it might look like success for a while, but in the long run, it breeds resentment and distrust."

3. Knowledge sharing is not rewarded

I acknowledge that many people have shared their knowledge with colleagues who eventually took over their jobs or edged them out in a job competition. Rather than serving as a lesson against knowledge sharing, the takeaway should be to practice political savviness. Those who feed on the "cheap advantage" don't get too far, as I discovered in the research for my next book on political savviness and project management.

People who share the most knowledge within our hyper-competitive workplace inspire me to expound upon the significance and efficacy of incentives, rewards, and recognition as a knowledge-sharing strategy for executing an enterprise KM.

Encourage employees to share knowledge by incentivizing the sharing. In some instances, project team members feel that they are being punished for sharing their knowledge, which they believe is their personal asset. During the developmental stages of our KM program at Texas DOT, I organized an enterprise knowledge fair and café that had 80 percent participation from all divisions and districts. As I was engaged with District Engineer John Speed in Odessa, Texas, he said, "I believe in the principles and methodologies of KM, and we practice it. I even make knowledge sharing a requirement for a promotion. If you want to get promoted, you start sharing your knowledge."

This is amazing! Employees should not be made to feel like they will be punished for sharing their knowledge. An atmosphere of reward and recognition should be created for the KM environment.

Some organizations such as Accenture perfected this act in what they called "gamification," which is an approach to a rewarding collaboration. It encourages and incentivizes its employees to display everyday work-related knowledge-sharing behaviors encapsulated in what is called the 3Cs:

- Connect to people and content
- Contribute their ideas, insights, experience, and knowledge
- Champion by encouraging their colleagues to go the extra mile

These behaviors are reinforced through employee performance-management processes, with performance factors linked directly to collaborating effectively. The company calculates a quarterly "collaboration quotient" for each employee as a means of motivating employees to engage more actively in effective collaboration and sharing. The score is based on over 50 activities tied to its 3Cs. Scores are weighted toward quality rather than quantity. For example, an employee who writes blog posts is rewarded more based on the number of views and downloads the blog receives, not merely the number of posts he or she has written. Scores are reviewed quarterly, and the program recognizes top collaborators. Leadership gives these employees a recognition letter, a small monetary award, and virtual badges to display on their internal People profiles; these awards are noted in their annual performance reviews (NCHRP, 2014).

While some people share their knowledge naturally, gamification incentives encourage sharing and collaboration that yields incredible results. Free coffee works, too.

4. Fear of sharing knowledge

Fear is the opposite of faith. Ignorance leads to fear. I encourage you to believe it! It is impossible to fear and believe in yourself or a higher being at the same time. People fear because of uncertainty, insecurity, the unknown, the future, and by nature. We all fear something. People ask me why I am excited about sharing my knowledge. My answer is because I'm a believer! I'm also a "possibilitarian!" American graffiti artist, speed-painter, and author, Erik Wahl (2019) said that "every child is an artist," but when we grow up, we are told that we can't. We can't disrupt the convention. Everyone has knowledge if you have ever said or done something and can share. How often do we deploy an enterprise application or buy a business tool and only use a few of its capabilities because of ignorance and fear? I believe everything is possible.

Not taking leaps of faith has consequences. For example, when Blockbuster faced or didn't face their fears of the early rise of Netflix, it cost them their business. Another example is the challenge Apple faces by retaining a proprietary closed operating system. When we work in an environment of fear, it is impossible to cross-fertilize and share knowledge.

Café is the opposite of fear! To remove fears and open the doors of knowledge sharing, it has to be okay to share one's knowledge— as well as your mistakes. Build organizational trust. The atmosphere of the café eliminates fears and builds confidence and trust.

5. Ignorance of the benefits of knowledge sharing

The hand that gives is always on top. People need the right information and knowledge to create the right attitude. We must acknowledge that the giver is not inferior to the receiver. A Knowledge Café brings enlightenment, creates space, and offers knowledge workers reasons to share what they know. As President Ronald Reagan said, "There is no limit to the amount of good you can do if you don't care who gets the credit." Small-minded people care a lot about who gets the credit.

6. Lack of understanding

Understanding is a fertile ground for knowledge, but understanding and knowledge are not the same things. You can have knowledge of something without proper understanding. You need to understand the knowledge that you possess and what should be shared.

According to the study of anatomy and physiology, "The cerebellum lies at the back of your brain and takes care of things like coordination, balance, and many more implicit functions that you don't even think about. We would consider our cerebellum as our 'intuitive brain'" (Wolf et al., 2009). The cerebrum lies in front of your brain and takes care of the movements you are consciously aware of. It is the part of your brain that can express ideas and direct your actions. It is your "intellectual brain" (Arnould-Taylor, 1998).

Your intellectual brain may know something, but your intuitive brain or your primitive brain may be on a different wavelength—not on the same page. Seek to understand the knowledge you have and the benefits of sharing what you know.

7. People shy away from sharing their failures

Some people ask if they should share knowledge of their failures. My answer is, yes, if the environment does not punish you for sharing your knowledge. Understanding vis-à-vis knowledge sharing means employing empathy; understanding something is to have a tested generalized insight, to comprehend, take in, or embrace. Understanding the place of knowledge sharing is key to answering this question. If you are insecure about your knowledge, you can't make much progress within the circumference of knowledge exchange. Understand the purpose of knowledge exchange at the café. Understand political savviness. Besides doing the actual job, sharing what you know is the only way to showcase what you know and how much you know. You should understand why, when, and how you should share your knowledge. Have fun sharing it.

So, does the knowledge of my job offer me job security? My counter-question will be, "Would you prefer to die with your knowledge—so no one remembers you for such knowledge, no one uses that knowledge, and no one knows what benefits that would offer to humanity?"

The experience from the projects, programs, and portfolios that I am managing right now and the knowledge that I possess in my current job will only suffice for this current job. There are two significant types of knowledge: tacit (noncodifiable) and explicit (codifiable) knowledge. Others have contended for four types of knowledge, including (1) classified knowledge (e.g., historical knowledge); (2) explicit knowledge (e.g., organizational knowledge); (3) implicit knowledge (e.g., knowledge discovery in databases); and (4) tacit knowledge associated with unexplainable knowledge.

Implicit knowledge or inarticulate knowledge is knowledge in the application of explicit knowledge—those skills and competencies that are transferable from one job to another and from one person to another. The knowledge that I will need for my next opportunity is not necessarily the knowledge I have for this current position. Politically speaking, you are not sharing the knowledge of the next position. You are sharing the knowledge of your current job.

I have practiced two principles in my career. First, whenever I have a new job, I tell my boss, "If your standards for me fluctuate around average, I will quit." Second, I affirm, "If someone needs to know anything about my current job, I will buy them lunch and explain everything I know. I will hold nothing back because I am working for the next position or promotion!"

There is a story of a couple who hated each other so much that they sold their house for $50 rather than the full market value after divorce. Neither of them wanted the other to profit from the house sale. This is what happens when we are not adept at sharing—everyone loses. We are better than that. Sharing is good. It's refreshing to give, teach, and share what you know. It shows that you have an asset. It's a way to build a legacy.

Epilogue

American entrepreneur, Emanuel James "Jim" Rohn said, "If you are not willing to risk the unusual, you will have to settle for the ordinary."

Stir your curiosity. Go for knowledge. Go for gold! Steven Wright, a comedian, was right when he said that "There's a fine line between fishing and just standing on the shore like an idiot."

> None of us—not you, not me—is here to stick a toe in the water. We're here to make waves.
> —Alan Weiss (2011)

Steward your personal knowledge and that of your organization today. Anyone can do this! Be a knowledge evangelist. Expand your relationships and your horizon. Watch power and wisdom invade your life!

MAKE IT HAPPEN! CAFÉ IT!

References

Abelin, J.-L. (2015). *What are the top challenges facing knowledge officers in large organizations?* Accessed on April 14, 2019, from http://www.kmworld.com/Articles /Editorial/ViewPoints/What-are-the-Top-Challenges-Facing-Knowledge-Officers -in-Large-Organizations-107576.aspx

Abramson, G. (1998, May 15). Measuring up. *CIO Magazine.*

Ackoff, R. L. (1989). From data to wisdom. *Journal of Applied Systems Analysis, 16,* 3–9.

Adoko, M. (2019a, July 11). *Lessons learned: Two tales of the Knowledge Management journey summer webinar* [Presentation]. Transportation Research Board's Task Force on Knowledge Management, Northeast Transportation Workforce Center.

Adoko, M. (2019b, July 11). *Lessons learned: Two tales of the Knowledge Management journey summer webinar* [Presentation]. The AASHTO Committee on Knowledge Management.

Alavi, M., & Leidner, D. (1999). Knowledge management systems: Issues, challenges, and benefits. *Communications of the Association for Information Systems, 1.* https://doi.org/10.17705/1CAIS.00107

Alithya. (2020). *2020 professional services industry trends: The importance of speed and agility in the digital age.* Accessed February 10, 2021, from https://www.alithya.com /hubfs/en/insights/reports-and-presentations/2020-professional-services-survey -report.pdf

Allee, V. (1997). *The knowledge evolution.* Butterworth-Heinemann.

Allee, V. (2001). *12 principles of Knowledge Management.* Accessed January 18, 2021, from http://www.providersedge.com/docs/km_articles/12_Principles_of _Knowledge_Management.pdf

American Association of State Highway and Transportation Officials (AASHTO). (2018, May 24). *American Association of State Highway and Transportation Officials Governing Documents.* https://www.transportation.org/wp-content/uploads/2018/07 /GovDocs-Update-Adopted-by-Board-of-Directors-5-24-18.pdf

American Association of State Highway and Transportation Officials (AASHTO). (2019, May 5–8). AASHTO Agency Administration Conference, Baltimore, MD.

American Association of State Highway and Transportation Officials (AASHTO) CKC. (2019). *Metrics that assess an organization's KM state.* American Association of State Highway and Transportation Officials, Special Committee on Research and Innovation, FY2021 National Cooperative Highway Research Program Problem Statement on Oral History Guidebook for Transportation Agencies.

American Productivity & Quality Center (APQC). (2019). *How human connections support digital transformation: General Electric case study.* Accessed October 18, 2019, from https://www.apqc.org/resource-library/resource-listing/how-human -connections-support-digital-transformation-general?mkt_tok=eyJpIjoiTW1KbFFppE STRZell4WVRkaSIsInQiOiJkNUNVWWJHenp6cFJGKohGcGxjaExjYUVP Wms3VUdSQ1dXb2lJNjcrelREUG9CdzdnNTQwVkJhc3dYYm9TTjlNUlJjRE FMZUN3eDEyakpBR254dEZZCUWZ2XC9PQndOUIwvU 3gwRHVSQXhQaHIzSnd5dXhHbzJ3ZXBvYYU5aTHRcL1oxZSJ9

Ang, A. (2018, January 26). Succession planning in real life: 3 major examples [blog]. *Technology Advice.* https://technologyadvice.com/blog/human-resources /succession-planning-real-life/

Arnould-Taylor, W. E. (1998). *A textbook of anatomy and physiology.* Stanley Thornes.

Arroway, J. (2019, May). *Setting the stage for knowledge management* [Conference presentation]. AASHTO Spring Administrative Conference, Baltimore, MD.

Artificial Intelligence. What is Artificial Intelligence? How does AI work? (n.d.). Builtin. Accessed February 2, 2021, from https://builtin.com/artificial-intelligence

Association for Talent Development (ATD). (2013, December 12). *$164.2 billion spent on training and development by U.S. companies.* ATD. https://www.td.org /insights/1642-billion-spent-on-training-and-development-by-us-companies

Association for Talent Development. (2019). *Determining impact and ROI for knowledge management, Bruce Aaron.* Accessed June 11, 2019, from https://www.td .org/newsletters/atd-links/determining-impact-and-roi-for-knowledge-management

Audi, R. (2003, November). The sources of knowledge. In *The Oxford handbook of epistemology*, Oxford Scholarship Online. https://oxford.universitypressscholarship .com/view/10.1093/0195130057.001.0001/acprof-9780195130058

Babcock, P. (2004, May 1). Shedding light on knowledge management. *HR Magazine*. https://www.shrm.org/hr-today/news/hr-magazine/Pages/0504covstory.aspx

Baldrige. (n.d.). Baldrige business, public sector and other nonprofit glossary. http://www.baldrige21.com/Baldrige_Glossary.html

Baskar, P., & Rajkumar, K. R. (2015, November). A study on the impact of rewards and recognition on employee motivation. *International Journal of Science and Research, 4*(11). https://www.ijsr.net/archive/v4i11/NOV151549.pdf

Beckman, T. J. (1999). The current state of knowledge management. In J. Liebowitz (Ed.), *Knowledge management handbook*, pp. 1.1–1.22. CRC Press.

Bedford, D. (2019, September 16). *Seeing and Living a Knowledge Culture* [Presentation]. Texas Department of Transportation, Austin, TX.

Bersin, J. (2012, June 13). New research unlocks the secret of employee recognition. *Forbes*. https://www.forbes.com/sites/joshbersin/2012/06/13/new-research-unlocks-the-secret-of-employee-recognition/#459398805276

Bohn, R. E. (1994). Measuring and managing technological knowledge. *MIT Sloan Management Review, 36*(1), 61–74.

Boisot, M. (1999). *Knowledge assets: Securing competitive advantage in the information economy* (rev. ed.). Oxford University Press.

Brooking, A. (1999). *Corporate memory: Strategies for knowledge management.* International Thomson Business Press.

Brown, J. S., & Duguid, P. (1996). Stolen knowledge. In H. McLellan (Ed.), *Situated learning perspectives* (pp. 47–56). Educational Technology Publications.

Brown, L. (2017, August 18). 50% of companies still in the process of implementing DevOps, report says. *TechRepublic*. https://www.techrepublic.com/article/50-of-companies-still-in-process-of-implementing-devops-report-says/

Buchanan, I. (n.d.). *Agile and DevOps: Friends or foes?* Atlassian Agile Coach. Accessed July 19, 2019, from https://www.atlassian.com/agile/devops#:~:text=%20Agile%20and%20DevOps%3A%20Friends%20or%20Foes%3F%20,that%20it%20helps%20to%20have%20two . . . %20More%20

Bukowitz, W. R., & Williams, R. L. (1999). *The knowledge management fieldbook.* Prentice Hall.

Burn, J., Marshall, P., & Burnett, M. (2002). *E-business strategies for virtual organizations.* Butterworth-Heinemann.

Centers for Disease Control and Prevention (CDC). (2006). *CDC unified process practices guide: Lessons learned.* Retrieved June 21, 2017, from https://www2.cdc.gov /cdcup/library/practices_guides/CDC_UP_Lessons_Learned_Practices_Guide .pdf

Christensen, T. (2013, January 21). The relationship between creativity and intelligence [blog]. https://creativesomething.net/post/41103661291/the-relationship -between-creativity-and

Cleveland, H. (1985). *The knowledge executive: Leadership in an information society.* Truman Talley Books/E. P. Dutton.

Close, J., & Close, C. (2018, June 8). The power of questions [blog]. *Close Team.* Accessed February 8, 2021, from https://upcloseteam.mykajabi.com/blog/the-power -of-questions

Cohen, D. (2009, June 1). Interview with Alexander Laufer. *ASK Magazine.* https://appel.nasa.gov/2009/06/01/interview-with-alexander-laufer/

Collison, C., & Parcell, G. (2005). *Learning to fly: Practical knowledge management from leading and learning organizations* (2nd ed.). Capstone.

Covey, S. R. (2004). *The 7 habits of highly effective people: Restoring the character ethic.* Free Press.

Datareportal. (2020, October). Overview of Global Internet Use. Accessed on January 20, 2021, from https://datareportal.com/global-digital-overview

Davenport, T. H. (1994, March–April). Saving IT's soul: Human-centered information management. *Harvard Business Review, 72*(2), 119–131.

Davenport, T. H., & Glaser, J. (2002, August 12). *Just-in-time delivery comes to knowledge management—Knowledge management just-in-time.* Harvard Business School. https://hbswk.hbs.edu/archive/just-in-time-delivery-comes-to-knowledge -management-knowledge-management-just-in-time

Davenport, T. H., & Prusak, L. (1998). *Working knowledge.* Harvard Business School Press.

Demarest, M. (1997). Understanding knowledge management. *Long Range Planning, 30*(3), 374–384.

Doepker, D. (2017, August 3). Steve Jobs systematically cultivated his creativity. You can too. *Entrepreneur.* https://www.entrepreneur.com/article/297167

Doyle, S. (2018, October 24). A critical leadership problem many companies don't even know they have. *Entrepreneur.* https://www.entrepreneur.com/article/322155

Drew, S. (1999). Building knowledge management into strategy: Making sense of a new perspective. *Long Range Planning*, 32(1), 130–136.

Edgerton, B. (2019, April 18). New research spotlights CEO succession challenges [blog]. *DD BoardTalk*. https://blog.nacdonline.org/posts/new-research-spotlights -ceo-succession-challenges

Encyclopaedia Britannica. (2020, February 19). Apprenticeship. In *Encyclopaedia Britannica*. https://www.britannica.com/topic/apprenticeship

Ernst & Young LLP. (2007). Profiting from experience. Accessed May 7, 2020, from https://digitalcommons.fiu.edu/cgi/viewcontent.cgi?article=3555&context=etd

Federal CIO Council. (n.d.). *KM in the government*. Accessed July 24, 2004, from http:// www.fgipc.org/02_Federal_CIO_Council/KMintheGov.htm.

Filev, A. (2017, October 28). *Leverage automation in your project management workflow: Applying key principles for operational excellence in project teams.* Paper presented at the Chicago PMI Global Conference.

FinancesOnline. (n.d.). *20 best knowledge management software for 2020.* Accessed February 8, 2021, from https://financesonline.com/knowledge-management/

Gartner. (n.d.). Gartner glossary. Accessed February 8, 2021, from https://www .gartner.com/it-glossary/knowledge-users

Garvin, D. A. (2000). *Learning in action: A guide to putting the learning organization to work.* Harvard Business School Press.

Ghosh, P. (2018, March 11). What happens when AI meets robotics? *BBC News.* https://www.bbc.com/news/science-environment-43215863

Girard, J. P., & Girard, J. L. (2015). Defining knowledge management: Toward an applied compendium. *Online Journal of Applied Knowledge Management, 3*(1), 1–20

Goldman, S. V. (1992). Computer resources for supporting student conversations about science concepts. *Sigcue Outlook, 21*(3), 4–7.

Gopnik, A. (2018, December 17). What cafés did for liberalism. *The New Yorker.* https://www.newyorker.com/magazine/2018/12/24/what-cafes-did-for-liberalism

Gregory, A. (2014, December 8). *What benefits increase employee loyalty and engagement?* Workforce 2020. https://addisongroup.com/about/in-the-news/news /workplace-study-shows-72-percent-of-employees-are-happy-at-work-but-are-still -looking-for-better-perks/

A guide to the project management body of knowledge (*PMBOK® Guide*). 6th ed. Project Management Institute, Inc.

Gurteen, D. (n.d.). *Conversational leadership*. Accessed on June 12, 2020, from https://conversational-leadership.net/punished-by-rewards

Gurteen, D. (1999, February). *Knowledge Management Magazine, 2*(5).

Gurteen, D. (2019, October). Knowledge Letter. *Gurteen Knowledge Letter* (232).

Gurteen D. (2020, August 14). *Conversation covenant: Creating a psychologically safer space for impossible conversations.* https://conversational-leadership.net/conversation-covenant/

Halawi, L. A., Aronson, J. E., & McCarthy, R. V. (2005). Resource-based view of knowledge management for competitive advantage. *Journal of Knowledge Management, 3*(2), 75–86.

Hall, J., & Sapsed, J. (2005). Influences on knowledge sharing and hoarding in project-based firms. In P. Love, P. S. W. Fong, & Z. Irani (Eds.), *Management of Knowledge in Project Environment* (pp. 57–80). Eddie England Elsevier Oxford.

Halme, K., Lindy, I., Piirainen, K. A., Salminen, V., & White, J. (2014). *Finland as a knowledge economy 2.0: Lessons on policies and governance. Directions in development—science, technology, and innovation.* World Bank. https://openknowledge.worldbank.org/handle/10986/17869

Hansen, M. T., Nohria, N., & Tierney, T. (1999, March–April). What's your strategy for managing knowledge? *Harvard Business Review*, March–April, 106–116.

Hiatt, J. M., & Creasey, T. J. (2003). *Change management: The people side of change.* Prosci Research.

Hofstede, G. (1997). *Cultures and organizations: Software of the mind.* McGraw Hill.

Holder, W. (n.d.) *KM thoughts: "KM is a journey, not a destination."* https://dms.nasc.org.np/sites/default/files/documents/Day_2_KM_Tools_Techniques.pdf

IDC latest survey ranks robotics as top priority for technology investment in 2017. (2017, August 31). Telecom TV. https://www.telecomtv.com/content/iot/idc-latest-survey-ranks-robotics-as-top-priority-for-technology-investment-in-2017-28116/

If you think education is expensive, try ignorance. (n.d.). Quote Investigator. Accessed January 21, 2021, from https://quoteinvestigator.com/2016/05/03/expense/#:~:text=For%20example%2C%20in%201902%20an,in%201978%20that%20credited%20him

Investopedia. (2020, December 25). Pareto Principle. Accessed February 1, 2020, from https://www.investopedia.com/terms/p/paretoprinciple.asp

Jafari, A., & Payani, N. (2013, August 28). A systematic approach for knowledge auditing. *African Journal of Management, 7*(32), 3159–3167. https://pdfs.semanticscholar.org/3c59/c62946441b7089b8221ffbf4300cc92bec5a.pdf

Jamrisko, M., Miller, L. J., & Lu, W. (2019, January 22). These are the world's most innovative countries. *Bloomberg.* https://www.bloombergquint.com/global -economics/germany-nearly-catches-korea-as-innovation-champ-u-s-rebounds

Jasimuddin, S. M., & Zhang, Z. (2014). Knowledge management strategy and organizational culture. *Journal of the Operational Research Society, 65,* 1490–1500. https://doi.org/10.1057/jors.2013.101

Kampioni, T., & Ciolfitto, F. (2015). *A practical guide to developing a knowledge management culture (KMC) in a non-profit organization (NPO).* In Proceedings of the 7th International Joint Conference on Knowledge Discovery, Knowledge Engineering and Knowledge Management (IC3K 2015) - Volume 3: KMIS, pp. 27–38. Accessed February 2, 2021, from https://www.scitepress.org/Papers/2015/55871/55871.pdf

Klimko, G. (2001, November 8–9). *Knowledge management and maturity models: Building common understanding.* Second European Conference on Knowledge Management, Bled School of Management, Bled, Slovenia, p. 270.

Knowledge Management Working Group of the Federal Chief Information Officers Council. (2001, August). *Managing knowledge @ work: An overview of knowledge management.* http://www.providersedge.com/docs/km_articles/KM_at_Work.pdf

Koenig, M. E. D. (2017). Your knowledge management should simplify, not complicate [blog]. *Panviva.* Accessed August 31, 2019, from https://staging.panviva .com/2017/02/knowledge-management-simplify/

Kohlbacher, F. (2008). Knowledge-based new product development fostering innovation through knowledge co-creation. *International Journal of Technology Intelligence and Planning, 4*(3), 326–346.

Kohn, A. (1993). *Punished by rewards: The trouble with gold stars, incentive plans, A's, praise, and other bribes.* Houghton Mifflin.

Kroenke, S. (n.d.). *Economics is about creating win-win situations.* BrainyQuote .com. Accessed February 9, 2021, from https://www.brainyquote.com/quotes/stan _kroenke_638069

Kronos Incorporated and Future Workplace. (2017). The employee burnout crisis: U.S. Survey Shows Burnout Is Undermining the Retail Workforce. Accessed on February 2, 2021, from https://www.kronos.com/resource/download/23811

Kumar, A. (2013, July 31). *Knowledge audit: Its learning lessons.* http://dx.doi.org/10 .2139/ssrn.2319723

LaFayette, B., Curtis, W., Bedford, D., & Iyer, S. (2019). *Knowledge economies and knowledge work (Working methods for Knowledge Management).* Emerald Publishing Limited.

Lave, J., & Wenger, E. (1991). *Situated learning: Legitimate peripheral participation.* Cambridge University Press.

Leonard, D. (2017, May 2). *Deep smarts and core capabilities.* https://www .knowledge-architecture.com/ka-connect-talks/deep-smarts-and-core-capabilities

Leonard, D., Swap, W., & Barton, G. (2015). *Critical knowledge transfer: Tools for managing your company's deep smarts.* Harvard Business Review Press.

Leonard, L. (2014, December 18). How to prevent experts from hoarding knowledge. *Harvard Business Review.* https://hbr.org/2014/12/how-to-prevent-experts-from -hoarding-knowledge

Liao, S. (2003). Knowledge management technologies and applications—literature review from 1995 to 2002. *Expert Systems with Applications, 25,* 155–164. https:// citeseerx.ist.psu.edu/viewdoc/download?doi=10.1.1.461.7500&rep=rep1&type=pdf

Liu, S. (n.d.). *Introduction to Knowledge Management.* The Wayback Machine website. Accessed March 25, 2021, from, http://web.archive.org/web/20070319233812/ http://www.unc.edu/~sunnyliu/inls258/Intro duction_to_Knowledge_Management .html

Lozep, C. (2020). *My greatest strength as a consultant is to be ignorant and ask a few questions.—Peter Drucker.* Independently published.

Lynch, L. (2020). 6 ways to encourage knowledge sharing at work. *LearnDash.* Accessed April 18, 2020, from https://www.learndash.com/6-ways-to-encourage -knowledge-sharing-at-work/

Manyika, J., Lund, S., Chui, M., Bughin, J., Woetzel, J., Batra, P., Ko, R., & Sanghvi, S. (2017, November 28). *Jobs lost, jobs gained: What the future of work will mean for jobs, skills, and wages.* McKinsey Global Institute. https://www.mckinsey .com/featured-insights/future-of-work/jobs-lost-jobs-gained-what-the-future-of -work-will-mean-for-jobs-skills-and-wages#

MarketsandMarkets. (2018, May). *DevOps market by type (solutions and services), deployment model (public, private, and hybrid), organization size, vertical (BFSI, healthcare, telecommunications & ITES, manufacturing), and region—global forecast to 2023.* https://www.marketsandmarkets.com/Market-Reports/devops-824.html ?gclid=CjoKCQiA14TjBRD_ARIsAOCmO9ZWlKOwLv1lvboNo2OMtdBQB1Az XThuxHrhzPcoi0139uHMjeOh76YaAjcCEALw_wcB

Marlin, M. (2008). Implementing and effective lessons learned process in a global project environment. Accessed February 9, 2021, from https://webcache .googleusercontent.com/search?q=cache:ivbuCHRsJ9YJ:https://pdf4pro.com/cdn

/implementing-an-effective-lessons-learned-1f7f65.pdf+&cd=3&hl=en&ct
=clnk&gl=us&client=firefox-b-1-d

Martin, R. (2019, October). Speaking at the PMI Global Conference in
Philadelphia.

Maxwell, J. (2014). *Good leaders ask great questions: your foundation for successful
leadership.* Center Street.

Mazur, E. (1997). *Peer instruction: A user's manual series in educational innovation.*
Prentice Hall.

Memari, E. (2017, December 11). *6 ways to create a knowledge sharing culture at
workplace.* Enterprise Communication Network. https://www.enterprise
-communication-hub.com/6-ways-to-create-a-knowledge-sharing-culture-at
-workplace/

Meza, D. (2016, May 19). Knowledge architecture: Its importance to an organization. https://appel.nasa.gov/wp-content/uploads/2016/06/Meza-David.pdf

Microsoft Corporation. (2019). *Everyday AI in Microsoft 365.* Accessed June 12, 2020,
from https://query.prod.cms.rt.microsoft.com/cms/api/am/binary/RE2AAob

Milton, N. (2017). *Knoco stories: The biggest barriers and enablers for knowledge
management.* Accessed of April 23, 2020, from http://www.nickmilton.com/2019/11
/the-biggest-barriers-and-enablers-for.html#ixzz6KRPX7XPJ

Mitchinson, A., & Morris, R. (2014). *Learning about learning agility* [white paper].
Center for Creative Leadership. https://cclinnovation.org/wp-content/uploads/2020
/02/learningagility.pdf

Mogg, T. (2018, March 6). Flippy the burger-flipping robot is now working
alongside humans at CaliBurger. *Digital Trends.* https://www.digitaltrends.com
/cool-tech/flippy-burger-flipping-robot-starts-work/

Mojibi, T., Hosseinzadeh, S., & Khojasteh, Y. (2015). Organizational culture and its
relationship with knowledge management strategy: A case study. *Knowledge
Management Research & Practice, 13*(3), 281–288, https://doi.org/10.1057/kmrp.2013.49

Morgan, S. (2017, November 14). Global ransomware damage costs predicted to hit
$11.5 billion by 2019. *Cybercrime Magazine.* https://cybersecurityventures.com
/ransomware-damage-report-2017-part-2/

Mueller, P. A., & Oppenheimer, D. M. (2014). The pen is mightier than the
keyboard: Advantages of longhand over laptop note taking. *Psychological Science,
25*(6), 1159–1168. https://doi.org/10.1177/0956797614524581

NASA ESMD Knowledge Café. (2010). May 4–6, 2010 Accessed May 22, 2020, from https://www.nasa.gov/pdf/463955main_aa_3-6_esmd_knowledge_café_menu.pdf

National Association of Corporate Directors (NACD). (2017). 2017–2018 public company governance survey executive summary. Accessed March 19, 2020, from https://www.nacdonline.org/files/2017%E2%80%932018%20NACD%20Public%20 Company%20Governance%20Survey%20Executive%20Summary.pdf

National Cooperative Highway Research Program (NCHRP). (2014, May). *NCHRP Project 20-68A, Scan 12-04, Scan team report: Advances in transportation agency knowledge management.* http://onlinepubs.trb.org/onlinepubs/nchrp/docs /NCHRP20-68A_12-04.pdf

New American Standard Bible (NASB). (1995). The Lockman Foundation.

New King James Version (NKJV). (1982). Thomas Nelson.

Nonaka, I. (1994). A dynamic theory of organizational knowledge creation. *Organization Science, 5*(1), 14–37. https://doi.org/10.1287/orsc.5.1.14

Nonaka, I., & Takeuchi, H. (1995). *The knowledge-creating company.* Oxford University Press.

Nonaka, I., and Takeuchi, H. (1996). The Theory of Organizational Knowledge Creation. *International Journal of Technology Management, 11*(7/8).

Northey, J., Meza, D., Bell, M., & Barnes, J. (2016, May 17). *APQC KM Working Group Update Critical Knowledge 2020.* Accessed on May 21, 2020, from https:// appel.nasa.gov/wp-content/uploads/2016/06/APQC-KM-Working-Group-Update -Northey-Meza-Bell-Barnes.pdf

Osterloh, M., and Frey, B. (2000). Motivation, knowledge transfer, and organizational forms. *Organization Science, 11*(5), 538–550.

Otto, N. (2017, August 9). Avoidable turnover costing employers big. *Employee Benefit News.* https://www.benefitnews.com/news/avoidable-turnover-costing-employers-big ?brief=00000152-14a7-d1cc-a5fa-7cffccf00000&utm_content=socialflow&utm _campaign=ebnmagazine&utm_source=twitter&utm_medium=social

Pasher, E., & Ronen, T. (2011). *The complete guide to knowledge management.* John Wiley & Sons, Inc.

Perrin, A. (2019, September 25). *One-in-five Americans now listen to audiobooks.* Pew Research Center. https://www.pewresearch.org/fact-tank/2019/09/25/one-in-five -americans-now-listen-to-audiobooks/

Project Management Institute (PIM). (2015, March). *Pulse of the Profession: Capturing the value of project management through knowledge transfer.* Larry Prusak. https://www

.pmi.org/-/media/pmi/documents/public/pdf/learning/thought-leadership/pulse
/capture-value-knowledge-transfer.pdf?v=bd4b8b5d-59b5-4c10-91c9-790133b7f376

Ramenyi, D. (2004). Knowledge sharing and collaboration: Knowledge Cafés: Do
it yourself knowledge sharing? In D. Gurteen (Ed.), *Conversational leadership*
[online book]. https://conversational-leadership.net/paper/knowledge-sharing-and
-collaboration/

Rao, A. S., & Verweij, G. (2019). *Sizing the prize: What's the real value of AI for your
business and how can you capitalise?* PwC. https://www.pwc.com/gx/en/issues
/analytics/assets/pwc-ai-analysis-sizing-the-prize-report.pdf

Sapsed, J. D. (2005). How should "knowledge bases" be organised in multi-technology
corporations? *International Journal of Innovation Management, 9*(1), 75–102.

Schroeder, D. M. (2019, October 7–8). *What makes CI in government successful? Is it
different from the private sector?* Washington State Lean Transformation Conference.
Accessed on December 5, 2019, from https://results.wa.gov/sites/default/files/2019
LeanConference/What%20Makes%20CI%20in%20Government%20Successful.pdf

Schwanenflugel, P. J., & Knapp, N. F. (2019, April 30). Why read when you can
listen? *Psychology Today*. https://www.psychologytoday.com/intl/blog/reading
-minds/201904/why-read-when-you-can-listen?amp

Senge, P. M. (1990). *The fifth discipline: The art & practice of the learning organization*. Doubleday Currency.

Serageldin, I. (2013, March 8). *The knowledge revolution and the future of libraries*.
Speaking at the Library of Congress, Washington, DC.

Sharma, T. (2019). Are chatbots replacing the call center? *Global Tech Council*.
Accessed on June 9, 2019, from https://www.globaltechcouncil.org/chatbot/are
-chatbots-replacing-the-call-center/

Shrestha, P. (2017, November 17). *Ebbinghaus Forgetting Curve*. Psychestudy.
https://www.psychestudy.com/cognitive/memory/ebbinghaus-forgetting-curve

Silver, Laura. (2019, February 5). *Smartphone ownership is growing rapidly around the
world, but not always equally*. Pew Research Center. https://www.pewresearch.org
/global/2019/02/05/smartphone-ownership-is-growing-rapidly-around-the-world-but
-not-always-equally/

Simon, H. A. (1976). *Administrative behavior: A study of decision-making processes in
administrative organizations* (3rd ed.). The Free Press.

The six most common types of meetings. (n.d.). MeetingSift. Accessed May 21, 2020,
from http://meetingsift.com/the-six-types-of-meetings/

Social collaboration. (2020, November 4). In *Wikipedia*. Accessed February 2, 2021, from https://en.wikipedia.org/wiki/Social_collaboration

Steinhage, A., Cable, D., & Wardley, D. (2017, March 20). The pros and cons of competition among employees. *Harvard Business Review*. https://hbr.org/2017/03/the-pros-and-cons-of-competition-among-employees

Stevenson, J., & Kaafarani, B. (2011). *Breaking away: How great leaders create innovation that drives sustainable growth—and why others fail*. McGraw-Hill.

Swanborg, R. W., Jr., & Myers, P. S. (1997, October 15). Wise investments. *CIO Magazine*.

Tett, G. (2015). *The silo effect: The peril of expertise and the promise of breaking down barriers*. Simon & Schuster.

Texas Department of Transportation (TxDOT). (2019). *Pocket Facts FY 2019 // CY 2018–2019*. Accessed January 23, 2021, from https://ftp.dot.state.tx.us/pub/txdot-info/gpa/pocket_facts.pdf

Top five things your customers really want in a café. (n.d.). SilverChef. Accessed April 6, 2019, from https://www.silverchef.com.au/blogs/resources/top-5-things-your-customers-really-want-in-a-cafe

UKEssays. (2018, November). *Knowledge-based organization*. Accessed February 9, 2021, from https://www.ukessays.com/essays/management/knowledge-based-organization.php?vref=1

U.S. Bureau of Labor Statistics. (2020, September 22). *Employee tenure summary*. https://www.bls.gov/news.release/tenure.nr0.htm

US Census Bureau. (2014, May 6). Fueled by aging Baby Boomers, nation's older population to nearly double in the next 20 years, Census Bureau reports. https://www.census.gov/newsroom/press-releases/2014/cb14-84.html

Verzuh, E. (2011). *The fast forward MBA in project management* (5th ed.). John Wiley & Sons.

Wahl, E. (2019, October). Speaking at the PMI Global Conference in Philadelphia.

Wammes, J. D., Meade, M. E., & Fernandes, M. A. (2016). The drawing effect: Evidence for reliable and robust memory benefits in free recall. *The Quarterly Journal of Experimental Psychology, 69*(9). https://doi.org/10.1080/17470218.2015.1094494

Wartzman, R. (2014, October 16). What Peter Drucker knew about 2020. *Harvard Business Review*. https://hbr.org/2014/10/what-peter-drucker-knew-about-2020

Weinberger, D. (2018, September 10). Computers, Internet, AI. *KM World.* https://www.kmworld.com/Articles/Columns/Perspective-on-Knowledge /Computers-Internet-AI-127236.aspx?pageNum=2

Weiss, A. (2011). *Million dollar coaching: Build a world-class practice by helping others succeed.* McGraw-Hill.

Weiss, S., Faris, B., & Sandy, B. (2021, January 29). *The new knowledge management: Mining the collective intelligence.* Deloitte Insights. Accessed February 10, 2021, from https://www2.deloitte.com/us/en/insights/focus/technology-and-the-future-of-work /organizational-knowledge-management.html

Wells, J. (2019). KMWorld 100 companies that matter in knowledge management 2019. *KMWorld.* https://www.kmworld.com/Articles/Editorial/Features/KMWorld -100-Companies-That-Matter-in-Knowledge-Management-2019-129903.aspx

Wenger, E. (1998). *Communities of practice: Learning, meaning, and identity.* Cambridge University Press.

Wenger, E. C., & Snyder, W. M. (2000, January–February). Communities of practice: The organizational frontier. *Harvard Business Review.* https://hbr.org/2000 /01/communities-of-practice-the-organizational-frontier

Whitley, B. (2019, July 10). *The rise of DevSecOps: Pushing security further back into Dev.* BrightTalk webinar. Accessed July 23, 2019, from https://www.brighttalk.com/webcast /16121/362801?utm_source=brighttalk-promoted&utm_medium=email&utm_term =Audience54063&utm_campaign=AUD-04594&utm_content=2019-07-14

Wiig, K. M. (1993a). *Knowledge management method.* Schema Press.

Wiig, K. M. (1993b). *Knowledge management foundations: Thinking about thinking– How people and organizations create, represent, and use knowledge.* Schema Press.

Wiig, K. M. (1993c). *Knowledge management foundations.* Schema Press.

Wiig, K. M. (1997). Knowledge management: Where did it come from and where will it go? *Expert Systems with Applications, 13*(1), 1–14.

Wiig, K. M. (2000). Knowledge management: An emerging discipline rooted in a long history. In C. Despres & D. Chauvel (Eds.), *Knowledge Horizons: The Present and the Promise of Knowledge Management* (pp. 3–26). Butterworth-Heinemann. https://doi.org/10.1016/B978-0-7506-7247-4.50004-5

Wilson, L. (2015, Spring). The inextricable connection between knowledge and experience. *Knowledge, Education, and Identity: Basic Problems of Philosophy.* Accessed June 11, 2019, from https://scholarblogs.emory.edu/basicproblems002/2015 /01/21/the-inextricable-connection-between-knowledge-and-experience/

Wolf, U., Rapoport, M. J., & Schweizer, T. A. (2009, July 1). Evaluating the affective component of the cerebellar cognitive affective syndrome. *The Journal of Neuropsychiatry and Clinical Neurosciences.* https://neuro.psychiatryonline.org/doi /full/10.1176/jnp.2009.21.3.245

Wong, M. (2014, April 24). Stanford study finds walking improves creativity. Stanford News. https://news.stanford.edu/2014/04/24/walking-vs-sitting-042414/

World Bank. (1998). *The world development report 1998/1999: Knowledge for development.* Oxford University Press. https://openknowledge.worldbank.org/handle/10986/5981

World Café. (2017, April 30). In *Wikipedia.* https://en.wikipedia.org/wiki/World _caf%C3%A9

Yeh, Y-J, Lai, S-Q, & Ho, C-T. (2006). Knowledge Management enablers: A case study. *Industrial Management and Data Systems, 10,* 793–810. https://doi.org/10.1108 /02635570610671489

Yelden, E. F., & Albers, J. A. (2004, August). The business case for knowledge management. *Journal of Knowledge Management Practice.*

Yip, J. Y. T., Lee, R. W. B., & Tsui, E. (2015). Examining knowledge audit for structured and unstructured business processes: A comparative study in two Hong Kong companies. *Journal of Knowledge Management, 19*(3), 514–529.

Youngren, D. (2017, July 20). *5 ways to increase knowledge sharing.* Bloomfire. https://bloomfire.com/blog/522359-5-ways-to-encourage-knowledge-sharing-within -your-organization/

Zimmermann, A. (2017, July 13). What is culture? *Live Science.* https://www .livescience.com/21478-what-is-culture-definition-of-culture.html

Knowledge Management Journals and Resources

- *Electronic Journal of Knowledge Management*
- *International Journal of Knowledge and Learning*
- *International Journal of Knowledge Management*
- *International Journal of Knowledge Management and Practices*
- *International Journal of Knowledge Management Studies*
- *International Journal of Learning and Intellectual Capital*
- *Journal of Intellectual Capital*
- *Journal of Knowledge Management*
- *Journal of Knowledge Management Practice*
- *Knowledge and Process Management*
- *Knowledge Management Research & Practice*
- *The Learning Organization*
- *Interdisciplinary Journal of Information, Knowledge, and Management* (Informing Science Institute)
- *Journal of Information & Knowledge Management* (World Scientific)
- *Journal of Organizational Knowledge Management* (IBIMA)
- *Knowledge Management for Development* (Taylor and Francis Online)
- *Online International Journal of Applied Knowledge Management* (The International Institute for Applied Knowledge Management)
- *Open Journal of Knowledge Management* (The Community of Knowledge)

Acknowledgments

I wish to acknowledge my employer, the Texas Department of Transportation (TxDOT), for allowing me to practice, develop, and implement some of the principles I espouse in this book, even though *all* the opinions expressed in this book are exclusively mine. I'm specifically indebted to David McMillian, director of Human Resources; Camille Thomason, former director of design; and Benito Ybarra, chief auditor, for the career guidance they provided me. It's worth mentioning the support from our leadership, the 50+ communities of practice (CoP) I mentor, and the entire project and KM community at TxDOT.

I'm particularly indebted to the Project Management Institute (PMI), especially the Austin Chapter, where I served in various capacities on the board, including president in 2018. Project-portfolio management is my base. I have extensive experience in project management that ran for decades and carried my skills into knowledge management. I'm thankful to the knowledge management community of the National Academy of Science, Engineering, and Medicine's Transportation Research Board (TRB) Information and Knowledge Management Committee and Association of Agency Highway Transportation Official's Committee on Knowledge Management. Some of the members of these communities contributed to the selection of the title of this book. I have learned a lot from these committees.

I would like to call out several leaders and project and portfolio managers in the Austin area who supported and participated in my

Leadership Cafés in Austin and tested my crazy ideas at the café. I'd also like to thank those who participate in my monthly Global Knowledge Café from around the world, including the Knowledge Management Community of Austin, which I co-founded with Cory Cannon.

The motivation and inspiration of Dr. Moses Adoka, chief knowledge officer at Goddard Spaceflight Center, Greenbelt, Maryland, and Sally Anderson, executive coach and change management expert, cannot go unnoticed.

A special acknowledgment goes to my friends Kimberly Thomsen, Monica Handy, Bruce Moore, and Joan Rylander, who helped with the manuscript editing at various stages and testing the café ideas. Also, I want to give a shout-out to the terrific project knowledge leaders, entrepreneurs, and friends across the globe who provided their case studies and shared their knowledge management experiences and challenges, including Theresa Luebcke, PMP, who was the PMI Region 6 Mentor for 26 chapters in the south-central United States; Tonya Hofmann, the CEO and Founder of the Public Speakers Association, BeeKonnected, and Wowdible Phone Application; Dr. Nidhi Gupta, PMP, who is a trained dentist and certified project manager; Dr. Monte Luehlfing, DHA, PMP, a senior IT project manager at the University of Mississippi Medical Center; and Koji Kodama, MBA, PMP (児玉光治), experientially multicultural, natively bilingual, technologically analytical, and strategically successful. Koji is a past president of the PMI Austin Chapter and currently the Global Executive Management (GEM) specialist in Saitama, Japan, Kodama Operations. Gabe Goldstein, MPM, served with me as the director of vendor relations on the PMI Austin board. Others deserving recognition include Ahmed Zouhai, PMP, who is a consultant with comprehensive global experience in project, program, and product management; Ram Dokka, PgMP, an Enterprise Agile Transformation Coach, senior IT portfolio/program/project manager, past president of the PMI Austin Chapter, and a board chair of the PMI Educational Foundation, award-winning project manager; Dr. Linda Agyapong, PhD, PMP, author and freelance PMP consultant and trainer for corporate institutions and higher education in

Newark, Delaware; Sandra Jackson, my successor as the president of PMI Austin 2019; and my Olympia and a smart 14-year-old daughter, Amara. They shared her perspectives on knowledge-sharing preferences for her generation.

Through the stories and café ideas you have just enjoyed, I seek to honor and acknowledge some inspirational colleagues, like Leni Oman, who reviewed the manuscript. I am incredibly honored to have the support and coaching of Dr. Denise Bedford, currently an adjunct professor at Georgetown University's Communication Culture and Technology program, adjunct faculty at the Schulich School of Business, York University, a Visiting Scholar at the University of Coventry, and a Distinguished Practitioner and Virtual Fellow with the U.S. Department of State for her constructive criticisms and guidance. She is a treasure!

I'm indebted to Eric Verzuh, the international bestselling author, and president of Versatile, for his encouragement, and David Gurteen, one of KM's fathers, for his friendship and inspiration for allowing me to bounce some of my ideas off him.

Finally, I'm deeply thankful to my family, my wife, Precious; my son, Benjamin; my daughter, Amara; and my mom, Ezinne Fidelia Anyacho, who visited often, for your patience with my writing period.

Index

Note: Information in figures and tables is indicated by page numbers in *italics*.

tool, 46; knowledge fair *vs.*, 45, *55–56*; knowledge workers in, 58–63, 129–134; Leadership Café and, 251–254; for learning organizations, 166–167; location, 60–61; meeting at, 49–54; meeting *vs.*, 54, *55–56*, 57–58; as melting pot, *43*; origin of term, 5; for pain from loss from change, 201–209; peer instruction *vs.*, 57–58; practice, 67–70, 198–201, 206–209, 227–229, 259–260; price, 61–62; project manager role in, 53–54; quality of, 60; questions, 102; racial reconciliation in, 191–193; service, 61; staff, 62; techniques, 127–128; World Café and, 47–49

knowledge capture, 233–234; defined, 77; departing employees and, 88; lessons learned and, 241; tools, 37

Knowledge-Creating Company, The (Nonaka and Takeuchi), 255

knowledge creation mechanisms, 11

knowledge creators, 48, 58, 67, 69–70, 80, 126–127, 220, 228, 236, 253–254

Knowledge Economies and Knowledge Work (LaFayette, et al.), 75

knowledge economy, 2–3, 46, 65, 88, 146–147, 182, 252

knowledge engineers, 257

knowledge exchange and transfer (KET), 96, 118, 134–135, 146, 150–151, 212, 241

knowledge fair, 44–45, *55–56*; design, 103–114; silos and, 85–89; techniques, 127–128

knowledge gaps, 13–19, *15*, 40, 61, 222, 228, 257–258, 267

knowledge leadership, 18; continuum, 248; importance of, 251–253; institutionalized knowledge and, 251–253; "lessons learned" and, 242;

roadmap, 247–251, *248*; wisdom and, 251–253. *See also* Leadership Café

knowledge management (KM): activities, 108; Agile implementation, 228–229; case study, 209–213, 257–259, *259*; challenges, 18–19; clearinghouse, 34; context and, 211; current, 80–85; defining, 71–80; discussions, 108; ecosystem, 76, 84; enablers, 30, 172–173; enterprise strategy for, 111–114; facilitator, 256; facts, 138–140; identification in, 77; information management *vs.*, 151, 211–232; institutionalization, 113–114; intellectual roots of, 81–85; intention in, 76, 96–99; investment in, 90; jargon, 98; as journey, 151; mechanism, 76; methods of, 233–234; middle managers and, 255–257; objectives, 223–224; opportunity and, 231–232; organizational excellence and, 231–232; organizational strategy, 222–225; origin of term, 80; past, 80–85; personal, 19–29, *20*, *24–28*, 37–38; personal growth and, 231–232; plan, 225–227; professional growth and, 231–232; program implementation, 220–222, *222*, 228–231; project, 159–163; in public sector, 84–85; software, 187–188; value, 216–220

Knowledge Management and Maturity Models: Building Common Understanding (Klimko), 225

Knowledge Management: An Emerging Discipline Rooted in a Long History (Wiig), 81

Knowledge Management Foundations (Beckman and Wiig), 81

Knowledge Management Institute (KMI), 165

knowledge officers, 257

About the Author

Benjamin Anyacho is passionate and engaging, a quintessential project and portfolio manager, expert, researcher, strategist, a knowledge management (KM) pedagogue, missionary, and proven servant-leader with decades of results-driven leadership experience in managing complex projects, programs, and portfolios. He has designed KM and organizational project management programs that have mentored hundreds of professionals. His works have been recognized nationally and internationally, and he has presented original content at several global conferences and forums, including PMI Global conferences and Leader-ship Institute Meetings, NASEM-TRB, AASHTO, university commencements, symposia, and so on.

He is the executive director of Apostolic Bridge Builders, Inc. in Austin, Texas. Benjamin is a voting member of various National Academies of Science, Engineering, and Medicine-Transportation Research Board committees, such as the Information and Knowledge Management Committee and NCHRP project panels, and he contributed to the design of AASHTO's Committee on Knowledge Management Chair of the AASHTO/TRB Knowledge

& Information Research Management Subcommittee. He is also a reviewer of the *Journal of Knowledge Management* and a board of trustee member of Juliana King University Houston, where he was honored with a doctorate in leadership, and he is a founding advisory board member of ADRN, the largest disaster-relief network in central Texas.

Benjamin initiated and guides the Texas Department of Transportation on Knowledge Management program development, designing several KM techniques and mentoring 50+ Communities of Practice. He was the charismatic president of the 3,500+ member Project Management Institute Austin Chapter in 2018 and led the board to increase its Net Promoter Score from 6.6 to 8.6 points. He served previously on the board as vice president of marketing. He is the founder of Leaders and Thinkers International and Non-Profit Management Professional—leadership networks that serve more than 40,000 global leaders.

Benjamin is a published author, a certified PMP, and has an MBA from St. Edward's University, Austin, Texas. He is a runner, and lives in Austin, Texas, with his wife, Precious, and two teenage children, Ben and Amara.

Dear reader,

Thank you for picking up this book and welcome to the worldwide BK community! You're joining a special group of people who have come together to create positive change in their lives, organizations, and communities.

What's BK all about?

Our mission is to connect people and ideas to create a world that works for all.

Why? Our communities, organizations, and lives get bogged down by old paradigms of self-interest, exclusion, hierarchy, and privilege. But we believe that can change. That's why we seek the leading experts on these challenges—and share their actionable ideas with you.

A welcome gift

To help you get started, we'd like to offer you a **free copy** of one of our bestselling ebooks:

www.bkconnection.com/welcome

When you claim your **free ebook**, you'll also be subscribed to our blog.

Our freshest insights

Access the best new tools and ideas for leaders at all levels on our blog at ideas.bkconnection.com.

Sincerely,

Your friends at Berrett-Koehler

Certified

Corporation